Critical Essays on Flannery O'Connor

Critical Essays on Flannery O'Connor

Melvin J. Friedman
and
Beverly Lyon Clark

G. K. Hall & Co. • Boston, Massachusetts

Library of Congress Cataloging in Publication Data
Main entry under title:

Critical essays on Flannery O'Connor.

(Critical essays on American literature) Includes bibliographies and
index.
1. O'Connor, Flannery — Criticism and interpretation — Addresses,
essays, lectures. I. Friedman, Melvin J. II. Clark, Beverly Lyon. III.
Series.
PS3565.C57Z64   1985   813'.54   84-27949
ISBN 0-8161-8693-6

CRITICAL ESSAYS ON AMERICAN LITERATURE

This series seeks to anthologize the most important criticism on a wide variety of topics and writers in American literature. Our readers will find in various volumes not only a generous selection of reprinted articles and reviews but original essays, bibliographies, manuscript sections, and other materials brought to public attention for the first time. This volume on Flannery O'Connor is a welcome addition to our list. Among the selections included are a number of pieces by other American writers, including Alice Walker, John Hawkes, Katherine Anne Porter, Caroline Gordon, Allen Tate, and Thomas Merton. There are reprinted articles by Alfred Kazin, Richard Poirier, Louis D. Rubin, Jr., and two of the most important French scholars of American literature, André Bleikasten and Michel Gresset. Michel Gresset's essay has been translated into English for the first time for publication in this volume. There are also original essays: an introduction by Melvin J. Friedman that outlines the critical history of O'Connor studies; an essay by Irving Malin on "The Partridge Festival"; an essay by Janet Egleson Dunleavy on O'Connor's portrayal of black characters; and an annotated bibliography of O'Connor scholarship by Beverly Lyon Clark and Caroline M. Brown. We are confident that this volume will make a permanent and significant contribution to American literary study.

Northeastern University   JAMES NAGEL, GENERAL EDITOR

CONTENTS

ESSAYS

PREFATORY NOTE

We were confronted with a vast gathering of critical commentary when making our decisions about the contents of the present collection. We decided, reluctantly, not to include sections of books entirely devoted to Flannery O'Connor. Thus we have not represented any parts of such seminal studies as Martha Stephens' *The Question of Flannery O'Connor*, Robert Coles's *Flannery O'Connor's South*, or Frederick Asals' *Flannery O'Connor: The Imagination of Extremity*. Readers of the present volume are urged to turn to these books and read them in their entirety — a gesture that is very much worth the effort.

In *Critical Essays on Flannery O'Connor* we have offered representative reviews of the two novels, the two collections of stories, the gathering of "occasional prose," and the 1971 collection of the thirty-one stories; these reviews are followed by four genuinely compelling tributes and reminiscences; then comes a chronological record of the critical response to the writing, with positive as well as negative soundings acknowledged. All of this material is reprinted except for the contributions of Irving Malin and Janet Dunleavy. Michel Gresset's essay appears in English for the first time.

The collection begins with an introduction, which tries to oversee Flannery O'Connor's career and the critical reaction to it, as well as to examine the most recent of the posthumous gatherings, *The Habit of Being* (1979) and *The Presence of Grace and Other Book Reviews* (1983). It ends with a lengthy bibliographical essay that assesses in depth some of the noteworthy commentary. The editors have silently corrected infrequent errors in detail but have not otherwise tampered with the interpretations of the reprinted material.

M. J. F.

B. L. C.

INTRODUCTION

I

Flannery O'Connor is in many ways the anti-Pynchon of post–World War II American fiction. (These are two names rarely coupled, even in an age when critics thrive on unlikely juxtapositions.) Richard Pearce accurately observed: "Thomas Pynchon has intellectually accepted and imaginatively confronted the multiplicity of the 'new world' and the acceleration of modern history."[1] Pearce makes him out to be—with his impeccable New England credentials—a legitimate heir to Henry Adams' vision and system expressed in *The Education of Henry Adams*. Several critics have persuasively shown that Pynchon has gone to modern science for the metaphors that offer his novels their foundation stones.[2]

Flannery O'Connor's orientation and worldview could not be more different. The domain of technology, expressed by such futile emblems as Rayber's hearing aid in *The Violent Bear It Away*, is something she aggressively resists, feels revulsion about. O'Connor's is essentially an Agrarian sensibility, nurtured on such militantly anti-industrialist, anti-scientific texts as the 1930 *I'll Take My Stand*. She affirms this somewhat in a letter she wrote to Shirley Abbott on March 17, 1956: "I like very much what you've done with the Agrarian business. I haven't seen it mentioned before in connection with my work and I think it should be."[3] She refers specifically to the 1930 Agrarian manifesto in a letter of February 15, 1964, and situates it nicely as "the only time real minds have got together to talk about the South . . ." (p. 566).

Flannery O'Connor was born in Savannah; moved to Milledgeville when she was twelve; and remained there through most of her lupus-shortened life. The only interruption in this devotedly Georgian existence was a five-year period spent partly at Iowa taking a Master of Fine Arts degree, partly on the eastern seaboard, with *séjours* at Yaddo, New York City, and the Connecticut home of Robert and Sally Fitzgerald. Ill health forced her to return to Milledgeville in 1951, to set up her workshop at the farmhouse with the regal sounding name—with its Hispanic vibrations—Andalusia. The mythology seems completed by the presence of peacocks

1

strutting about the farm, which O'Connor once identified as "the bird of Hera, the wife of Zeus." Her final thirteen years were passed in these surroundings where she fine-tuned those elegantly crafted stories and those intricately patterned short novels.

This brief sketch of her life—which was in the main quite sedentary—establishes her credentials as rural Southerner, Agrarian-nurtured. It does not, however, account for her Roman Catholicism, which was indispensably linked to her "habit of being" and to her art. If *The Education of Henry Adams* is a central text in explaining Thomas Pynchon so must Jacques Maritain's *Art and Scholasticism* be seen as crucial to Flannery O'Connor's vision.[4] Or at least to one side of that vision. Coupled with the rigors of the Scholastic mode is a darker strain in her Catholicism, which Warren Coffey, in a review of *Everything That Rises Must Converge* which appears in this volume, has identified as Jansenist. (See also Allen Tate's piece in our collection for the same suggestion.) This "harsh theology" with its "melancholy effect," as Jean-Jacques Rousseau spoke of it in the sixth book of his *Confessions*, seems indeed to have informed her belief and partly shaped the contours of her work. Her lean, understated prose offers a determined stylistic accompaniment to her grim, Augustinian faith. (Frederick Asals offers some inspired pages on these matters in his *Flannery O'Connor: The Imagination of Extremity* [University of Georgia Press, 1982].)

Her brief life in letters extended over less than two decades—between 1946, the year she published her first story, "The Geranium," and 1964, the year she died. Much has been written about her, including some twenty-five books. There have been disturbed rumblings of late about this proliferation of commentary on a writer who managed just two novels and thirty-one stories during her lifetime. Even Robert Coles, one of the wisest and most patient of her critics, expressed some discomfort in his *Flannery O'Connor's South*: "How much more critical attention can a couple of dozen stories and two quite slim novels, however brilliantly and originally crafted, manage to sustain—without some recognition from all of us that the time has come for a bit of a pause?"[5] The chorus of dissent included Jerome Klinkowitz, who offered melancholy, unencouraging remarks in his contribution to *American Literary Scholarship: An Annual / 1980*, suggesting that "the most useful work" on her had "been done several years ago," with the order of the day now being "mediocre and repetitious criticism."[6] The seeming justness of these observations has apparently not frustrated or dispirited O'Connor interpreters. A recent issue of *Studies in American Fiction* (Autumn 1983) offers two essays on her work. The lead article in the Fall 1983 *Southern Humanities Review* has the provocative title "Flannery O'Connor and the Manichean Spirit of Modernism." (Coles and Asals have already touched on the Manicheanism in her work.) Recent issues of other journals as different as *Modern Fiction Studies, American Literature, Studies in Short Fiction,* and *The Mississippi Quarterly* have featured articles on her work. And *The Flannery O'Connor Bulletin*, which was launched in 1972 at Georgia College (O'Connor's alma mater), is alive and well.

Flannery O'Connor would probably have viewed all this with incredulity, if not with amused delight, if she had lived to see this swelling of commentary. Gilbert Muller begins his *Nightmares and Visions: Flannery O'Connor and the Catholic Grotesque*: "I have been told that Flannery O'Connor read *The Pooh Perplex* with glee, and that subsequently she referred to the act of criticism as the perplex business."[7] Her letters reflect this distrust of the critical function especially when directed at her own work. Her favorite word of derision is "interleckchul," that calculated misspelling that threads its way through *The Habit of Being*; it has something of the quality of Samuel Beckett's "Crritic!" which Estragon mouths, "(*with finality*)," in *Waiting for Godot*. Flannery O'Connor's discomfort with northern intellectuals—with the exception of an elite gathering of writer friends, which included Robert Fitzgerald, Robert Lowell, Elizabeth Hardwick, John Hawkes, Robie Macauley, and Richard Stern—is evident in many of her epistolary exchanges. While a number of the Agrarians who gathered at Vanderbilt in the years before 1930 were able to move north, reassess their values, and adjust to new cultures and settings, it is difficult to imagine Flannery O'Connor managing such a radical and permanent displacement. Milledgeville and environs seem almost essentially her ambience.

Twenty years after her death (the occasion was recorded at a symposium in Sandbjerg, Denmark, of all unlikely places, in August 1984), a number of things can be established about her life and work. She brought her career to a stunning climax at a rather comfortable interregnum in American letters. The deities of modernism were gone, with their tidily finished, neatly patterned, mythically ordered texts, like *The Great Gatsby, A Farewell to Arms*, and *Absalom, Absalom!* The "disruptive" gestures of the so-called postmodernists, who brought with their experiments an irreverence and uncertainty about even the function of print on the page, were not yet in focus (although Pynchon's *V.*, a sacred text for the new generation, appeared a year before O'Connor's death). Thus her career was managed with an immaculate avoidance of the "interleckchul" maneuverings of the modernists, who wrote in the wake of new theories about consciousness and time by William James, Henri Bergson, and Sigmund Freud, which produced an inward turning, personal fiction that accommodated the rough edges of the psyche and of "human time." She also sidestepped that increasing concern with a technological world and its dehumanizing consequences which was to haunt the careers of Pynchon, Donald Barthelme, Robert Coover, and their contemporaries. While Pynchon probably took seriously Henry Adams' symbol of the Dynamo and his "Grammar of Science," Flannery O'Connor felt comfortable only with Adams' Virgin. She wrote understated, orderly, unexperimental fiction, with a Southern backdrop and a Roman Catholic vision, in defiance, it would seem, of those restless innovators who preceded her and who came into prominence after her death.

II

When she died in 1964, her various "constituencies" seemed united in praise of her work. The Winter 1964 issue of *Esprit* (published at the University of Scranton) was devoted entirely to her memory, with a substantial section turned over to tributes by writers, critics, and theologians of widely different backgrounds and persuasions. The chorus of assent included fiction writers like Saul Bellow, J. F. Powers, John Hawkes, and Eudora Welty; poets like Elizabeth Bishop, Robert Lowell, and Allen Tate; professor-critics like William Van O'Connor, Ray B. West, Frank Kermode, and Louis D. Rubin; churchmen like Thomas Merton, Harold C. Gardiner, S. J., and Nathan A. Scott. This extraordinary gathering of talent crosses geographical, religious, and generic boundaries, to honor a Southern Catholic writer who essentially "stayed home" to write about her region.

The Habit of Being is filled with O'Connor's ill-tempered responses to reviewers, critics, and even friends who she believed misunderstood her work. Yet except for early misreadings, unfounded accusations of her fiction shamefully indulging in the "gratuitous grotesque," she generally fared rather well with her commentators. The first serious dissenting voice was that of John Hawkes, who raised some disturbing questions in his "Flannery O'Connor's Devil" (which appears later in this volume). O'Connor had been exchanging letters with Hawkes for four years when *Sewanee Review* brought out his essay in the Summer 1962 number, so she was quite prepared for his outburst; in fact, she wrote to Robert Fitzgerald on this subject on August 3, 1962: "I have argued with him [Hawkes] for years about his Devil, which he don't know is an unfallen spirit of some purely literary kind" (*The Habit of Being*, p. 486). Hawkes was questioning her vision rather than her craft and remained faithful to his 1962 *Sewanee Review* position when he remarked in his statement in the Winter 1964 *Esprit* that she was a "brilliant but highly disturbing visionary writer" who wrote "amazingly detached and often marvelously distorted fictions." He ended with the lovely sentence: "She leaves us the beauty of the paradox, which is a great gift" (p. 30).

Hawkes's seeming irreverence about the darker side of her inspiration unnerved a number of O'Connor's apologists, including her friend Brainard Cheney, who answered Hawkes's 1962 essay with a stern riposte in the Autumn 1963 *Sewanee Review*, "Miss O'Connor Creates Unusual Humor Out of Ordinary Sin," pointing to, among other things, Hawkes's "invincible ignorance (it seems) of the Christian view of things." O'Connor herself appeared less disturbed and, fortunately, did not allow Hawkes's reading of her work as being "happily on the side of the devil" to interrupt a long-standing friendship and epistolary relationship. (Her letters to him are among the finest things in *The Habit of Being*. One can hope eventually for both sides of the correspondence, producing a small volume of literary exchange of the order, say, of the recent Nabokov-Wilson letters.)[8]

More disconcerting than the Hawkes essay for the O'Connor faithful was Josephine Hendin's *The World of Flannery O'Connor*. In this book the author simply refuses to accept the gospel according to Stanley Edgar Hyman, Robert Drake, Sister M. Bernetta Quinn, and other O'Connor critics who subscribe to what she calls the "religious interpretation." Hendin proceeds almost immediately to force Flannery O'Connor onto the psychiatric couch and raise questions about her personal life: Why did she leave New York to settle on the Connecticut farm of the Robert Fitzgeralds? Why could she only be "comfortable when alone in an insulated and protected world"?[9] Why did she have to play the role of the Southern hick mocking the northern "interleckchul"? Mrs. Hendin tries very hard to classify O'Connor's "essential malaise" before turning to the fiction. She clearly emerges from her study as the very type of the northern "interleckchul" whom O'Connor felt so uncomfortable with.

It would be difficult to place Martha Stephens in this camp since she is a Southerner (born in Waycross, Georgia) who was educated at O'Connor's alma mater, Georgia College. Yet her *The Question of Flannery O'Connor*, perhaps the best book on the Georgia writer, joins the rank of the nay-sayers. While Hendin worries about such things as the reversal of the roles of hero and villain to the point at which O'Connor becomes "the pure poet of the Misfit," Stephens is disturbed by the "inadequate tonal resolutions." She is the first to suggest that "we cannot be the readers the stories require us to be,"[10] thus indicating an unfortunate disjunction between reader and text. She joins Hawkes in acknowledging the grim, forbidding side of Flannery O'Connor while admiring the craft, especially of "some nine or ten nearly perfect short stories" (p. 144).

Carol Shloss would place the number below nine or ten. In her *Flannery O'Connor's Dark Comedies: The Limits of Inference* (Louisiana State University Press, 1980), she also worries about reader response; she is concerned that the Georgia writer does not always anticipate "fictionally" the needs and assumptions of her readers. Shloss's uncertainties are in certain ways akin to those of Martha Stephens although they are expressed in somewhat different terms. Instead of the "tonal dilemma" that bothered Stephens, Shloss is preoccupied with "heavy ambiguities." She feels, rightly, that the text is the proper place for communication between writer and audience; she sees a serious disequilibrium between the "anagogic" responses O'Connor, the Catholic writer, expected and the interpretations rendered by readers of more secular persuasions. Only in "The Artificial Nigger," O'Connor's favorite story, does Shloss view the ideal coming together of authorial anticipation and reader response.

Claire Kahane (née Katz) and André Bleikasten, each of whom is represented by an essay in this collection, offer additional voices of dissent. Kahane is a skilled feminist and psychoanalytic critic who seems weary of the Christian perspective O'Connor demanded of her readers. Bleikasten is one of that new breed of French critic—along with Michel Gresset and Claude Richard—who has taught us so well how to read American fiction from Faulkner through O'Connor and Styron. (His studies of *As I Lay Dying* and *The Sound and the Fury* are among the handful of best books ever written on Faulkner.) He issued a valuable warning in a recent essay on O'Connor: "To refresh our perception and appreciation of her work, what is probably needed now is a freer, less timorous and less pious approach, focusing on the multiple meanings produced by the interplay of signifiers rather than on a unique, unequivocal transcendental signified equated with ultimate truth."[11]

These spirited objections raised in the past two decades by critics ill at ease with the "pieties" preached by O'Connor and her apologists have helped to restore some balance to the critical enterprise. It has become clear of late that analysis of her work is not the unique province of Roman Catholics and a handful of gifted Southerners reared in the Agrarian tradition. (The collection that follows tries to represent the dissenters as well as the orthodox accepters; we have tried not to stray too far in either direction, but to record some of the soundest and most critically incisive judgments on each side.)

All is clearly not as peaceful in O'Connor country as it was when the author died twenty years ago. The eulogies following her death have given way to some serious questionings of her habits of art if not of her habits of being. Commentators are beginning to despair of the accumulation of criticism about a writer with an exceedingly modest output. Josephine Hendin briefly described her visit to Andalusia in the early pages of *The World of Flannery O'Connor*, but unlike most of the other pilgrims she noticed such unpleasant things as "the squirrels have lately begun to eat her dogwood buds" (p. 6). This observation might serve as a metaphor for the present uncertainties, the present disenchantment and disrepair.

I have no intention of entering the controversy or of contributing further to "the perplex business." My remaining remarks will be directed toward the two recent volumes, *The Habit of Being* and *The Presence of Grace and Other Book Reviews*. I shall resist the temptation of writing yet another essay on the two novels and the thirty-one stories!

III

The Habit of Being attracted an uncommon amount of attention, mostly favorable, when it appeared in 1979. Reviewers anxiously tried to establish its essential place in the epistolary canon; fairly typical are these high-sounding words from *The Chronicle of Higher Education:* "*The Habit of Being* is one of the great collections of letters in American literature, equal in range and quality to those of Hawthorne and Melville and comparable, in what they tell us about the craft of fiction and writing, to the notebooks and prefaces of Henry James and the journals of Henry David Thoreau."[12] The letters, if not "one of the great collections of letters in American literature," are at least blessedly free of the "tonal dilemmas" and "heavy ambiguities" of the fiction. They contain a toughness and forthrightness that should delight all but the occasional subjects of O'Connor's barbed and ill-tempered responses. Like Flaubert's correspondence, the contents of *The Habit of Being* offer an essential passageway to the art. When Flaubert famously warned in a letter to his favorite correspondent, Louise Colet, that "the artist must appear no more in his work than God in nature," he could have been offering advice to a devoted twentieth-century disciple, Flannery O'Connor. Indeed her approach to fiction profits from the Flaubertian notion of the invisibility of the author. So the letters—as in the case of Flaubert—are the place to go for revelations about craft and temperament. (*Mystery and Manners*, of course, also affords some intimate glimpses into O'Connor's workshop.)

Thus while the fiction has been looked at with increasing uncertainty and irreverence, *The Habit of Being* has been greeted with enthusiasm and even awe. Here is Clara Claiborne Park looking at the collection three years after its publication: "For the letters shine. They are a cornucopia of pleasure, a day-by-day encounter, not only with a surpassing intelligence, but with a resilient and humorous virtue that converted intelligence into a premature and touching wisdom."[13] This is more than empty lyricism. Park convinces us of her sincerity when she brings the fiction together with *The Habit of Being* and makes the following unexpected judgment:

> To profit fully from the immense body of writing that Flannery O'Connor produced in her years in the country of the sick we must put the letters first. I do not mean merely to read them first, although there is every reason not to postpone the pleasure, but to *put* them first. To understand the whole that is more than the sum of its parts, let us take the letters as primary and the fiction as a gloss upon them, the black repository of all that the letters do not say, of the rebellion and disappointment and anger which the letters show so thoroughly surmounted that we might almost believe they were never felt.

She reinforces the position, with a quiet eloquence, later on the same page: ". . . for it is in the letters, not the fiction, that grace is enacted" (p. 254). The stories "shrink" before Park's gaze; the letters carry us to areas where the fiction fears to tread.

It is almost unprecedented to enter literary history through one's epistolary gestures. The cases of a number of women like Caroline von Schlegel, Bettina von Arnim, Rahel Varnhagel, and Madame de Sévigné come to mind. I have to feel that Clara Claiborne Park is somewhat overstating the case for O'Connor, although Park's essay makes for compelling reading. The letters of Flannery O'Connor do not, I think, belong in the company of the masters of the form, like Flaubert, Madame de Sévigné, Virginia Woolf, John Keats, or Thomas Mann.

The Habit of Being, in all fairness, does not disappoint. Neither does it offer any particular surprises. Readers of the fiction and *Mystery and Manners* should be prepared for virtually everything.

Letter writing clearly mattered more to O'Connor than to most writers, especially in the period from early 1951 until her death in August 1964 — when lupus gave her life a decisive sedentary turn. She explained her special circumstances in a letter written to a priest friend: "I never mind writing anybody. In fact it is about my only way of visiting with people as I don't get around much and people seldom come to see us in the country" (p. 139).

Certainly the large number of letters she sent to "A." (a woman "who wishes to remain completely anonymous," we are told by Sally Fitzgerald), which cover the period from July 20, 1955, through July 25, 1964, have quite special properties. They are usually more formal and serious, with something more of a "high" style, than the correspondence with other friends. A remark made in one of these letters, dated November 25, 1960, "the human comes before art," sets the tone for this epistolary exchange. O'Connor is concerned not only with her own but with her friend's spiritual dimension, her "habit of being," and worries when "A." seems to be turning away from the Church in favor of the gospel according to Iris Murdoch. This gathering of letters to "A." seems "overflowing with theology," to use the words of Carl Ficken.[14] It is perhaps the closest thing we have to an *apologia pro vita sua* on Flannery O'Connor's part, a kind of spiritual history with a nod to Cardinal Newman.

O'Connor is also upset somewhat at "A." 's inability to get published and encourages her own agent, Elizabeth McKee, to circulate two of her novels. But O'Connor is quick to point out that she, too, benefits from the relationship: "Your writing me forces me to clarify what I think on various subjects or at least to think on various subjects and is all to my good and to my pleasure" (p. 103).

As I read through this trove of letters to "A." I was reminded several times of the correspondence between Jacques Rivière and Alain-Fournier. The spiritual and the literary mingle in the same happy way in this other epistolary *crise de conscience* which, incidentally, also went on for nine years (1905–14) and ended abruptly also with the early death of one of the letter-writers (Alain-Fournier). The Roman Catholic Church is at the nerve center of the Jacques Rivière–Alain-Fournier exchange and it seems to magnify the tortured presence of two tormented souls. (The gifted critic of French literature Martin Turnell once characterized Rivière as a "professional *tourmenté*"; there are suspicions of O'Connor's being some-

thing of the same in her letters to "A.") The principal difference between
these epistolary transactions is that we have both sides of the correspondence between Rivière and Alain-Fournier while we have only O'Connor's
contributions in *The Habit of Being*. We can hope someday Farrar, Straus
and Giroux will bring together both ends of the exchange in a single
volume, something akin to the recent gathering A *Late Friendship: The
Letters of Karl Barth and Carl Zuckmayer* (Eerdmans, 1983).[15] The
writing to "A." loses something now by being crowded in upon by so many
other letters — most of which rarely achieve the same tone and dimension.

I do not mean to suggest that the remainder of the correspondence is
unworthy of serious consideration. It is just that no other block of it has
quite the staying power, quite the urgency of the letters to "A." Sally
Fitzgerald, in her interlinear commentary, found something special in the
letters to Maryat Lee ("none so playful and so often slambang" [p. 193]),
but many of them seem ungenuine, even forced. The attempts at humor —
such as addressing Maryat Lee as "Dear Raybat" and signing off as
"Tarfunk" in the last letter Flannery O'Connor ever wrote — have a hollow,
almost incongruous ring.

The letters to Cecil Dawkins, a Catholic writer of modest reputation
born in Alabama, come closest, I think, to the "A." group. (O'Connor
seemed to display an admirable concern for writers conspicuously less
successful than herself. This almost singular dedication to advancing their
careers brings to mind Joyce's herculean efforts on behalf of Italo Svevo,
Edouard Dujardin, Valery Larbaud, and others.) In fact, it is to Dawkins
that O'Connor first reveals her uncertainties and anxieties about "A." 's
leaving the Church. While most of the "A." correspondence tips the
balance in favor of the spiritual, the Dawkins cluster leans more toward
the literary. Cecil Dawkins finally intruded on O'Connor's oeuvre in a
unique way by producing a play called *The Displaced Person*, made up of
several O'Connor stories, which was put on in 1965 at the American Place
Theatre in New York; this project apparently had the blessings and even
the enthusiasm of Flannery O'Connor — who rarely put up with any kind
of tampering with her work. Some of her most trenchant judgments turn
up in the Dawkins letters, such as the following: "I have just read a review
in the Chicago *Sun* about *Wise Blood* in which I am congratulated for
producing a *Lolita* five or six years before Nabokov — so Freud is dogging
my tracks all the way. I really have quite a respect for Freud when he isn't
made into a philosopher. If I can lay hands on it, I will send you an article
about him and St. Thomas in which they are rowing in the same boat. You
probably hear a lot about Freud at Yaddo. To religion I think he is much
less dangerous than Jung" (p. 491). O'Connor's uneasiness with Freud, by
the way, is felt intermittently throughout the correspondence. On one ill-
tempered occasion, for example, she chides her friend William Sessions:
"I'm sorry the book [*The Violent Bear It Away*] didn't come off for you
but I think it is no wonder it didn't since you see everything in terms of sex

symbols, and in a way that would not enter my head—the lifted bough, the fork of the tree, the corkscrew. . . . The Freudian technique can be applied to anything at all with equally ridiculous results" (p. 407).

In a letter to John Hawkes the preoccupation surfaces again: "I'm not skittish about Leslie Fiedler. He doubtless knows a good thing when he sees it, even if he does have to wrap it up in Freud" (p. 413). (The context here is that the author of *Love and Death in the American Novel* had been asked to write the introduction for Hawkes's *The Lime Twig* and O'Connor offers some guarded reservations about the choice.) There are a good number of letters to Hawkes in *The Habit of Being* and, as I remarked above, they are among the finest in the collection; they have their own tone, their special integrity. We are in the presence of two young writers of approximately equal stature, both born in 1925 and both literary descendants of Nathanael West, but of widely different temperaments and beliefs, having a go at each other's convictions and artistic habits. O'Connor, although somewhat ill at ease with the New Englander who once said that he "began to write fiction on the assumption that the true enemies of the novel were plot, character, setting, and theme," offers nothing but praise for his work. Respect rather than warmth might be said to characterize her epistolary responses to Hawkes. The Hawkes-O'Connor relationship obviously depended a good deal on mutual admiration but the foundation stones always seemed a bit unsteady.

Respect is also an essential ingredient of the letters O'Connor wrote to Caroline Gordon, her longtime friend and mentor. While there are oddly few letters to Gordon in *The Habit of Being* (four in all), there are an immense number of references to her in correspondence with other people. One can trace the curious twists and turns of a literary friendship, based on differences in age and temperament, when one views O'Connor's responses to this older Southern Catholic writer. O'Connor, from her earliest letters, insists on the crucial presence of Allen Tate's wife in the shaping of her work and her career. The name *Caroline* has an almost magical ring in some of the early letters as it is invoked kindly and lovingly to prove a point or to express thanks for help. The help obviously continued through the remainder of O'Connor's life—Caroline Gordon read her work and offered suggestions until the end—but the tone of gratitude altered in a subtle way. It seemed somehow to become more an obligation than a pleasure to send her stories and novels on to the older writer. We have this kind of equivocation expressed more and more frequently: "Caroline read it but her strictures always run to matters of style. She swallows a good many camels while she is swatting the flies— though what she has taught me has been invaluable and I can never thank her enough" (p. 328). She chides her on one occasion, following the publication of Gordon's essay on *Wise Blood* in the Fall 1958 *Critique*, for having erred in several details (p. 305).

A psychologist might argue that O'Connor's letters reveal an unconscious attempt to rid herself of an authority figure, Caroline Gordon. Perhaps this is too easy an explanation, but the growing disenchantment is certainly evidenced in rather telling asides like "as I have learned a great deal from her, I preserved more or less a respectful silence" (p. 434), which seem to occur with greater frequency in the later letters.[16]

The Habit of Being also contains letters written to scores of other people, including authors of the prominence of Robert Lowell, Elizabeth Hardwick, Elizabeth Bishop, Robie Macauley, and J. F. Powers; no group of them, however, seems to offer quite the fascination as the letters discussed above. While I cannot agree with Clara Claiborne Park that "it is in the letters, not the fiction, that grace is enacted," I find *The Habit of Being* to be of unusual consequence in reassessing the stories and the novels.[17]

The Presence of Grace and Other Book Reviews, a 1983 arrival, is considerably less crucial. O'Connor made clear how she felt about the reviewer's craft in a letter to "A." in *The Habit of Being*: ". . . but to tell you the truth, I hate to write reviews and can never think of anything intelligent to say about the book" (p. 363). She exaggerates surely her being unable ever to "think of anything intelligent to say about the book." Indeed, between 1956 and 1964 she wrote 120 reviews, presumably in those periods of the day when she was, as it were, off duty from her fictional labors.

Miles Orvell, in his *Invisible Parade: The Fiction of Flannery O'Connor* (Temple University Press, 1972), was the first to establish the essential yet ancillary position of the book reviews. He dutifully offers a list of the "major books" she reviewed, in chronological order, toward the end of his study. In the same year, in her *Flannery O'Connor: Voice of the Peacock* (Rutgers University Press), Kathleen Feeley alerts us to the existence of a handful of reviews while establishing the contours of O'Connor's personal library. Ralph C. Wood, in a revealing essay, "The Heterodoxy of Flannery O'Connor's Book Reviews," treats the matter at length, offering the knowing judgment that the reviews "have a decidedly occasional tone, and they lack that sinewy perfection which characterizes her fictional prose."[18] Lorine M. Getz, in her *Flannery O'Connor: Her Life, Library and Book Reviews* (Edwin Mellen Press, 1980), appreciably advances the enterprise, by reprinting more than seventy of the reviews and offering introductory material as well as an alphabetical list of books reviewed. David Farmer, in his *Flannery O'Connor: A Descriptive Bibliography* (Garland, 1981), gives the reviews a permanent place in the canon by listing them in Section C, "Contributions to Periodicals," in the midst of her other magazine and newspaper publication.

After this brief history of the scholarly stages in making the reviewing habits known and the reviews themselves available, we should turn to *The*

Presence of Grace, a collaborative effort by Leo J. Zuber, who died before the completion of the work, and Carter W. Martin, who saw it through its final stages and wrote the introduction and editor's note.

Martin, the author of *The True Country: Themes in the Fiction of Flannery O'Connor* (Vanderbilt University Press, 1969), is very good, in his prefatory remarks, at characterizing the special properties of what O'Connor once referred to as "notices" rather than reviews; the extreme brevity of these critical pieces never permits the kind of straying or playful divagation that most reviewers allow themselves. Indeed, as Martin tells us, "her forte is spare precision" (p. 7). He usefully offers a number of elegant examples to show how her prose works in this savagely reduced form. One can fault Martin's introduction only because it fails to acknowledge the important efforts of Orvell, Feeley, Wood, Getz, and Farmer as crucial touchstones on the way to *The Presence of Grace*.

A reading of the 120 reviews — which are arranged chronologically as much as possible and interrupted now and then by a number of letters not included in *The Habit of Being* — is an experience akin to making one's way through Pascal's *Pensées*, La Bruyère's *Les Caractères*, or La Rochefoucauld's *Maximes*. (There is perhaps something of the flavor of France's neoclassical century in O'Connor's reviewing habits.) The *Pensées* is especially to the point since Flannery O'Connor's belief, as Warren Coffey tells us, is not far removed from Pascal's seventeenth-century Jansenism.

Carter Martin correctly observes in his introduction "that reviewing for her was an obligation, a serious part of her life in the Church . . ." (p. 5). In fulfilling this commitment she fortunately is not inattentive to lapses in taste and shoddy working habits; she insists with the books she reviews that belief is inseparable from a devotion to craft. Thus in commenting on Paul Horgan's *Humble Powers*, she remarks poignantly: "This is not to say that Mr. Horgan is writer first and Catholic second, but simply that, so far as can be judged from these three stories, he is, as every Catholic writer must be at least in desire, completely both" (p. 20). She echoes this sentiment in reviews of other Catholic fiction writers she admires, like J. F. Powers, François Mauriac, Julien Green, Caroline Gordon, and Evelyn Waugh. Invariably the test of quality is as seriously imposed as the test of religious conviction. Lives of saints were never very much to O'Connor's liking. She began her introduction to *A Memoir of Mary Ann* with this revealing sentence: "Stories of pious children tend to be false."[19]

The theologians and other systematic thinkers who genuinely matter to Flannery O'Connor and generally receive her blessing in *The Presence of Grace* are Teilhard de Chardin (four reviews; two different ones of *The Phenomenon of Man*), Romano Guardini (six reviews), William Lynch, S. J. (three reviews), Edith Stein (two reviews), Eric Voegelin (three reviews), Jacques Maritain (one review), and Étienne Gilson (two reviews). All of them, incidentally, receive prominent mention in *The Habit of Being*.

Her admiration for Teilhard de Chardin is evident at almost every turn. She sees in him the unlikely combination of theologian, scientist, poet, and mystic—the first, one might say, with these credentials since Pascal. O'Connor is at her most lyrical when discussing the person who gave her the title for her posthumous collection of stories, *Everything That Rises Must Converge*:

> Because Teilhard is both a man of science and a believer, the scientist and the theologian will perhaps require a long time to sift his thought and accept it, but the poet, whose sight is essentially prophetic, will at once recognize in this immense vision his own. Teilhard believed that what the world needs now is a new way to sanctity. His way, that of spiritualizing matter, is actually a very old way, one which throughout history is always being obscured by one form of heresy or another. It is the path which the artist has always taken to his particular goals, but which is set before our minds now in a scientific expression. (pp. 87–88)

She does, however, finally draw back somewhat and display a certain uneasiness because of a warning issued about Teilhard by the Holy Office (see pp. 160–61). Ralph C. Wood, in his "The Heterodoxy of Flannery O'Connor's Book Reviews," is very convincing on this matter.

A more irreverent tone is evident in a good many of the other reviews. Clever and barbed turns of phrase are not uncommon. Thus when reviewing the Catholic magazine the *Critic*, she is quick to point out: "The poetry will probably be tolerated, though not read, and the fiction read but not tolerated" (p. 115). She begins her review of Julien Green's *The Transgressor* quite memorably: "Spokesmen for the deliver-us-from-gloom school of Catholic cricitism have found that this novel commits the unpardonable sin: it is depressing" (p. 55). She ends a review of a novel she finds especially distasteful: "The result, fictionalized apologetics, introduces a depressing new category: light Catholic summer reading" (p. 73). These examples and others reveal that Flannery O'Connor had the gift of aphoristic turn. O'Connor would have regarded this as high praise; indeed in one of her reviews she remarked that "the ideal form for unadulterated wisdom is the aphorism" (p. 39).

The Presence of Grace, like those seventeenth-century French works by Pascal, La Bruyère, and La Rochefoucauld, mentioned above, should be read in small doses. At its best it might serve as a reviewer's primer, suggesting how to deliver over the contents and importance of a book in a few hundred words.

The letters—which are printed in italics—are less interesting than the reviews. Most of them are clearly not up to the epistolary standards set in *The Habit of Being*. One that is worthy of our attention was sent to "A." on September 8, 1956, when O'Connor was still a fledgling reviewer. It defines the new form she has ventured upon: "These aren't reviews, just notices, and what you need to develop for them is something I call Church

Prose (from Church Mouse) — lean spare poor and hungry. It's no great question of art here though you can say one or two pertinent things with 200 words. Me, I have a hard time making some of my reviews even that long" (p. 26).

These "notices," then, reveal an ancillary, perhaps less realized side of her talent. They indeed have the "decidedly occasional tone" that Ralph C. Wood found in them. (The prose here is perhaps even more "occasional" than that found in *Mystery and Manners: Occasional Prose.*) *The Presence of Grace* is one of those gatherings that offer reassurances rather than surprises. Few would care to exchange this collection — or *The Habit of Being* and *Mystery and Manners* either, for that matter — for those two novels and thirty-one stories. But the reviews, letters, and essays have that magical touch that urges a return to the fiction.

MELVIN J. FRIEDMAN

Notes

1. Richard Pearce, Introduction to *Critical Essays on Thomas Pynchon* (Boston: G. K. Hall, 1981), p. 10.

2. See especially Alan J. Friedman and Manfred Puetz, "Science as Metaphor: Thomas Pynchon and *Gravity's Rainbow*," in *Critical Essays on Thomas Pynchon*, pp. 69–81.

3. See *The Habit of Being: Letters of Flannery O'Connor*, ed. Sally Fitzgerald (New York: Farrar, Straus & Giroux, 1979), p. 148. All subsequent references, included parenthetically in the text, will be to this edition. See also P. Albert Duhamel, "The Novelist as Prophet," in *The Added Dimension: The Art and Mind of Flannery O'Connor*, eds. Melvin J. Friedman and Lewis A. Lawson (New York: Fordham University Press, 1977), second edition, pp. 88–107.

4. Sally Fitzgerald remarks in her Introduction to *The Habit of Being*: "It was from this book [*Art and Scholasticism*] that she first learned the conception of the 'habit of art,' habit in this instance being defined in the Scholastic mode, not as mere mechanical routine, but as an attitude or quality of mind, as essential to the real artist as talent" (p. xvii).

5. Robert Coles, *Flannery O'Connor's South* (Baton Rouge and London: Louisiana State University Press, 1980), p. xxiii.

6. Jerome Klinkowitz, "Fiction: The 1950s to the Present," in *American Literary Scholarship: An Annual/1980*, ed. J. Albert Robbins (Durham: Duke University Press, 1982), p. 317.

7. Gilbert H. Muller, *Nightmares and Visions: Flannery O'Connor and the Catholic Grotesque* (Athens: University of Georgia Press, 1972), p. vii.

8. For a discussion of the relationship, see my "John Hawkes and Flannery O'Connor: The French Background," *Boston University Journal*, 21 (Autumn 1973), 34–44.

9. Josephine Hendin, *The World of Flannery O'Connor* (Bloomington and London: Indiana University Press, 1970), p. 11. All subsequent references, included parenthetically in the text, will be to this edition.

10. Martha Stephens, *The Question of Flannery O'Connor* (Baton Rouge: Louisiana State University Press, 1973), p. 11. All subsequent references, included parenthetically in the text, will be to this edition.

11. André Bleikasten, "Writing on the Flesh: Tattoos and Taboos in 'Parker's Back,' " *Southern Literary Journal*, 14 (Spring 1982), 10.

12. Michael True, "The Luminous Letters of a Writer of Genius," *The Chronicle of Higher Education*, April 16, 1979, p. R6.

13. Clara Claiborne Park, "Crippled Laughter: Toward Understanding Flannery O'Connor," *The American Scholar*, 51 (Spring 1982), 252. All subsequent references, included parenthetically in the text, will be to this edition.

14. See Carl Ficken, "Theology in Flannery O'Connor's *The Habit of Being*," *Christianity and Literature*, 30 (Winter 1981), 57.

15. The title "a late friendship" applies nicely also to the epistolary relationship between O'Connor and "A." which was started only nine years before O'Connor's death. Karl Barth, by the way, was a Protestant theologian who much interested Flannery O'Connor; his name appears three times in *The Habit of Being*. She reviewed his *Evangelical Theology: An Introduction* in the October 24, 1963, *The Southern Cross*. (See *The Presence of Grace and Other Book Reviews*, compiled by Leo J. Zuber, edited and with an introduction by Carter W. Martin [Athens: University of Georgia Press, 1983], pp. 164–65. All subsequent references, included parenthetically in the text, will be to this edition.)

16. Shortly after the publication of *The Habit of Being*, Sally Fitzgerald brought out "A Master Class: From the Correspondence of Caroline Gordon and Flannery O'Connor," *Georgia Review*, 33 (Winter 1979), 827–46. The exchange of letters is weighted heavily on the side of Caroline Gordon, who manages in a long letter to O'Connor a full-scale critique of *Wise Blood*, with useful side references to Flaubert, Henry James, Chekhov, Kafka, Proust, and other writers. In another letter, which Gordon wrote to Robert Fitzgerald, she gets to the nerve center of O'Connor's art very quickly: "At any rate, she is already a rare phenomenon: a Catholic novelist with a real dramatic sense, one who relies more on her technique than her piety" (p. 828). This early correspondence which Sally Fitzgerald makes available here underscores the classic relationship between a generous teacher and a willing pupil.

17. Substantial portions of my discussion of *The Habit of Being* are taken from my " 'The Human Comes Before Art': Flannery O'Connor Viewed Through Her Letters and Her Critics," *Southern Literary Journal*, 12 (Spring 1980), 114–20.

18. Ralph C. Wood, "The Heterodoxy of Flannery O'Connor's Book Reviews," *Flannery O'Connor Bulletin*, 5 (1976), 3.

19. See Flannery O'Connor, *Mystery and Manners: Occasional Prose*, eds. Sally and Robert Fitzgerald (New York: Farrar, Straus & Giroux, 1969), p. 213.

REVIEWS

Wise Blood

A Case of Possession
John W. Simons*

This is the first novel of a twenty-six-year-old Georgia woman. It is a remarkably accomplished, remarkably precocious beginning. Written in a taut, dry, economical and objective prose, it is an important addition to the grotesque literature of Southern decadence. It is also a kind of Southern-Baptist version of "The Hound of Heaven."

Hazel Motes, recently mustered out of the U. S. Army, sets his mind on becoming an itinerant evangelist after the manner of his grandfather. Tennessee swarms with these circuit preachers, whose motives and origins are dubious. But Motes' gospel is to be revolutionary. He is to preach "the Church without Christ." The symbols of what I should call his "ordination" are a black preacher's hat and a second-hand Essex car. The hat is a symbol of a kind of interior anointing. The car is a symbol both of his "otherworldliness" and of his mechanism of escape from Christ.

Motes encounters several characters who are important to him and to the novel. They are Asa Hawks, a preacher whose simulated blindness becomes for Hazel a temptation and a challenge; Hawks's daughter, Sabbath Lily, whose body cries for Hazel's; Enoch Emery, a demoniac whose washstand is the altar of his Black Mass; and Onnie Jay Holy, who is Hazel's disreputable *alter ego*. After a series of macabre events, Hazel kills his *alter ego* and wrecks his car. He gives up his career as preacher and spends his remaining years as a kind of urban anchorite, submitting himself to penances of an incredibly harsh nature. His death is laconic and terrible.

Wise Blood receives its title from Enoch Emery's Satanic charism. His blood is "wise," that is, it warns him, like the alleged pricking of witches' thumbs, of an unnamed evil which is imminent and which is to use him as its involuntary engine. What is true of Emery is true in a less pronounced way of all the characters in the novel. All are driven; all are possessed. They live, like animals, according to some anonymous law of the blood. Not one of them exhibits the capacity to think or even to feel humanly.

*Reprinted, with permission, from *Commonweal*, 27 June 1952, pp. 297–98.

19

Their world is not a society at all. There is no fellowship that we recognize as human. Motes is possessed too, but in the Dostoievskian sense. Christ somehow sings in his blood.

Motes' rejection of Christ, or apparent rejection of Christ, can be explained simply. His childhood was fed on a crude evangelism which luridly associated Christ with sin. Christ was involved in a man's life in proportion to a man's involvement in sin. Even as a boy Motes had "a deep black wordless conviction that the way to avoid Jesus was to avoid sin." The proposition is reversible: the way to avoid sin is to avoid Jesus. This is the essence of the Motesian gospel. If he sometimes indulged in sin, he did so listlessly, so as to prove that he did not believe in it.

It is Sabbath Lily Hawks, the degenerate, who sees Motes for what he really is. "I seen you wouldn't never have no fun or let anybody else because you didn't want nothing but Jesus." When he ceases to be a preacher and abandons his car (the instrument of his flight from Christ), and when he blinds himself as a ritual gesture of his guilt, we may assume, if we wish, that Christ has gained a wordless victory.

This is a possible reading of the main intention of *Wise Blood*. It is not, however, the whole of the novel, which is rich in secondary themes. Metaphor is almost always deeply imbedded in the factual narrative, but there are times when the symbols become detached and seem to be indulged for their own horrendous sake.

The style is bare and almost reportorial. The author is, so to speak, nowhere in sight, a virtue which is perhaps overvalued in the contemporary novel. (An anonymous style tends, by an inner logic, to be the non-existence of style.) The stifling world which emerges from these pages is an animalistic world. The author's predilection for zoological symbolism is more than a trick of style. There is more crude animalism in Taulkinham than in the fictional zoo of its outskirts. Nobody here is redeemed because there is no one to redeem. It is doubtful, for all my own high-minded scansion of symbol, that even Motes is redeemed.

Young Writer With a Bizarre
Tale to Tell
Sylvia Stallings*

Flannery O'Connor, in her first novel, has taken on the difficult subject of religious mania, and succeeds in telling a tale at once delicate and grotesque. For it fulfills the first and most important requirement of any work of the imagination, which is to convince the spectator of the total reality of something outside his experience.

*Reprinted from *New York Herald Tribune Book Review*, 18 May 1952, p. 3, by permission of Sylvia Stallings Lowe.

Very few readers of *Wise Blood* will have suffered from an obsession like that of Hazel Motes, the lanky Tennessean who sets out to free his fellow men from their enslavement to a redeeming Jesus. Hazel's grandfather had preached salvation for sinners but Hazel, remembering the old man's finger levelled accusingly at him, concluded that with no redemption there would be no need for Jesus and so he determined to convert people to the Church Without Christ where there were no sins and no sinners. How the world received him and how he came to die in a ditch with broken glass in his shoes and barbed wire wrapped around his chest and both his eyes put out with quicklime is Miss O'Connor's story, and it is a strange one.

For Haze in his career touched also on the lives of Enoch Emery, who stole a mummy out of its glass museum case to provide this peculiar prophet with a new jesus, and of Asa Hawks and his perverse daughter, Sabbath Lily, who ought by rights to be comic figures straight out of Dogpatch and who yet come to life with all the soft-spoken villainy of Dostoievsky's men and women—except that in this curiously vivid world good and evil seem to have lost their cutting edge. Haze brought uneasiness to the fat whore, Leora, as well, and to the gorilla who shook the hands of the first ten children in line at the picture show, and to his landlady, who thought that life had at last found her a friend: even if he was a blind man he could learn to play the guitar and they could sit on the porch in the evenings behind the rubber plants; the two of them, he strumming the guitar.

Some of the power of Miss O'Connor's writing comes from her understanding of the anguish of a mind tormented by God, and some from her ability to anchor the fantastic in the specific, so that her characters go about their preposterous lives in a way that parodies with a horrible fascination the actions of a sensible man. She understands also how to drive home a telling metaphor: few boys could forget having had for grandfather "a waspish old man who had ridden over three counties with Jesus hidden in his head like a stinger."

The only doubt Miss O'Connor leaves in the mind is where, after an opening performance like this one, she has left herself to go.

A Good Man
Is Hard to Find

With a Glitter of Evil

Caroline Gordon*

This first collection of short stories by Flannery O'Connor exhibits what Henry James, in "a partial portrait" of Guy de Maupassant, called "the artful brevity of a master." James added that Maupassant was "a 'case,' an embarrassment, a lion in the path." The contemporary reviewer, called upon to evaluate the achievement of the young American writer, may well feel that a lioness has strayed across *his* path. Miss O'Connor's works, like Maupassant's, are characterized by precision, density and an almost alarming circumscription. There are few landscapes in her stories. Her characters seem to move in the hard, white glare of a searchlight — or perhaps it is more as if the author viewed her subjects through the knot-hole in a fence or wall.

James complained that Maupassant's work lacked a dimension, because he "took no account of the moral nature of man. . . . The very compact mansion in which he dwells presents on that side a perfectly dead wall." This charge cannot be laid at Miss O'Connor's door. The difference lies in the eye that is applied to the crack in the wall of her "very compact mansion." Miss O'Connor, for all her apparent preoccupation with the visible scene, is also fiercely concerned with moral, even theological, problems. In these stories the rural South is, for the first time, viewed by a writer whose orthodoxy matches her talent. The results are revolutionary.

Miss O'Connor has an unerring eye in the selection of detail and the most exquisite ear I know of for the cadences of everyday speech. The longer, statelier sentence which has come down to us from the great masters of English prose and which, in the hands of a writer like Joyce, throws into such dramatic relief his mastery of the vernacular, is not as yet in her repertory. She is, like Maupassant, very much of her time; and her stories, like his, have a certain glitter, as it were, of evil, which pervades them and astonishingly contributes to their lifelikeness.

In "A Good Man Is Hard to Find" an American family, father, mother, three children and grandmother, set off on a vacation motor trip,

*Reprinted from *New York Times Book Review*, 12 June 1955, p. 5. © 1955 by The New York Times Company. Reprinted by permission.

their aim being to cover as much ground as possible in the time allotted for the vacation. "Let's go through Georgia fast, so we won't have to look at it much" is the way 8-year-old John Wesley puts it. Before they are through they have all six confronted eternity — through the agency of a gunman escaped from a penitentiary who employs the interval, during which his two henchmen are off in the wood murdering the father and mother and three children, in discussing the problem of death and resurrection with the grandmother.

In "The Displaced Person" Mrs. Shortley, the wife of a dairyman, reads the Apocalypse and communes with her soul so long and earnestly that she has visions. Mrs. McIntyre, the owner of the dairy farm, being more sophisticated than Mrs. Shortley, does not have as easy access to spiritual comforts and, when hard pressed, turns to the memory of her late husband, "the Judge." She sometimes sits and meditates in his study, which she has kept unchanged since his death as a sort of memorial to him.

Mrs. McIntyre married the Judge because she thought he was rich — and wise. His estate proved to consist of "fifty acres and the house." His wisdom is still embodied in pithy vulgarization of proverbs: "One fellow's misery is the other fellow's gain." "The devil you know is better than the devil you don't."

Miss O'Connor is as realistic and down to earth a writer as one can find. Yet many people profess to find her work hard to understand. This may be because she uses symbolism in a way in which it has not been used by any of her young contemporaries. Mrs. Hopewell in "Good Country People" is thrifty, kind-hearted and optimistic, abounding in aphorisms such as "A smile never hurt anyone," "It takes all kinds to make a world." She cannot understand why her daughter Joy is not happy. Joy, who had her leg blown off when she was ten years old, has a doctor's degree in philosophy, a bad complexion and poor eyesight and at 32 is so joyless that she has changed her name to "Hulga" because she thinks that is an ugly name. It is not hard to find in the two women figures of the "Old" and the "New" South.

Perhaps a profounder symbolism underlies "The Displaced Person." The judge, a "dirty, snuff-dipping courthouse figure," may also — for the orthodox — symbolize the "Old" South, his study, "a dark, closet-like space as dark and quiet as a chapel," the scanty provision which the "Old" South was able to make for the spiritual needs of her children.

Two Ladies of the South   Louis D. Rubin, Jr.*

Katherine Anne Porter, Elizabeth Madox Roberts, Caroline Gordon, Carson McCullers, Eudora Welty, more recently Flannery O'Connor, Elizabeth Spencer—the list of women writers who have helped to make the Southern renascence of the past several decades so remarkable a literary flowering is a distinguished one. Miss Porter has written little of late, and Miss Roberts is dead now, but Miss Gordon continues to produce a new novel every few years, while Miss Welty, who is somewhat younger than several of the others, seems only to be gaining momentum. This array of writers has produced an imposing fiction, and the end is not yet. This year, within two months' time, we have been given a new collection of Eudora Welty's short stories, and a first collection by Flannery O'Connor. To read the first is to be assured that a sensitive, discerning artist is steadily extending her range; to read Miss O'Connor's volume is to watch the emergence of a clear-sighted and sure talent. . . .

The short stories of Miss Flannery O'Connor, here collected for the first time, are as unlike those in Miss Welty's new book as it is possible for two Southern authors to be. Where Miss Welty's fiction hovers, where her style is veiled, shimmering, elusive, Miss O'Connor's approach is direct, precise, bounded. Evelyn Waugh is quoted as saying of Miss O'Connor's novel *Wise Blood* that "if this is the unaided work of a young lady it is a remarkable product." An odd way to put a compliment, and yet the stories of *A Good Man is Hard to Find* represent a much greater success in conception and execution than her novel did. *Wise Blood* had fine things in it, but as a novel it did not sustain the promise of several of its parts. In the short story form, however, Miss O'Connor seems to have found the vehicle in which her literary attack would be at its surest and most congenial.

Something about Miss O'Connor's work is reminiscent of the best work of another Georgia writer, Erskine Caldwell. Perhaps it is subject matter most of all. Though in no sense concerned with the pornography and lasciviousness to which Caldwell often resorts, she too goes in for the miseries of the poor whites—faith healers, a one-armed vagrant who weds a deaf-and-dumb girl to steal her mother's old car and then abandons her on their wedding trip, hermaphrodites at the fair, country cousins mystified by the city's ways, a Bible salesman and a girl with a wooden leg, displaced tenant farmers. Perhaps the similarities are enhanced, too, by the style of Miss O'Connor's stories—realistic, plain, literal:

> The ugly words settled in Mr. Shiftlet's head like a group of
> buzzards in the top of a tree. He didn't answer at once. He rolled

*Reprinted from *Sewanee Review*, 63 (1955), 671–81, by permission of *Sewanee Review* and Louis D. Rubin, Jr.

himself a cigarette and lit it and then he said in an even voice, "Lady, a
man is divided into two parts, body and spirit."

The old woman clapped her gums together.

"A body and a spirit," he repeated. "The body, lady, is like a house;
it don't go anywhere; but the spirit, lady, is like a automobile; always on
the move, always. . . ."

There is much dialogue; Miss O'Connor has an outrageously keen ear
for country talk. There is also considerable humor. The incongruous, the
hilarious, the absurdly comic (the man doing the preaching above is the
one who marries the deaf-mute in order to steal the family car) are grist to
Miss O'Connor's mill. She relishes the ridiculous:

"I told you you could hang around and work for food," she said, "if
you don't mind sleeping in that car yonder."

"Why listen, Lady," he said, with a grin of delight, "the monks of
old slept in their coffins!"

"They wasn't as advanced as we are," the old woman said.

In the first, title story of the collection, an escaped killer engages in
platitudinous conversation with an old woman while his henchman kills
her son, daughter-in-law, and children. Finally the grandmother too is
exterminated. "Some fun!" the henchman remarks. "Shut up, Bobby Lee,"
the killer declares. "It's no real pleasure in life."

Where Miss O'Connor's art differs — profoundly — from Caldwell's is
not in language or subject matter so much as in the attitude of the author.
Caldwell is the naturalist, out to make a social point, preoccupied with
the poor farmer's oppressed economic condition. Flannery O'Connor has
no such intention, no such simple approach to people. More kin to the
Bundrens of As I Lay Dying, her people confront spiritual and moral
problems, not economics. There is in her characters a dignity, a human
worthiness, that shows the real respect Miss O'Connor has for them. All of
them are, in their own times and situations, responsible agents, not
trapped automatons.

Miss O'Connor is in essence a religious writer. Knowledge of good
and evil is at the heart of her stories. A most powerful, ironic tale is that
called "Good Country People," in which the central figure is a young
woman with a wooden leg and a Ph.D. in philosophy, who lives on a farm
with her mother. Along comes a seemingly starry-eyed Bible salesman,
and the girl, who is avowedly an atheist who believes in "nothing," decides
to seduce him. They retire to a barn, climbing the ladder to the hayloft. As
a proof of her love, the Bible salesman persuades her to remove her
wooden leg. He quickly seizes it, and takes from his satchel a bottle of
whiskey, a pack of pornographic cards, and a tin of contraceptives. She
repulses his advances then, whereupon as she watches in horror he places
the wooden leg in the satchel:

"I've gotten a lot of interesting things," he said. "One time I got a
woman's glass eye this way. And you needn't to think you'll catch me

because Pointer ain't really my name. I use a different name at every house I call at and don't stay nowhere long. And I'll tell another thing, Hulga," he said, using the name as if he didn't think much of it, "you ain't so smart. I been believing in nothing ever since I was born!"

The Bible salesman disappears down the ladder, leaving the helpless girl atheist sitting on the straw. She has learned a little more, now, about what it means to believe in "nothing."

Still another useful comparison for these stories is with the work of another Georgia lady, Miss Carson McCullers. For one thing, both Miss O'Connor and Miss McCullers seem to share a strong artistic sympathy for the wretched, the deformed, the physical and mental misfits. Some of the people in *A Good Man is Hard to Find* remind one forcibly of those unhappy folk who are described in *The Heart is a Lonely Hunter*. The significant difference has to do with the matter of pathos. Through all of Carson McCullers' writings runs the strain of the sentimental, of a vague, undefined yearning. As a novel, *The Heart is a Lonely Hunter* is marred by the unresolved attitude on the part of the author. She is not sure whether to be ironic over the lonely plight of her misfits and adolescents, or to yearn with them for better things. At different times she does both. Flannery O'Connor, on the other hand, knows exactly where she stands, and so does the reader. Never once is she sentimental about a character: this is the situation, this is the person, this is what happens. There is a great deal of compassion in her work, but it is always compassion for characters because they are human beings with human limitations, not because they have limbs missing or have lost their jobs or are otherwise discomfited. The moral consciousness that runs throughout the stories of *A Good Man is Hard to Find* can accept evil, but not try to find excuses for it.

The longest, most ambitious story in Miss O'Connor's volume is a fiction in three parts entitled "The Displaced Person." It is the story of what happens on a Southern farm when a displaced person is brought in from Europe to work on it. The efficiency of Mr. Guizac, the D. P., his tireless energy, his complete ignorance of Southern rural mores—he proposes that a Negro farmer bring over his young cousin and marry her—all combine to wreck things on the hitherto inefficient, lackadaisical farm. First the Shortleys, the family of white farm workers, are displaced. Then the satisfaction of the proprietor, Mrs. McIntyre, over the farm's vastly increased efficiency, changes into an increasing sense of insecurity over the strangeness of the foreigner's ways. Finally she decides to give him his notice. But the Southern white worker, Mr. Shortley, has returned with word that his wife died of a stroke the day they left the farm. "I figure that Pole killed her," he remarks. "She seen through him from the first. She known he came from the devil. He told me so." Before Mrs. McIntyre can notify Mr. Guizac that he is to leave, he is "accidentally" crushed to death by a tractor which Mr. Shortley had been driving.

Knowing that she is somehow responsible for all this, Mrs. McIntyre collapses, and soon goes to pieces, developing a nervous affliction, giving up her farm. Finally she loses her speech and sight, and can only lie in bed while the old priest who had suggested Mr. Guizac to her in the first place, and who is the only one who still remembers her, comes once a week to sit by her side and explain the doctrines of the church. She is now the displaced person; the things she had been taught to believe and the things she knew had failed to permit her to cope with the world.

Told with precision and with a tasteful economy of word and phrase, the story shows the author's convincing grasp of a social and moral situation. Mr. Shortley, the farm hand, is in his own lights "justified" in having killed the intruder, Mr. Guizac. Mrs. McIntyre was in her own lights "justified" in preferring the D. P.'s vastly more efficient labor, which for the first time permitted her farm to operate at a profit. Mr. Guizac himself was doing no harm; he was acting only according to his training and knowledge. Yet Mrs. Shortley is dead, Mr. Guizac is dead, and the Southern farm society has collapsed before the unaccustomed, the new.

"The Displaced Person" is an original story. Miss O'Connor's is a distinct, original talent. In comparing her work with that of others I have not intended to slight her authentic, creative individuality of conception and performance. There are certainly elements in her work that draw upon the books she has read, but not to Miss O'Connor's disadvantage. In force and insight her work can stand by itself; *A Good Man is Hard to Find* is a book of solid artistic attainment.

The Violent Bear It Away

Flannery O'Connor's Violent
View of Reality
P. Albert Duhamel*

Everyone talks about reality as if it were beyond man's powers to change to suit his whims, yet almost everyone acts as if it could be changed — at least a little — to conform to his expectations. With the publication this month of her second novel, *The Violent Bear It Away*, Flannery O'Connor sums up her earlier work and challenges comparison with the greatest in her exploration of the consequences of man's refusal to see things as they really are and act accordingly.

Her control character, Francis Marion Tarwater, like many of his contemporaries tarred with the brush of sin and redeemed by the water of baptism, tries "to keep his vision located on an even level, to see no more than what was in front of his face and to let his eyes stop at the surface of that." Symbolic of modern man he refuses to let his eyes rest on anything longer than is absolutely necessary to identify it, for he is afraid that if he does "the thing would suddenly stand before him strange and terrifying, demanding that he name it and name it justly and be judged for the name he gave it."

Francis Marion Tarwater, who responds only to his last name, has a long line of intellectual ancestors, including Macbeth, who delayed as long as they could calling things by their right names and resisted "this threatened intimacy with creation." Although never as comic as Don Quixote tilting at the creations of his own imagination, nor as tragic as Ahab, determined that Moby Dick will be what he wants it to be, Tarwater is one of the most challenging symbols of modern man who tries to see only the part of reality that he wants to see. His creator has won the right to be considered among the most creative critics of our time.

Robert McCown's brief essay on the reality of sin as portrayed in Flannery O'Connor's collection of short stories entitled *A Good Man Is Hard to Find* appeared in *The Catholic World* of January, 1959. Until that time critics had disguised their uncertainty over just what she could be up to by falling back on the condescending categories of the over-worked

*Reprinted from *Catholic World*, 190 (1960), 280-85, by permission of *New Catholic World*.

29

reviewer and labeling her "an interesting Southern stylist," or "promising young woman writer." With the publication of her third book there is now the very real possibility that they will go to the opposite extreme and disregard her art and concentrate excessively on her ideas.

There is also an even greater danger that Catholic critics, always on the lookout for the Catholic novel by a Catholic novelist, may be tempted to paraphrase her work into a piece of apologetics. The Southern critics, Tate, Ransom, Warren and others with whom Miss O'Connor has already been identified, have labored to define the heresy of the paraphrase, the belief that any paraphrase of the thought content of an art work can substitute for the work itself. This is a heresy to which the Catholic critic is particularly susceptible, and it would be particularly unfortunate if it were to crop up in the evaluation of Miss O'Connor's work for she has already said in print that the Catholic artist must adapt himself to the demands of art and not attempt to adapt his art to suit his propaganda. It is as a creative artist that she has worked out her techniques and her intuitions of the modern scene, and it is as an artist that she must be read and evaluated.

All of the South, as every average reader knows, is like Gaul, divided into three parts: the Magnolia South of the Civil War, costume romance; the Bayou South of decadent honor and Krafft-Ebing sin; and that last great battle ground of cultural conflict, Yoknapatawpha County. Miss O'Connor's South cannot be located anywhere on this distorted literary map, but it does seem typical of large sections of real-life Georgia and Tennessee — and of large sections of many other parts of the world where real people struggle with real emotions. It is the typical and essential which interest her, not the unique of abnormal psychology nor the encyclopedic detail of photographic realism. If in the past it has been possible to attribute her economy in the use of characters and setting to the demands of the short story form, some other explanation must now be found for her self-imposed limitations in this story to four main characters and three settings.

The important characters in *The Violent Bear It Away* are Tarwater, a kind of latter-day Huck Finn; his great-uncle Mason Tarwater, a kind of latter-day prophet; Rayber, a very up-to-date schoolteacher; and his son Bishop, an idiot. The story moves from Powderhead, a remote clearing in the Georgia hills where Tarwater has been reared by his great-uncle and preserved from the contamination of civilization, to the city where Rayber lives, and it reaches its climax at a run-down lakeside resort.

Miss O'Connor quickly involves her few characters in violent actions as she had in most of her short stories, but notably in "A Good Man Is Hard to Find." If she omits all the trivial acts of her main characters to concentrate on their important decisions and actions, it is because she wants to make her readers see to the essence of things, not stop at the outside. She is not afraid to call things by their right names because she has not avoided the "threatened intimacy of creation."

Her current novel begins at the point where Tarwater must decide on how he is going to see things, the way his great-uncle taught him or the way the schoolteacher says things are. The old man guaranteed the purity of his upbringing by keeping him out of school and teaching him "figures, reading, writing and history beginning with Adam expelled from the Garden and going on down through the presidents to Herbert Hoover, and on in speculation toward the Second Coming and the Day of Judgment." These were the things the old man claimed one had to know in order to understand the "hard facts of serving the Lord." All other knowledge was nothing. He felt about science the same way that Mr. Shiftlet, a character in Miss O'Connor's story "The Life You Save May Be Your Own," did about the doctor who had cut into the living heart: "Why, if he was to take that knife and cut into every corner of it, he still wouldn't know no more than you or me." True knowledge is intuitive, emotional as well as intellectual, not clinical and aseptic.

In an essay on "The Church and the Fiction Writer," published in *America* on March 30, 1957, Miss O'Connor quoted with approbation a remark which she attributed to Monsignor Romano Guardini to the effect that "the roots of the eye are in the heart." This is what the great-uncle has tried to teach Tarwater in the hope that he would grow up a prophet who would burn the schoolteacher's eyes clean. Just before he died he laid upon Tarwater the symbolic obligation of going forth and baptizing Rayber's idiot son.

Rayber is a more horrible reincarnation of Hulga, the female Ph.D. and self-professed scientist in Miss O'Connor's short story "Good Country People." Like Hulga he claims that he believes in nothing but the scientifically demonstrable, and they both discover that those who claim to have no illusions have the most. Rayber thinks of himself as the supreme rationalist who has so cauterized himself of all sentimentality that he can take pride in having procured for his sister her first lover—so that she could gain some self-confidence. Everything that goes into his head, and it must first pass through a hearing aid, symbolic of his contact with reality only through science, comes out quantified, a chart or a figure.

The old man had first tried to teach the teacher that there were some things that could not be quantified, that you couldn't grind "the Lord into your head and spit out a number." He thought he was making some headway until he discovered that the only reason the schoolteacher was interested in him was to write him up for a schoolteacher's magazine as an example of a nearly extinct breed of religious maniacs who thought they had a mission. The schoolteacher thought he had succeeded in his attempt to explain the old man away, "grind him into his head and spit out a number," when he wrote: "This fixation of being called by the Lord had its origin in insecurity. He needed the assurance of a call so he called himself." When the old man read this he gave Rayber up for lost and concentrated on rearing Tarwater to continue his mission.

This statement of the conflict between Rayber's quantitative view of reality and the old uncle's intuitive view of things is reminiscent of another Southern critic's interpretation of *King Lear*. In *This Great Stage*, Robert Heilman interprets the tragedy as the result of an attempt to impose on the world a rationalistic standard of values instead of recognizing the necessity of imaginative insight to an understanding of people.

At first Tarwater struggles to preserve his own identity and he does his best to avoid seeing things as his great-uncle saw them, for this would only force him to fulfill his symbolic mission and baptize Bishop. His main reason for holding out is that he cannot understand what happiness the old man hoped for after death. As soon as he died he wanted to "hasten to the banks of the Lake of Galilee to eat the loaves and fishes that the Lord had multiplied." Tarwater sensed that this was at the core of his great-uncle's madness and he was afraid that he might inherit it "so that nothing would heal or fill his stomach but the bread of life."

At the end of his adventure floating down the Mississippi, Huck Finn returns to Aunt Polly's civilization only with great reluctance because "I been there before." In her short story, "The Artificial Nigger," Miss O'Connor told of a trip a boy, Nelson, made to Atlanta with his grandfather. At the end of their adventures Nelson says, "I'm glad I've went once, but I'll never go back again." Like Huck and Nelson, Tarwater had been to the city of civilization before he flees there at his [great-uncle's] death. On his first trip he had "realized almost without warning, that this place was evil." His return is a proof of his desperate desire to avoid submission to his great-uncle's mission and testament. All through his stay he is unsatisfied with city food, "and his hunger had become like an insistent silent force inside him."

Rayber is delighted to take Tarwater in and to have an opportunity to refashion "the brand of independence the old man had wrought – not a constructive independence but one that was irrational, backwoods, and ignorant." This is the kind of independence grandparents try to teach their grandchildren in many of Miss O'Connor's stories.

Rayber plans to re-educate Tarwater. He decides to start at the very beginning "by introducing him to his ancestor the fish, and to tell the great wastes of unexplored time." His efforts to get close to the boy are pathetic, and he tries to rationalize the unbridgeable gulf between them in the same terms that had almost succeeded in explaining away the old man. He believes to the end that Tarwater is suffering from a false sense of guilt because he has thus far failed to baptize Bishop and that all he has to do is wait and Tarwater will come around. Little by little however Tarwater senses the sterility of Rayber's point of view and he taunts him for his scientism by referring to his hearing aid and asking, "Do you think in the box . . . or do you think in your head?" Rayber grows desperate and [begins] to use his idiot son as a lure to keep Tarwater around.

The portrayal of Bishop is as sympathetic as Miss O'Connor's portrayal of children in all her other stories. Children, like the unloved child in "The River," have a way of seeing things with a directness and simplicity which poses problems for adults who want to see reality just a little bit different from the way it really is. Bishop himself is a problem about which there can be two points of view. "Precious in the sight of the Lord," says the great-uncle; "a mistake of nature," says Rayber who once went so far as to attempt to rectify nature's error by trying to drown his son.

Rayber's normal way "of looking on Bishop was as an X signifying the general hideousness of fate. He did not believe that he himself was formed in the image and likeness of God but that Bishop was he had no doubt. The little boy was part of a simple equation that required no further solution, except at the moments when with little or no warning he would feel himself overwhelmed by the horrifying love."

It was a surge of this love which had come over him while he was trying to drown the idiot. This love, which was strong enough "to throw him to the ground in an act of idiot praise," cannot be accounted for in Rayber's philosophy. To him, "It was completely irrational and abnormal." Yet there it is, a part of reality which he cannot explain and which he could [not] change or deny.

But, as Tarwater comes to realize this is not the weakest part of Rayber's view of things. What finally turns him against the schoolteacherview is the realization that Rayber has not got the guts to do anything. All he has the guts for is not to do something. He cannot drown the child. All he can do is not baptize him. Just before the climactic event of the novel Tarwater sums up his indictment of Rayber and all he stands for. " 'You can't just say NO,' he said. 'You got to do NO. You got to show it, you got to show you mean it by doing it. You got to show you're not going to do one thing by doing another. You got to make an end of it. One way or the other.' "

Tarwater "does No," and makes an end of it just as forcefully as the Misfit in the author's story, "A Good Man Is Hard to Find." In any encounter between a merely verbal, distorted and distorting view of things, and an intuitive, committed view of reality—the violent bear all before them.

This time it is doubtful if any reviewer will refer to Tarwater's action as a "garish climax," as the *Saturday Review* once did to the climax of her story, "Greenleaf"; or as an act of "sardonic brutality," as *Time* did of the action of "A Good Man Is Hard to Find." It is now obvious that there is nothing "garish," "gratuitous," or "grotesque," about this novel, or about any of her other works for that matter.

Many aspects of her writing which have puzzled critics—her directness of phrasing, her reduction of character and setting to essentials, her avoidance of any hint of sentimentalizing—can now be understood as the direct consequence of the application to art of what might be called a "violent" view of reality. It is not really violent, but must only seem so to those accustomed to taking ambiguous positions or rationalizing all committed points of view away in Rayber terms. *Time* laughed off "A Good Man Is Hard to Find," as "slam-bang humor," and her first novel, *Wise Blood*, as "arty fumbling." Critics may try to get Miss O'Connor into their heads again and grind out some classification, but they will have as much trouble as Rayber did with great-uncle Tarwater.

In the end Tarwater learns what Miss O'Connor believes every artist and Catholic must, and humbles himself in the face of what is and what cannot be revised in the interests of any abstraction. He becomes convinced that the prophetic or violent view of reality is the only one which will satisfy his hunger and he accepts his mission to "go warn the children of God of the terrible speed of mercy." He returns for a third time, "toward the dark city, where the children of God lay sleeping," his "singed eyes, black in their deep sockets, seemed already to envision the fate that awaited him."

The best guarantee of remaining mediocre is to remain content with the vision of the eye which sees only the surface of things and tries to change what it cannot account for to suit itself. The best way to avoid mediocrity is to accept the violent consequences of the prophetic view of things as they are. Tarwater may fail to reawaken the sleeping children of God; the artist may fail to make people see into the nature of things as they are, but neither will ever be mistaken for mediocrity. The prophetic vision will never allow the shadow to fall "Between the conception / And the creation / Between the emotion / And the response" as it does in those whom T. S. Eliot—so long ago it seems—called "The Hollow Men." If there are enough of the violent to bear it away, then there is hope that the way the world ends is not with a whimper—nor a bang.

A Vision Deep and Narrow   Frank J. Warnke*

Flannery O'Connor's latest novel is built around a fairly complete collection of the stock materials of contemporary Southern fiction—the back-country farm, the fanatic old man, the twisted adolescent, even, God help us, the idiot child. It is in the line of Southern literary tradition in its general mode as well—psychological realism leavened by a pervasive allegorical potentiality. In short, it is very deeply a work of convention.

*Reprinted from *New Republic*, 14 March 1960, pp. 18–19. Reprinted by permission of the *New Republic*, © 1960, The New Republic, Inc., and of Frank J. Warnke.

The convention, however, is one which apparently matches Miss O'Connor's vision of life, and within it she creates a work of compelling power.

In a run-down shack in a forest clearing, the 14-year-old orphan Francis Marion Tarwater lives with his great-uncle, a religious fanatic who feels that he is a prophet called by the Lord to announce to the world its imminent doom. Old Tarwater has stolen the boy as an infant from his uncle, an atheist schoolteacher. When the prophet dies, at the beginning of the novel, he bequeaths to the boy the burden of his vocation, the duty of giving him Christian burial, and the task of baptizing the schoolteacher's idiot son. Young Tarwater, however, with no desire to play Elisha to the old man's Elijah, affirms his freedom by setting fire to the shack which he believes still holds the corpse and by running away to the city and his uncle.

Tarwater's quest for his own identity requires that he triumph in the two conflicts which then face him—conflict with Rayber, his uncle, who wants to re-make him in the image of his own sterile secularism, conflict with himself because of his irresistible compulsion to baptize the child. He wins the first battle decisively; he loses the second when, in a last desperate existential assertion, he drowns the child but finds the words of baptism spilling from his helpless mouth. Doomed already, he learns that his great-uncle has actually been given burial by a Negro neighbor, and the call to prophecy descends on him.

The "Southernness" of Miss O'Connor's work lies not only in her choice of materials and in the ritualistic resolution through violence but also in an intensely theological orientation. Like writers as diverse as Faulkner and R. P. Warren, Miss O'Connor is concerned above all with the misery of man without God. Her development of the theme is not simple: Rayber's atheism is presented as empty and futile, but at the same time the prophetic vocation of the old man and the boy is seen as destructive and mad. The old man has, as Rayber says, "called himself," and Miss O'Connor's prose suggests in his calling an alienation from divinity almost as complete as Rayber's: "He proclaimed from the midst of his fury that the world would see the sun burst in blood and fire and while he raged and waited, it rose every morning, calm and contained in itself, as if not only the world, but the Lord Himself had failed to hear the prophet's message." The cruelly distorted symbols of blood and fire which permeate the novel suggest further horrors in the old man's obsession, and the allegorical implication of the book's climax—a mad and murderous John the Baptist baptizing an idiot Christ—embodies an almost unbearable view of the predicament of modern man.

The vision, however distressing, is a powerful and deeply-felt one. It would be more powerful if the cards were distributed a bit more fairly. For, if we can accept the Tarwaters as a convincing version of certain desperately driven religious men (and it is hard not to accept such vigorous and finely-detailed characterizations), we cannot really accept Rayber as anything, least of all as the embodiment of secular humanism — a creed which, whatever its aesthetic shortcomings, does not lead inevitably to paralysis of the emotions. One suspects, in Rayber, a straw man, and his dry rustlings do not make it any easier to go along with Miss O'Connor's persistent suggestion — that the Tarwaters, however misled and doomed they are, are somehow closer to the vital principles of freedom and passion than is the atheist. It won't work.

Flannery O'Connor's gifts as a novelist go beyond stylistic felicity. She penetrates the tortured minds of her characters with sympathy and, occasionally, even rueful humor. But the final impression the book leaves, for all its great virtues, is one of crankiness and provincialism. Why? Does it have something to do with a national conviction that only violent actions performed by ignorant and underprivileged people are "real" enough to write about? Does it have something to do with that vision which has always haunted our imagination — of a man utterly alone trying to discover his relationship to God and reality? Does it perhaps suggest that our culture itself is cranky and provincial? The questions are pertinent, but I suppose it's ungrateful, when there are so many bad novels around, to let them be raised by a good one.

Everything That Rises Must Converge

Flannery O'Connor   Warren Coffey[*]

We now have all the work by which Flannery O'Connor will be remembered in the world. Of her last stories, collected in *Everything That Rises Must Converge*, it is certainly the just praise, and maybe the highest after all, that they are up to her first ones. She wrote best in the short story and has left a handful of them at least that are likely to last as long as literacy. When she died at thirty-nine last year, it was with her work done, I think, and work of an imaginative order and brilliance rare in the world at most times, perhaps always in American writing. Her friend, Robert Fitzgerald, has added to the book an introduction that gives at once an intelligent assessment of her work and a view of the harrowing human cost that always has to be paid for writing with the grainy toughness and originality of Flannery O'Connor's. She died of lupus, the blood disease that had also killed her father. Her doctors diagnosed it in 1950 when she was twenty-five and were able to stop it for a time, first with ACTH and then with something even newer than that. But she was forced to go and live on her mother's farm in Milledgeville, Georgia, and in her last years, it was hospitals, ACTH, crutches, gradual wasting, the hospital, a coma, and on August 3, 1964, death. In what appears to have been her one concession to the literary personality, she raised peacocks. But more than any other writer of her generation, she went her own way, and she sent out of Georgia in those years two collections of stories, *A Good Man Is Hard to Find* in 1955, and now *Everything That Rises Must Converge*, that contain some of the surest and most original comic writing ever done by an American.

Her novels are another matter. They suffer, I think, from an excessive violence of conception. They are the children of a rape or, better, of a five-months birth, on their way to being something perhaps very fine, but not there yet. *Wise Blood*, which she brought out in 1952, seems more the work of somebody who has a Master's degree in creative writing from the University of Iowa in pocket — as she had — than a book that has seen its

*Reprinted from *Commentary*, November 1965, pp. 93–99, by permission; all rights reserved. Also by permission of Kathleen M. Coffey.

way to saying something. Though the early train scenes have some wildly comic writing, the book as a whole seems as much a product of the determination to write a full-length novel as of anything more august. Ford Madox Ford used to say that nobody should be permitted to write a novel before forty. He was right, of course, and somebody should see to the whole matter, perhaps the Congress. Mistakes about it cost dearly. (Norman Mailer comes to mind, who is now ready to write *The Naked and the Dead*.)

Flannery O'Connor's other novel, *The Violent Bear It Away*, has passages of great and strange beauty—the scenes toward the end, for example, leading up to young Tarwater's walk back to the city—but it makes a mistake that the stories never make: the vehicle plainly does not fit the tenor. The whole novel is based on the idea that young Tarwater has inherited a compulsion to baptize from his mad preacher uncle. At the level of metaphor, the idea is entirely sound: large numbers of people do wish to convert us to their beliefs, i.e., to *baptize* us. But concretely and physically, where metaphor should have its base, it ceases entirely to work, for nobody inherits, I think, and very few acquire, this compulsion to push other persons under water. And it is on a physical drowning, a literal baptizing, that all of *The Violent Bear It Away* centers. I honor the Flannery O'Connor novels. They are mistakes of a promise that nobody else could have managed, and they have passages of great brilliance. But her strength was at the epiphany (a term of Joyce's now unfortunately become jargon), the leading of the reader up to a dazzling revelation in a moment of time or away from that moment on the waves of its resonance. "Good Country People" is an example of the one and "Revelation" of the other. For the longer stretches of time and the wider range required of the novel, she did not have the gift.

Aside from her years at the University of Iowa and a short time in New York and Connecticut, Flannery O'Connor lived her whole life in Georgia, though it is well to remember that the lupus had a lot to do with keeping her there toward the end of her life. She once expressed a desire to go out to California to press her researches into vulgarity, but on the whole she was a rooted Southerner. Louis D. Rubin saw her once at a meeting of writers where she was asked "how she felt, as a Southerner, to be writing in the shadow of William Faulkner." And he has recorded her wonderfully laconic reply: "Well, nobody likes to get caught on the tracks when the Dixie Flyer comes through." Faulkner's *As I Lay Dying* was apparently one of a few books she pressed on friends. And her debt to Faulkner is plain, mainly I should say in her refusal to deal with life in abstractions and in her power with regional detail—clay roads, stands of pine, barns, and so forth—and the gritty concreteness of language that are the badge in narrative and in style of that refusal. Her "major" at the Woman's College of Georgia had been the social sciences, and yet in her books to speak the bright language of those studies is infallibly the sign of the fool and generally of the knave as well. In this way, Flannery O'Connor was, I suppose, a Southern writer. The South gave her her terrain and the people she wrote about first and last. And William Faulkner gave her a start at a way of treating them. But her way of seeing them was her own and would have been the same, I think, if she had lived in North Dakota or Nova Zembla. Her writing is so different from that of the other Faulknerians — so different from that of Capote, for example, or the even more girlish Williams — that one is taken even less far than usual by labels like "Southern" or "Faulknerian" when talking about her books.

She owed almost as much, I should say, to Ring Lardner and Nathanael West as to Faulkner. To Ring Lardner, the satirist's trick of catching cliché as it falls and freezes the banality of a life or mind. ("If I can help a person, all I want is to do it. I'm above and beyond simple pettiness," one of her social workers says.) What we hear is the oiliness of that. We hear our attitude. The satirist hears and freezes on the page what is said. Much of Ring Lardner's writing is journeyman stuff, but in four or five stories he proved what nobody would have ventured to imagine: that the methods of classical English satire, the methods of Swift, worked for American life too. He proved that if you let those ball-players and song-writers and movie-stars talk in their own accents for very long they would explode themselves more shatteringly than anybody could hope to do from the outside. Starting from there — and it tells us something of her independence that she should have started with somebody as much out of fashion as Ring Lardner — Flannery O'Connor went on to make merry with the pretensions of social workers and intellectuals and anxious mothers and wives of Dixie hog-farmers. With an ear as fine as Lardner's own for dialect and for the way of a man with a cliché, Flannery O'Connor had what is even rarer, a conscious and austere control of the art of the story. She avoids the wandering and the sprawl that are the inherent dangers of Lardner's method — however racily the ball-player talks, he often becomes tedious in his brainlessness and illiteracy — by always telling her stories in her own person and thus staying on top of her matter.

Nathanael West's *Miss Lonelyhearts* was another of the books, Robert Fitzgerald tells us, that Flannery O'Connor used to press on her friends. And her debt here, though not plain, is again extensive. To extreme and painful situations she brought, as West did, a great deal of mocking ironic poise. If she has no girls without noses, she has them with artificial legs and with acne-blued faces. She has one-armed men and men covered with tattoos, and she is fond of thrusting this grotesque part of humanity into confrontations with characters more comfortably housed in the flesh. Her purpose in all this, and West's, is not, I think, that of the Fat Boy in Dickens: "I wants to make your flesh creep." Rather, these violent confrontations and the violent action that grows out of them show her willingness to take a chance on the assertion that behind the grotesquerie and violence a God presides. West, using the same surreal methods, questioned that assertion. Miss O'Connor's success in making hers stick in a literary way varies a good deal, from stories like "A Temple of the Holy Ghost," which strikes me as rather pat and wan, up through such later brilliant successes as "The Enduring Chill" and "Revelation." The latter is, oddly, her most Westian story. It takes place in a doctor's waiting room and involves a righteous hog-farmer's wife and a fat Wellesley girl with a messy case of acne and an anxious mother. The farmer's wife rattles on, for all the world like Robert Burns's Holy Willie, about God's special favors to her: "If it's one thing I am . . . it's grateful. When I think who all I could have been besides myself, and what all I got, a little of everything, and a good disposition besides, I just feel like shouting, 'Thank you, Jesus, for making everything the way it is.' " The Wellesley girl listens to many minutes of this and then breaks down all over the room, exploding into manic pain and hatred and screaming, "Go back to hell where you came from, you old wart hog." For her pains, she gets a shot in the arm and a trip to the mental ward. This much is out of Nathanael West, but the resolution of the story is Flannery O'Connor's own. The hog-farmer's wife is brought to ask for the first time if 180 pounds of flesh as comfortably appointed as hers can really be headed for hell. The story ends with her being carried out on the waves of that question. Nathanael West has greater range and greater knowledge of the world, but he does not, I think, cut this deep. Flannery O'Connor had from him the daring to face big questions and part of the technical dash to get them stated in fiction, but her way of resolving them was her own.

She was — that rare thing among Catholic writers in this century — a Catholic born. The Catholicism never gets stated in her stories, but it is always assumed, and it always glimmers in the distance as a kind of unwritten and implied *Paradiso* for the dark comic goings-on in the stories themselves. As an American Catholic, Flannery O'Connor was, of course, a Jansenist. (In America, an occasional Italian escapes this, but not enough to count; the Irish never, at least in my experience — though the late President Kennedy seems to have carried very dashingly whatever Jansenist scars he might have had.) At the end of her life, she liked to read the books of Teilhard de Chardin, one of which provided the title for *Everything That Rises Must Converge*. But her mind and imagination were formed long before this and by teachers less bland. The intellectual source of Catholic Jansenism, so far as it has one, is Pascal, the greatest mind the Catholic Church produced in its last encounter with the world. In order to attack the scientific rationalisms of his century, he had to point to the abyss of spirit they had blithely opened, and in order to attack the pride that he thought animated them, he had to carry further than most Catholic thinkers had done the idea of human depravity. Man's intellect was an abyss of pride and the affections of his heart corrupt. He was saved from his puniness in a universe vaster than he dared to imagine only by the wonderful mercy of God, on whom Pascal is driven to make his desperate wager of faith. This Jansenism has taken many forms in the world and got around in it a good deal. The most famous variant of it is the Irish one, and the most plausible explanation of how it spread and took hold there is that of Sean O'Faolain, who sees it as having been brought over by exiled priests of the *ancien régime* at the time of the Revolution and installed in Irish seminaries such as Maynooth, with the connivance of the British masters of Ireland and in return for assurances of the political conservatism of the clergy. There, supposedly in response to something in the Irish character itself, depravity becomes identified with sex and sin almost coextensive with sexual sin. And in this form Jansenism reached America with the immigrants. I have gone a long way from Flannery O'Connor and Milledgeville, Georgia, in all this, and yet I think that Jansenism, more than anything else, explains both her very considerable power at the short story and her limitations. The pride of intellect, the corruption of the heart, the horror of sex — all these appear again and again in her books, and against them, the desperate assertion of faith.

Out of these themes grows the paradigm story, for Flannery O'Connor, like most authors, had a paradigm story which she wrote again and again, in her case a kind of morality play in which Pride of Intellect (usually Irreligion) has a shattering encounter with the Corrupt Human Heart (the Criminal, the Insane, sometimes the Sexually Demonic) and either sees the light or dies, sometimes both. "The Lame Shall Enter First," which is perhaps a better paradigm than story anyway, will illustrate. We meet a social worker named Sheppard — *shepherd*, I suppose, though the author once wrote to a professor of English who had asked about the symbol-value of one of her characters' names, "As for Mrs. May, I must have named her that because I knew some English teacher would write and ask me why." Sheppard, who disbelieves in God and the devil, has undertaken to rehabilitate the thieving club-footed Rufus Johnson by taking the boy into his own household, buying a new shoe for the bad foot, and providing access to the *Encyclopaedia Britannica*. Johnson, who at fourteen boasts of his possession by Satan, is the corrupt human heart that Flannery O'Connor saw as beyond the reach of any therapy but the grace of God. He steals, peeps into windows, lies, smashes up houses, dances in Sheppard's dead wife's girdle, and — just at the point where Sheppard admits the failure of therapy — drives his would-be benefactor's son to suicide and goes off insisting to the police that Sheppard had made sexual advances to him.

That is the paradigm, and though not all the stories are written to it, not even all the best ones, a good many are and the point, I think, is that God gets asserted out of the abyss of the human heart. "The Lame Shall Enter First" is itself a reworking of *The Violent Bear It Away*, where the paradigm may also be seen. Variations of it appear in "Revelation" and "The Enduring Chill," where Irreligion appears as mere Conventional Religiousness — low-on-the-hog Protestantism in the one and high-tea

Catholicism in the other. The Corrupt Heart can become a pathological killer—the Misfit in "A Good Man Is Hard to Find," or a shifty Bible salesman in "Good Country People" or a whore in "The Comforts of Home." In a somewhat lower key, the redneck grandfather in "The Artificial Nigger" is appalled to discover himself capable of telling a lie denying kinship with his own grandson.

Though I have dwelt at some length on the horror of sex as an element in American Jansenism and in Flannery O'Connor's books, I do not wish to overstate this, because it seems to me that her record in the whole matter is better than that of almost any Catholic writer of the century. "Good Country People" is a story a man would give his right arm to have written. Manley Pointer, an itinerant Bible salesman, leads Hulga Hopewell, a thirty-two-year-old Ph.D. in philosophy—she tells him she is only thirty, a great stroke—into a barn, where, after not quite seducing her, he steals her wooden leg. Sex here is both terrible and wildly funny. Yet "Good Country People" alone among the Flannery O'Connor stories explodes out of the kind of encounter between a man and a woman that Chekhov thought of as the most basic of human and fictional situations. For the rest, she has so many stories about households with feuding mothers and daughters or mothers and sons that her work, read in the aggregate, begins to take on the repressed, house-bound quality that life has in that Irish Jansenism I have talked about, the exact thing that Joyce planted a bomb under in *Portrait of the Artist* and sent a burying party to deal with in "The Dead." Outside of "Good Country People," even in it for that matter, sex generally has something of the demonic about it for Flannery O'Connor—the homosexual attack on young Tarwater in *The Violent Bear It Away*, for example, or the club-footed boy leering in at windows in "The Lame Shall Enter First."

In talking of her obsession with human corruption, I have not wanted to suggest that Flannery O'Connor spent all her evenings or even any of them with the volumes of Pascal. She often insisted, though, that she was Catholic of the old school and made no bones about her disdain of those who would make of religion a set of symbols with perhaps a certain literary use in the world. Her mind and imagination were formed in the Catholicism preached from American pulpits, taught in parochial schools, and whispered in confessionals. Her story, "The Enduring Chill," has a wry, affectionate portrait of a Father Finn which hits off beautifully the type that American Jansenism has so often produced. He is the type that American seminaries appear for many years to have bred and, on the whole, it was not a bad choice. Father Finn is half-blind and half-deaf, and has a grease-spot on his vest. He has no intellectual attainments, but he is kindly and morally serious. Men like him kept the faith and dispensed the sacraments, the offices in which they chiefly shine, through the wreck of faith in the 19th century when even so great a collector of lost causes as Matthew Arnold abandoned that of religion as impossibly lost.

When they have tried to raise this Jansenism to intellectual expression, however, they have generally fared less well. The books of the American Jesuit critic Fr. Harold Gardiner are an example. Writers are all right with Fr. Gardiner, or mostly so, if they observe the Sixth and the Ninth Commandments.[1] This is sometimes called Fr. Gardiner's Range. Writers observe these two Commandments when they represent copulation as taking place on weekdays, outside of Lent, in months with an R in them, with one's wife in a received Western position, without looking. I may have left something out, but it is many years since I have been able to get through any of Fr. Gardiner's books. The scheme seems overly simple, and I admit there is an element of caricature in it, but what has always astonished me about Catholic writing in this century is that, despite the subtle minds it has produced (Mauriac, for example) and the formidably accomplished writers (Waugh, for example), it has always taken essentially Fr. Gardiner's view of sex (with Ford Madox Ford the one considerable exception). More than anything else, this horror of sex has robbed Catholic writing of the range, the sanity, and the shrewd and generous humanity that it had when Geoffrey Chaucer rang for the last time the great Catholic bell and rang it in plague-time too.

Some years ago, and before he went on to higher things, Conor Cruise O'Brien wrote an acute book of literary criticism, *Maria Cross*, in which he dealt with recurring "imaginative patterns" in eight Catholic writers — Mauriac, Bernanos, Greene, Waugh, and others, all of them worlds removed from Flannery O'Connor. Her writing in general owes almost nothing to theirs, though Manley Pointer has something perhaps of Waugh's Basil Seal about him. So it is the more remarkable to find behind Miss O'Connor's writing the exact pattern that O'Brien has found behind that of her European fellow Catholics and near contemporaries: a pattern of intense and incommunicable pain arising from sex and transformed by religion into art. It is, of course, a Jansenist art, and it arises this way: "Man remains nailed to his mother. When he seeks to break loose, to find 'paradise' in loving another woman, he becomes aware of his crucifixion. Crucifixion — in which the cross [the woman] suffers equally with the sacrifice [the man] — is punished for being the cross, is the only form of love." All the writers that O'Brien was talking about were men, but when the necessary changes have been made, his idea will work for Flannery O'Connor's books too. O'Brien says further of these writers: "Through their acceptance of the holy mysteries, of the cross, they turn what might have been — what is, perhaps, in many — a private and incommunicable suffering, into public utterance and communion with others. . . . The individual's private suffering partakes of, is the same as, the general sufferings of humanity. The sense of history reaches the writer not intellectually, through the acceptance of a program — as with a Stalin prizeman — but from below, through all the deepest feelings which animate his work." As surely as it is behind the comic writing of Waugh, this pattern is also behind the comic writing of Flannery O'Connor. The pain and the acceptance of pain are behind the art, which is where they surely belong, not in it. This it is that enables Waugh to take the long view, to write with immense comic assurance of the most painful kinds of human experience — death itself, for example, or cannibalism for that matter. In the same way, Flannery O'Connor fits into a comic view of the world such things as manic killers, deformed bodies, intense hatreds, and violent deaths. With all of this, her comic art, like Waugh's, is able to live as merry as cup and can. The one thing that both of them find too terrible in the world to contemplate is ordinary sexual experience, love as anything other than a crucifixion — though it must be granted that both writers are admirably open when put against a Mauriac or a Graham Greene.

Lawrence Durrell has written somewhere that D. H. Lawrence had one important idea, the idea of a good lay, but had made the mistake of trying to build the Taj Mahal around it. James Joyce had more than one idea but nonetheless built *Ulysses* around the same one, the *yesses* at the end. To spiritualize sex, as Lawrence does, or to give it an importance it does not have, as Joyce does, is no less a mistake than the Jansenist insistence that it is not there at all, or if it is, that it is too painful to contemplate. Henry Miller is closer to sanity in the whole matter, I think, and I mean specifically the low comedy sex episodes in a few of his books, not the lowing that arises when he begins to think world thoughts. We have here the spectacle of three writers variously gifted but all in full flight from historical Christianity — Joyce from Irish Jansenism, Lawrence from English Dissenting Protestantism, and Miller from German-American Lutheranism. What they are all fleeing is the Jansenist or Calvinist — and they come to much the same thing — nightmare of sex. It is more than a remarkable fact that they found it necessary to do so. To do their work, they needed to connect with ordinary life over a range of experience that the Christianity they knew did not permit. They have surely made their own mistakes, but Catholic writing has much to learn from them. Pascal himself has a sentence that fits the case: "Greatness is not displayed by standing at one extremity but rather by touching both ends at once and filling all the space between." A Chaucer managed it, for a time at least, but of course there are not many of those. On the other hand, there is no reason to close off the possibility. *Ab esse ad posse* is an argument that keeps its force. Catholic writing has often had in this century great austerity and control, as it has again in the stories of Flannery O'Connor. It can never make peace with the world, but I think at last it is going to have to make its peace with Henry Miller. The cost of not doing so is the loss of range and humanity and the retreat to an ever more waspish perfection in ever smaller literary forms. That is the direction in which Flannery O'Connor's writing sometimes fails. "The Comforts of Home," for example, does "Good Country People" over in reverse gear, which is more ingenious than efficient. And *Everything That Rises Must Converge*, which has excellent and varied stories, has none as raucously funny as "The Artificial Nigger" or "The Life You Save May Be Your Own" in her earlier collection. She would not go wider than her ground, and nobody could have gone deeper there.

She had done her work, I think, when she died and done it very well. It is all native stone of her own quarry. She found the human heart a pretty dark place, as most writers have done who have cared to look very long. But she was not a hater, and she never trafficked in despair. She did much of her writing with death more or less in the next room but went on until she had sent into the world the tough and brilliant comic stories of which all readers now become, in an old formula, the heirs and assigns forever. "Nothing is here for tears . . . nothing but well and fair."

Note

1. According to Jewish and Protestant teaching, these would be the Seventh and Tenth Commandments. [*Commentary* ed.]

If You Know Who You Are You Can Go Anywhere
Richard Poirier*

Short of any posthumous publication, these are the last stories we shall have from Flannery O'Connor. She died last summer at 39 in Milledgeville, Ga., a town where her family, old Georgian Catholic, has lived since before the Civil War. The introduction by her friend Robert Fitzgerald is thus understandably dedicatory, and yet it makes none of the excessive claims for her place in contemporary American literature that are always the anticipated embarrassment on such occasions. With respect to her work, the introduction observes what she herself would have considered a fitting humility. "To know oneself," she remarked in 1957, "is, above all, to know what one lacks. It is to measure oneself against Truth, and not the other way around. The first product of self-knowledge is humility." "Measuring" of this kind is characteristic of her Catholicism, and of Mr. Fitzgerald's too, who tells us of their going daily to Mass during the months in 1949–50 when Miss O'Connor lived with the Fitzgeralds in Connecticut. His essay has clarity braced against exaggeration — which, as much as anything else, is evidence of his affectionate knowledge of the person and her work.

Humility in the claims made for oneself, for what one knows and

*Reprinted from *New York Times Book Review*, 30 May 1965, pp. 6, 22. © 1965 by The New York Times Company. Reprinted by permission. Also by permission of Richard Poirier.

values, is in fact the operative standard within the stories. Pride makes a fool at some time or other of nearly all of her characters. It gets expressed not grandly but within the grotesqueries of daily, mostly Southern life, and within simple people who are aware of no alternatives to that life, once pride is destroyed, except death or a strange God.

Everything that rises must indeed converge, joining the anonymity either of oblivion or the blessed. The pride of her characters may be for a new hat, a bit of money, a college degree or clean hogs; it is her particular genius to make us believe that there are Christian mysteries in things irreduceably banal. And in this too there is an aspect of Catholicism, most beautifully exemplified in the penultimate stanza of the "Paradiso," where Dante likens his poetic efforts in fashioning a vision of God to the work of a "good tailor."

Her characters seem damned precisely to the degree that they lack Miss O'Connor's own "measure" of their trivialities. They have no measure for them *but* pride, and they can therefore appeal for authority only to mundane standards that never threaten it, to platitudes and to prejudices, very often racial ones. Necessarily, she is a mordantly comic writer. She offers us the very sounds of platitude ("If you know who you are you can go anywhere," remarks the mother to her intellectualist son in the title story), or of prejudice (as in the imagined dialogue with God of the pretentious lady in "Revelation," who would have asked Him to make her anything but white trash: " 'All right make me a nigger, then — but that don't mean a trashy one.' And he would have made her a neat clean respectable Negro woman, herself but black.")

Except for sloth, pride is of all human failings the one that can be most difficult for a writer to translate into actions. Most often it expresses itself in a smugness of *in*action, the hostilities it creates in others being the result merely of the tones of voice, the gestures, the placidities which are its evidence. Miss O'Connor can produce as much violence from a quiet conversation as can other writers from the confrontations of gangsters or fanatics, though she can manage that, too.

The action in the best of these stories, "Revelation," is to a large extent dialogue, in which the veritable sounds of people talking gently in a doctor's office about everything from the heat to the ingratitude of children leads to a sudden but somehow expected flare-up of violence and disaster. With very little room for maneuver — most of her stories are about 20 pages long — she achieves transitions and even reversals of tone with remarkable speed, and she can show in people who have been almost preposterously flat a sudden visionary capacity. This absolute sureness of timing is, I think, what makes the reader assent to the religious direction which her stories take: from involvement in the most common stuff they move toward the Heaven and the Hell weirdly apprehended by her characters.

Miss O'Connor's major limitation is that the direction of her stories tends to be nearly always the same. [Caring almost nothing for secular destinies, which are altogether more various than religious ones, she propels her characters toward the cataclysms where alone they can have a tortured glimpse of the need and chance of redemption.] The repetitiousness inherent in her vision of things is more bothersomely apparent in this collection than anyone would have guessed who read the various pieces over the interval of their periodical publication.

Story after story here and in her other fiction — "Wise Blood," "A Good Man is Hard to Find," "The Violent Bear It Away" — involves a conflict between parental figures and recalcitrant, precocious, generally snotty children aged anywhere from 8 to 36. The local result of this conflict is dialogue that comically mixes the parent's cant of "understanding" with muttering from children that has the velocity of a thrown knife. The ultimate result is usually the murder or suicide of one of the conflicting parties, often bringing with it some sort of distorted religious vision.

Of the nine stories in this present volume the casualty list is heavily parental. In "Everything That Rises Must Converge," a mother dies in the arms of her remorseful son. In "Greenleaf," a mother is killed by a bull — not with the connivance but partly because of the irresponsibility of her bachelor sons.

In "A View of the Woods," a grandfather dies of a heart attack after physical combat with a 9-year-old granddaughter whom he can subdue only by strangulation. In "The Enduring Chill," a son comes home to die but is kept alive, much to his distaste, by a mother who will probably kill him with her conversation.

In "Judgement Day," a father, staying with his daughter in New York, wants to die so that he can be taken back to Georgia — and achieves this ambition, partly by provoking a Negro into abusing him much as does the woman in "Everything That Rises." In "Revelation," an older lady is struck on the head by a book and then assaulted by a Wellesley girl, home from vacation, while she is telling the girl's mother that sometimes "I just feel like shouting, 'Thank you, Jesus, for making everything the way it is!' " In "The Comforts of Home," a mother is shot by her bachelor son who is aiming instead, maybe, at the convict girl whom she has introduced into the household. In "The Lame Shall Enter First," a son, wanting to find his dead mother in the heavens, hangs himself at the instigation of a convict boy to whom his father is proud of showing "kindness."

In one sense, Miss O'Connor's repetitiousness is an indication of how serious a writer she is. As against what might be called writers by occupation (who can of course always "pick" their subjects) she was obsessed by arrangements of life and language in which she saw some almost eschatological possibilities. [And her religious commitment is the more powerful in determining the shape of her stories precisely because it is never made overt merely in rhetoric.] It exists, as strong commitments often do, in a form unspoken, inseparable from the very processes of her sight and feeling. She may be the only writer of English or American fiction in this century whose style, down to the very placing of a comma, is derived from a religious feeling for the simplest actualities. Obviously, being a religious writer in this way is different from anything in, say, Graham Greene, who merely lugs theological rhetoric into stories that were by nature best left as mildly entertaining adventures.

I cannot describe her very rare distinctions in this vein more clearly than she did in an essay called "The Fiction Writer and His Country": "I see," she wrote, "from the standpoint of Christian orthodoxy. This means that for me the meaning of life is centered in our Redemption by Christ and that what I see in the world I see in relation to that." To see the world from such a standpoint means caring about the possibilities of Redemption literally in what one sees, in the grossest things, and it is no wonder, therefore, that she has such a sharp eye for the grotesqueness and the pathos of the most ordinary vanities. But the test is in the reading and for that nothing better illustrates her intensely applied power than the story "Revelation." It belongs with the few masterpieces of the form in English.

Mystery and Manners

[The Limits of Explanation]

Frederick Asals*

Flannery O'Connor was no critical theorist and had no pretensions to being one. Her essays and lectures, gathered together by Sally and Robert Fitzgerald from both published and (apparently with exasperating difficulty) unpublished material, witness as strongly to her distrust of the pure intellect, wrapped away in abstraction, as do her stories and novels. Neither, on the other hand, was she given to commentary on her fellow writers, living or dead. All but one of these essays is about fiction, but fiction as seen from the standpoint of the practicing writer with her own particular concerns and problems. Their most interesting ideas are the fruit of reflection on her imaginative struggles to turn the convergence of Catholicism, the South, and her own ruthlessly comic eye into the stuff of art.

She once spoke of herself as a writer "congenitally innocent of theory," but of course she operated on certain assumptions about the nature and demands of fiction, assumptions that are readily identifiable as post-Jamesian or modernist. This seems clear enough from the fiction itself, but her remarks to writing classes and secondary school teachers make it explicit: fiction is essentially dramatic, it must show and not tell, meaning is inseparable from form, which in all good stories arises organically, and so on. Given the nature of the audiences and the fact that these pieces were not intended for general publication, it would be unfair to O'Connor to tote up the commonplaces and charge them against her. Even these lectures are frequently leavened by her wit and good sense and insight, and only the churlish might suggest that the editors, who were at pains to cull them from the chaos of her manuscripts, should not have bothered. It is good to have all the occasional works between two covers, but, with some significant exceptions, the finest and most stimulating remain her article on peacocks, "The Fiction Writer and His Country," "Some Aspects of the Grotesque in Southern Fiction," and the Introduction to A Memoir of Mary Ann, all available previously.

*Reprinted from "Flannery Row," Novel, 4 (1970), 92–96, by permission of Novel and Frederick Asals.

That these essays have not lacked readers is evidenced by much of the critical commentary on O'Connor. It has become depressingly commonplace to use her own words to account for her fiction, to assume that she is not only the creator of her works, but the final authority on them as well. A rather unfortunate example is Carter W. Martin's *The True Country*, the first book-length study of the fiction. . . .

Now there is some reason for such subservience, which is by no means limited to Martin's book. Aside from the caution one exercises in dismissing or reversing any writer's comments on his own work, O'Connor's public pronouncements are so direct and unpretentious, so free from cant and filled with quiet assurance, that they fairly disarm our native suspiciousness. These essays often glow with her fine awareness, and many of their passages *are* genuinely illuminating of the fiction. Unlike Faulkner, she did not (to use the polite term) "mythologize" her role or her works in her remarks on them. Still, there are limits to an undiscriminating reliance on any writer's self-explanations. What is more, the careful reader of *Mystery and Manners* will discover that at different times she takes quite different positions on the same topic, positions which, if they are not precisely contradictory, at least lead in very different directions. The critic needs to do some sorting out.

A case in point is the crucial issue of the grotesque in her work. In her best known essay, "The Fiction Writer and His Country," published in 1957, she attributes the "distortions" in her fiction to her need to disturb the uncomprehending slumber of a secularized and therefore "hostile" audience: "When you can assume that your audience holds the same beliefs you do, you can relax a little and use more normal means of talking to it; when you have to assume that it does not, then you have to make your vision apparent by shock — to the hard of hearing you shout, and for the almost-blind you draw large and startling figures." This is only the earliest of several passages in these essays that dismiss the violence and grotesqueness of the fiction as rhetorical strategy, a mere "means of talking to" one's audience. Flannery O'Connor is the first of the defenders of her work — the followers have been legion — who seem to feel that its wildness needs explaining away, or at least tidying up, as an "inessential" feature attributable to an unsympathetic audience rather than to the exigencies of her own imagination.

No doubt she was mistrustfully conscious, perhaps at times overly conscious, of an audience she assumed to be "hostile," yet her real relation to that audience seems more accurately expressed by some later passages in these lectures. Considering the problem of how to please both the "average" and the "intelligent" reader, she suddenly remarks, "actually, both of these readers are just aspects of the writer's own personality, and in the last analysis, the only reader he can know anything about is himself. We all write at our own level of understanding. . . ." One writes as one must; the serious fiction writer "writes neither for everybody, nor for the special few, but for the good of what he is writing . . . the writer whose vocation is fiction sees his obligation as being to the truth of what can happen in life, and not to the reader — not to the reader's taste, not to the reader's happiness, not even to the reader's morals." That any writer is deeply and inevitably affected by the entire fabric of his age, including the quality and expression of its religious beliefs, is a truism, but it is also quite another matter from attributing the essential properties of his work to the projected nature of an assumed audience. As an accounting for the grotesqueness of O'Connor's fiction, the reader-in-need-of-shock-therapy hypothesis explains both too much and too little.

Two passages, near the beginning and end of *Mystery and Manners*, allow for some rather obvious general reflections on the grotesque. At the opening of her article on peacocks, she recalls that when she was five years old Pathé News had sent a photographer to take pictures of a chicken of hers which could walk both forward and backward. She continues: "From that day with the Pathé man I began to collect chickens. What had been only a mild interest became a passion, a quest. I had to have more and more chickens. I favored those with one green eye and one orange or with overlong necks and crooked combs. I wanted one with three legs or three wings but nothing in that line turned up. I pondered over the picture in Robert Ripley's book, *Believe It or Not*, of a rooster that had survived for thirty days without his head; but I did not have a scientific temperament." For all its amused tone, this reminiscence surely makes unmistakable what should not need pointing out: that beyond and beneath any uses or meanings she turned it to, the grotesque was native to the grain of Flannery O'Connor's imagination, not an incidental excrescence or a rhetorical device, but the heart of her vision, a part of the very way in which she perceived the world. The unerring eye for the off-center, the delight in the vulgar, the cool fascination with the horrifying and inexplicable, which is suddenly flicked to a comedy even more frightening in its extensions — brief as it is, the passage suggests the distinguishing features of the fiction.

It is perhaps worth stressing the relish, the delight — the zest — in her apprehension of the grotesque, for another passage from "The Fiction Writer and His Country" has been the source of further misunderstanding: "My own feeling is that writers who see by the light of their Christian faith will have, in these times, the sharpest eyes for the grotesque, for the perverse, and for the unacceptable." The clear implication here (reinforced by the context of this sentence) is that the final three terms are interchangeable. *Ergo*, any O'Connor character who can be identified as grotesque is as good as hung with a placard proclaiming "Irreligious Sinner." Matters are of course neither so mechanical nor so simple, as even the briefest glance at the fiction shows: Hazel Motes is as grotesque in his penitential devotions at the end of *Wise Blood* as he was in his earlier blasphemy, and the recognition that *all* of the major characters of *The*

Violent Bear It Away are "grotesques" does not even begin to sort out their various significances in that novel. And this leads us to the second exemplary passage, the single clause that opens the final selection of *Mystery and Manners:* "We're all grotesque." Between the basic observation that the grotesque vision is a part of O'Connor's native equipment as a writer and this most sweeping of all "meanings" that denies the human condition wholeness this side of the grave lies almost everything interesting that she made of the grotesque in her work, but these seem to me to mark off the terrain within which profitable discussion can take place.

Lawrence warned us to trust the tale, not the teller, and the wary reader of these essays need point only to the remarks she made in 1963 about her well-known "A Good Man Is Hard to Find" to justify his skepticism. One can easily pass over her hope that the grandmother's final gesture to The Misfit might have begun a process which would "turn him into the prophet he was meant to become"; that, as she firmly says, is another story, and it would be a reckless piety indeed which would see it even suggested by the one we have. But her astonishing description of the grandmother herself as a woman who "lacked comprehension, but . . . had a good heart" cannot be disposed of so simply. The comment reflects the mellowing that seems to have taken place in O'Connor's later years (and which can be detected in her stories of the 1960's), but it is ruinous if applied seriously to the earlier tale.

As with individual matters, so with the larger issues: discrimination is essential. Perhaps the most suggestive passages are not those in which she stands squarely on her Catholicism or her Southernness or even the rigors of her art, but those that hint at some of the tensions that inform the fiction. In the stories and novels, the eye is O'Connor's pre-eminent sensory touchstone, the quality of a character's "vision" a revelation of his deepest commitments, and in these essays the metaphor of sight recurs again and again in passages of varying illumination. "I see from the standpoint of Christian orthodoxy," she stated flatly in "The Fiction Writer and His Country," which for all its quiet eloquence is the most dogmatic of the essays. Later, however, she admitted that for the writer who considers himself also a Christian, the problem of vision is not so immediately settled, for he has in fact two pair of eyes, his own and those of the Church. She goes on this way:

> It would be foolish to say there is no conflict between these two sets of eyes. There is a conflict, and it is a conflict which we escape at our peril, one which cannot be settled beforehand by theory or fiat or faith. We think that faith entitles us to avoid it, when in fact, faith prompts us to begin it, and to continue it until, like Jacob, we are marked. . . . The tensions of being a Catholic novelist are probably never balanced for the writer until the Church becomes so much a part of his personality that he can forget about her — in the same sense that when he writes, he forgets about himself.

This is the condition we aim for, but one which is seldom achieved in this life, particularly by novelists.

One may perhaps be permitted the speculation that the conflict spoken of here is one that Flannery O'Connor experienced intimately, that the struggle to keep in a single focus these two sets of eyes was a wrenching one which finds expression in the fiction not only in the fierce characters and actions she created, but in the energy of the narration itself, that intensity of feeling that drives the stories to their violent climaxes. At the very least, this fear of the Manichean separation — of fact from mystery, judgment from vision, nature from grace, reason from imagination, as she notes the divisions in "Catholic Novelists and Their Readers" — is transformed into an essential part of her material in the form of the "double" motif which pervades her work from her first novel to her last published story. In desperate defense of their limited visions of reality, the characters in story after story who furiously confront one another stare into distorting mirrors, and the heroes of the two novels, as well as finding their own strange reflections in the figures they encounter, carry the Manichean division deep within themselves. "Does one's integrity ever lie in what he is not able to do?" she asked. "I think that usually it does, for free will does not mean one will, but many wills conflicting in one man." Flannery O'Connor's integrity as a writer lies in her ability to project her own conflicting "wills" into the action of the fiction while holding with tense poise to a single vision that transcends all of them. It is in her novels and stories rather than in these essays that she most richly showed what she had to give, but anyone at all interested in her fiction will not want to ignore *Mystery and Manners*.

On Flannery O'Connor   Saul Maloff*

Even if these "occasional" pieces — lectures, less formal talks, some critical essays and reviews, and miscellaneous articles — were not buttressed by the authority of the late Flannery O'Connor's fictions and thoroughly established reputation, they would be eminently worth collecting. Miss O'Connor could not have intended a collection; and her devoted friends and editors, the Fitzgeralds, tell us of their labors in cutting and pruning and splicing together fragments, in some instances, to make wholes of overlapping talks on the same or related subjects. Yet, remarkably, there is no oppressive sense of redundancy or padding; but rather a liberating one, of themes and variations, accretion and accumulation, a

*Reprinted from *Commonweal*, 8 August 1969, pp. 490–91, by permission of *Commonweal* and Saul Maloff.

steady expansion of implication and statement to the point where the ideas essential to her life and art gathered toward the makings of something like a system.

Each piece—from those that seem little more than extended asides to those that clearly intend a summation of views—is singular, finely wrought and deeply felt; each bears the unmistakable imprint of her mind and play of her wit; and in each—how rare this is in expository prose—there is audible always the sound of her voice speaking; never the sound of a machine clattering. Except for the marvelous opening memoir of her life with the peacocks she raised, this volume records her lifelong preoccupation with the making of literature, the meaning and value of fiction.

Miss O'Connor wrote not as a theorist, nor even as a critic in any of the usual senses—nowhere in the volume does her attention come steadily to rest on a particular work or author. She wrote, as a writer of fiction reflecting on craft and art who in perfect confidence took herself and her work as sufficient instances of general problems about which universal assertions can be made; and when, in violation, almost, of her native temperament, she addressed herself to more theoretic questions—of regionalism, of being a Southern writer, of the "grotesque" in fiction, and especially of the vexed problem of religious belief, particularly Catholic belief and its relations to literature—she did so, one feels, as much because no one else could, or cared to, as because of the great pressures they exerted upon her as she practiced and sought to perfect her distinctive, recalcitrant art.

So to describe the book is to make it seem a writer's book aimed at other writers (which it is); but it is also to miss its special pleasure. "Special" because, though she provides it on every page, in every paragraph, it is not of the ingratiating kind. She does not court the reader; she doesn't seek to amuse or cajole or flatter so that she will be loved. Fiction was her life, its value transcendent. She is never consoling or reassuring. The defining quality of her mind was toughness, even harshness, impatience. She could be cranky, petulant, hectoring. She speaks with the wonderful arrogance of a writer who had come to know the exact dimensions of her powers—both scope and limitations; and who knew that though she had written relatively little, she was already among the American writers.

There was no doubt in her mind that she was born to write; that (in her terms) a gift had been given her; that it was her vocation, her calling; and that therefore to write at anything less or other than the intense pressure at which art is forged was sinful. From a writer less gifted, this would be intolerable pride; from her, we accept the terms in all their severity. The formidable claims are an altogether just estimate. Good fiction is hard to find: a good writer spares neither himself nor his readers. Not everyone can write; in fact few can: no one chose them though they may think they were called, though they may think that "anyone's unrestrained feelings are . . . worth listening to because they are unrestrained and because they are feelings." To "intrude upon the timeless" requires "the violence of a single-minded respect for the truth." Her truth, of course, was special and non-transferable; but shift the terms appropriately and it applies everywhere.

Exacting as all this sounds, Flannery O'Connor was never high-flown. She was pleased without the slightest condescension when a down-home countrywoman remarked of some of her stories, "Well, them stories just gone and shown you how some folks *would* do"; she was pleased not only because the response was an honest one but because it is sound literary criticism, because, she remarks, it is "right": "when you write stories, you have to be content to start exactly there — showing how some specific folks *will* do, *will* do in spite of everything."

But for the "little old lady in California" who informed her that when the tired reader comes home at night, he wishes to read something that "will lift up his heart" — for her, she has no time at all. And not because "it seems her heart had not been lifted up by anything of mine she had read," but because "if her heart had been in the right place, it would have been lifted up" — which can stand as an instance, at once, of her wit and critical self-knowledge, contempt for sentimentality, and her way of lifting up an extinct cliché bodily, standing it on its head and then on its feet again, fully alive.

God, alas, knows, the lady from California, whose name is Mrs. Legion, may have been Jew or Gentile, animist or Buddhist, or, serially, all; but one suspects she was Catholic, for the reason that Miss O'Connor reserved her finest wrath for those closest to her heart, her co-religionists (a term she would have hated), who like all other Americans with hearts in the wrong place wanted them lifted up. For her part, as a writer and a Catholic, as a Catholic writer, her aim in art was simply put: her "subject in fiction," she wrote, "is the action of grace in territory held largely by the devil." But she was a writer and not a theologian, and for a writer that is not sufficient knowledge. The "fiction writer," she wrote, and the statement, which recurs again and again with slight variation throughout the book, is virtually her motif, "presents mystery through manners, grace through nature, but when he finishes there always has to be left over that sense of Mystery which cannot be accounted for by any human formula." Of course there has to be no such thing. For "fiction writer" read "serious Catholic fiction writer"; but lower the case on Mystery and modify the final phrase, and it can stand as well as any other as a general statement about literary art, and, for herself, as credo. Only the most serious writer, of whatever kind, can venture to talk this way without disgracing herself and creating a scandal; and only a first-rate one can deliver the goods, which she did, again and again. She was simply describing not only the ideal she strove for but the end she actually achieved.

Now, this view of art has far more in common with the *serious* work of any real artist—of wavering, atrophied, vestigial, or no faith at all—than it does with the aggressive Philistinism of the canting letter-writers who reproach the writer for not lifting up their hearts; or (more to the point) the "pious trash" that passes for fiction among those who, hating art, batten on trash and do so in good conscience so long as trash breathes pieties and quotes Scripture. Miss O'Connor cites Cardinal Spellman's *The Foundling*—too obvious an example to be interesting; one trembles to think of others she had in mind when she spoke of pious trash—some, no doubt, masquerading as serious fiction.

The assault is devastating. What makes it of far more than parochial interest is its sweep of implication. Change the terms of immediate reference and the strictures apply exactly to all bogus constructions, soft at the edges as at the center, which seek to uplift, edify, hearten, instruct, to "tidy up reality"—which seek all purposes that are not those of art, which has no purpose other than to be faithful to itself. Pious trash is not only trash; it is, to put a strict construction on it, also impious. Bad art, whatever its purity of intention, is bad politics, too; and bad morals; and bad theology. It is all these for the fairly simple reason that bad art necessarily lies; and good art, whatever its impurities, finally breaks through and transcends them to significant truths.

The range of Flannery O'Connor's occasional prose—which was not after all her métier—is necessarily limited, and many of her readers will take exception (as I do) to this or that formulation—on the South, on "pornography" and "obscenity," on some marginal matters; but at this distance from her death these no longer seem important. What is important is the luminosity and intensity of her best pages on the nature of fiction—the suppleness and radiance of her intelligence and the acerbity of her wit; and what is of lasting importance is the body of work that underlies and amplifies them.

The Complete Stories

Flannery O'Connor: The Canon Completed, the Commentary Continuing

Melvin J. Friedman*

Flannery O'Connor remarked in one of the composite pieces included in *Mystery and Manners:* "It's always necessary to remember that the fiction writer is much less *immediately* concerned with grand ideas and bristling emotions than he is with putting list slippers on clerks." She said this after examining a sentence from *Madame Bovary* and marvelling at its economy and powers of suggestiveness. She perhaps saw a special kinship between Flaubert's controlled methods of composition, realized through his famous *style indirect libre*, and her own "habit of art" (an expression she was particularly fond of).

There is much of Flaubert's attention to detail and untiring search for the best possible turn of phrase in evidence in *The Complete Stories of Flannery O'Connor*. All thirty-one of these stories — even those six which were originally part of her Iowa master's thesis — seem splendidly finished. There is no sense of any of them being prematurely removed from the drawing board. The O'Connor stories need no props or critical underpinnings, although the collection is clearly enriched by a discreet introduction and helpful bibliographical notes by Robert Giroux. One never has the uncomfortable feeling (such as one has with the recent Carson McCullers miscellany, *The Mortgaged Heart*) of a patchwork quilt of short pieces, stitched together with finesse and devotion by an editorial hand.

Even the early O'Connor stories, quite simply, are finished pieces and point with assurance to her best work in the shorter form, like "Revelation," "Everything That Rises Must Converge," and "Judgement Day." Her earliest story, "The Geranium," in fact proves to be a first draft of her last story, "Judgement Day" (which gives *The Complete Stories* an intriguing symmetry); the characters are renamed, the situation is altered, the vision is deepened, but, in the end, the O'Connor of 1946 has curiously much of the wisdom, finesse, and narrative control of the O'Connor of 1964. Flannery O'Connor seems not to have passed through the painful apprenticeship of so many other writers.

*Reprinted from *Southern Literary Journal*, Spring 1973, pp. 116–20, by permission of *Southern Literary Journal*.

One can see the six stories which comprised Flannery O'Connor's master's thesis moving toward her first published book, *Wise Blood*. The last of these stories, "The Train," in fact, is an early version of the opening chapter of this first novel. There are the usual O'Connor name changes — Hazel Wickers becomes Hazel Motes, Mrs. Wallace Ben Hosen becomes Mrs. Wally Bee Hitchcock — and the necessary adjustments of narrative focus from story to novel. But "The Train" has its own pace and movement, its own identity, and deserves to stand by itself as the sixth in order of composition of Flannery O'Connor's complete stories. The same can be said about the seventh, eighth, and tenth stories, "The Peeler," "The Heart of the Park," and "Enoch and the Gorilla," all of which were finally revised to become chapters of *Wise Blood*.

One sees, I think, how the first ten of *The Complete Stories*, all written before the publication of *Wise Blood*, directly or indirectly make us ready for Flannery O'Connor's first novel. There is nothing like the startling and radical leap from the apprenticeship stories of *The Mortgaged Heart* to Carson McCullers' first novel, *The Heart Is a Lonely Hunter*. Indeed there is no great distance separating an early piece like "Wildcat," with its creative writing course origins, from *Wise Blood*. One ends up by feeling that everything is worth preserving in *The Complete Stories of Flannery O'Connor*. Flannery O'Connor apparently never wrote any fugitive pieces; there was clearly no emptying of waste baskets or raiding of cobwebbed attics to fill out the pages of her *Complete Stories*.

The notion of arranging the stories chronologically in their order of composition (retaining the sequence she followed in her thesis for the first six stories) might prove unsettling to those who view the two collections, *A Good Man Is Hard to Find* and *Everything That Rises Must Converge*, as following some inviolable pattern or design. Indeed rearranging the stories might be likened by some critics to the heresy of reordering Joyce's *Dubliners* or Sherwood Anderson's *Winesburg, Ohio*. It does seem odd, for example, to place "A Stroke of Good Fortune" (the fourth story in *A Good Man Is Hard to Find*) between "The Heart of the Park" and "Enoch and the Gorilla," early versions of parts of *Wise Blood*. This gesture, determined entirely by chronology, breaks up a four-part narrative sequence ("The Train," "The Peeler," "The Heart of the Park," and "Enoch and the Gorilla") which traces Hazel Wickers-Weaver-Motes's[1] train ride to Taulkinham, his first encounter with Enoch Emery, a subsequent meeting between the two, and Enoch's confrontation with "Gonga, Giant Jungle Monarch." Hazel dominates the first two stories, Enoch the latter two. Ruby Hill's unwillingness to face up to her pregnancy in "A Stroke of Good Fortune" clearly has no place between the two Enoch Emery-controlled stories.

Yet there is a certain value in having the chronological arrangement; it lets us in on the subtle and gradual maturing of a remarkable talent. When Flannery O'Connor remarks in *Mystery and Manners* that "a story really isn't any good unless it successfully resists paraphrase, unless it hangs on and expands in the mind," we have a reliable index for measuring her development. The possibilities for effective paraphrase are surely better in the early stories; the lines of their narrative strategies are much more clearly drawn. They do not, however, linger on quite so long. The vintage O'Connor story, as Carter Martin suggested in *The True Country: Themes in the Fiction of Flannery O'Connor*, has the effect of good poetry with its oblique devices, with its economy of means, and with its density. An early story like "The Barber" has certain decisive regional and tall-story properties: the self-righteous liberal confronts the bigoted hangers-on at the local barber shop and loses control in the face of their mockery. The humor results partly from the incongruity between the intellectual's[2] precise speech and the regionalisms of his taunters. The taunters, predictably, win the day. The humor is much darker and grimmer in the later stories and the effects are arrived at through much less obvious devices. Our laughter is quite muted as Sarah Ruth screams "Idolatry!" when her husband bares his tattooed back to her ("Parker's Back"), or as Mrs. Turpin approaches the pig pen and "remained there with her gaze bent to them as if she were absorbing some abysmal life-giving knowledge" ("Revelation").

    The Complete Stories, then, points to the subtle, slow, and not always obvious growth of a major short-story writer who deserves a place beside her friend Katherine Anne Porter. The Flaubertian way in which Flannery O'Connor went about her work apparently prevented these startling and rather terrifying leaps from apprenticeship to early prime to full maturity to later manner—which so many writers go through. We are grateful for *The Complete Stories* also because it includes such a fine uncollected piece as "The Partridge Festival," which was previously available only in the pages of *The Critic.* . . .

Notes

    1. He is called Hazel Wickers in "The Train," Hazel Motes in "The Peeler," and Hazel Weaver in "The Heart of the Park." He does not appear in "Enoch and the Gorilla."

    2. The intellectual is called Rayber and he is clearly a model for the character of the same name in *The Violent Bear It Away*.

Flannery O'Connor: The Complete Stories

Alfred Kazin*

The title sums up author, book and life: *Flannery O'Connor: The Complete Stories*. She died in 1964 at the age of 39; she published 31 stories, of which 12 have been uncollected until now. Now they are all in one book, arranged in chronological order from the stories she wrote for her master's thesis at the University of Iowa to "Judgement Day," a harrowing version of her brilliant early story about an elderly Southerner's exile in New York, "The Geranium." Since the stories here include the original openings and other chapters of her two novels *Wise Blood* and *The Violent Bear It Away* and since stories were more natural to her than novels, we do have almost all of Flannery O'Connor "complete" here. Especially when you reflect that the driving characteristic of her style, her mind, her particular faith, was to find people "complete" in the smallest gesture, or in a moment's involuntary action that could decide a life forever.

She could put everything about a character into a single look, everything she had and knew into a single story. She knew people with the finality with which she claimed to know the distance from hell to heaven. For her, people were complete in their radical weakness, their necessarily human incompleteness. Each story was complete, sentence by sentence. And each sentence was a hard, straight, altogether complete version of her subject: human deficiency, sin, error — ugliness taking a physical form.

I met her during the McCarthy period, under circumstances that persuaded me that she — or her friends — would have considered Jefferson Davis a Communist. I later visited her and her famous peacocks at her home in Milledgeville, Ga., in the company of her parish priest, who found her formidable in her fierce disapproval of his literary tastes. To tell the truth, what I liked most about her was her stories. She was not just the best "woman writer" of this time and place; she expressed something secret about America, called "the South," with that transcendent gift for expressing the real spirit of a culture that is conveyed by those writers (they are not necessarily the greatest, but neither do they ever die out of our minds) who become nothing but what they see.

Completeness is one word for it; relentlessness, unsparingness would be others. She was a genius. A mark of nongenius in story telling is to be distracted, to hint there are things to say that the author will get down to someday. Nongenius is nonconcentrating, and no matter how nasty it may be to people in the story, it is genial to itself. There is laxness in the air, self-conscious charm, a pensive mood of: What should come next?

O'Connor, as I must call her, was in story after story all there,

*Reprinted from *New York Times Book Review*, 28 November 1971, pp. 1,22. © 1971 by The New York Times Company. Reprinted by permission.

occupying the mind and the whole life of a character who was as solidly on the page as if impaled on it. Her people were wholly what they were, which wasn't much in "humane" terms. But they were all intact of themselves, in their stupidity, their meanness, their puzzlement, their Southern "ruralness." The South was her great metaphor, not for place but for the Fall of Man. Life for O'Connor was made up of absolutes; people were absolute, sharp, knives without handles. Hazel Motes all too believably blinds himself in *Wise Blood*. Old Mr. Fortune, in "A View of the Woods," loves his granddaughter so deeply and identifies her with himself so wildly that of course he kills her without meaning to when she amazes him by balking his wishes. The young son of the dissolute city couple in "The River" is taken by his baby-sitter to see a country baptism, goes back by himself and drowns trying to find his new friend Jesus in the river.

The people were complete because the reader, not they, knows all about them. They were nothing but their natures, and since there was nothing to life but people's natures, this made life moral. O'Connor's sentences, as ruthless as Stephen Crane's but less literary, always more objective than Hemingway's at his would-be toughest, measured like a rule, and came down flat. People in her stories are always at the end of their strength. They are at the synapse between what they are (unknown to themselves) and what they do. And these synapses, these flashes of connection, are so "complete," immediate, right, irreversible, that a particular feature of O'Connor's style is that a sentence is exact — not showily, as is the nature of rhetoric, but physically, the way different parts of a body fit each other. No one ever wrote narrative with more secret cunning, coming up with the minute differences that excite us in reading and cause us to respond. Yet no one ever wrote less "beautifully" in the contemplative, lyric Hemingway fashion. She was more devoted to the synonym than to the metaphor, for what she saw was the non-human that people always reminded her of:

> He seemed mute and patient, like an old sheep waiting to be let out.
>
> The rest of his face stuck out like a bare cliff to fall from. . . .
>
> On the porch there were three little boys of different sizes with identical speckled faces and one tall girl who had her hair up in so many aluminum curlers that it glared like the roof.
>
> When he finished, he was like something washed ashore on her, and she had made obscene comments about him, which he remembered gradually during the day.

Then there was the deadliness of observation without cruelty, funny because the different items "fit." "Mrs. Watts's grin was as curved and sharp as the blade of a sickle. It was plain that she was so well-adjusted that she didn't have to think any more." "He was chewing gum slowly, as if to music." " 'He has a ulcer,' the woman said proudly. 'He ain't give me a minute's peace since he was born.' " Her sentences are more often disturbing in their laconic rightness than smart. She was not looking around her as she wrote. She was herself impaled on what her people were doing. There was nothing but that: one small circle.

Though she would have been only 46 by now, her stories already seem non-contemporary in their passion for the art of fiction. One realizes how diffuse and subjective the practice of fiction has become since O'Connor wrote the first stories in this book for her master's thesis at Iowa, which read as if she were going to be examined by Willa Cather and Stephen Crane. We live in such an age of commentary now! She had the dread circulatory disease of lupus from the time she began to write — her short career was a progress by dying — and I wonder if the sourness, the unsparingness, the breath-taking perspective on all human weakness in her work need as many translations into theology as they get in contemporary American criticism. As Josephine Hendin pointed out in *The World of Flannery O'Connor*, there was an unreal and even comic gentility to her upbringing in Milledgeville that must have given O'Connor a wry sense of her aloneness as a woman, artist and Southerner who happened to be an Irish Catholic.

On the other hand, she was so locked up in her body that one can understand why life as well as her faith made her think of "this is my body, this is my blood." She touched the bone of truth that was sunk in her own flesh. Thus she lost herself in a story. And this was grace. Reading her, one is aware above all of a gift blessedly made objective, a giftedness reading the world. Words became true in her dramatic world, in action, gesture, death. That too was completeness of a kind, resting its weight perfectly in story after story. But fiction depended for her on an unyielding sense of our limits, and the limits could be raised only by death.

In "Greenleaf," the great story of a woman killed by the bull that her impossibly inefficient farmhand, Greenleaf, is always letting out, the woman stares at the "violent black streak bounding toward her as if she had no sense of distance, as if she could not decide at once what his intention was, and the bull had buried his head in her lap, like a wild tormented lover, before her expression changed. . . . She had the look of a person whose sight has been suddenly restored but who finds the light unbearable."

REMINISCENCES
AND TRIBUTES

Gracious Greatness

Katherine Anne Porter[*]

I saw our lovely and gifted Flannery O'Connor only three times over a period, I think, of three years or more, but each meeting was spontaneously an occasion and I want to write about her just as she impressed me.

I want to tell what she looked like and how she carried herself and how she sounded standing balanced lightly on her aluminum crutches, whistling to her peacocks who came floating and rustling to her, calling in their rusty voices.

I do not want to speak of her work because we all know what it was and we don't need to say what we think about it but to read and understand what she was trying to tell us.

Now and again there hovers on the margin of the future a presence that one feels as imminent — if I may use stylish vocabulary. She came up among us like a presence, a carrier of a gift not to be disputed but welcomed. She lived among us like a presence and went away early, leaving her harvest perhaps not yet all together gathered, though, like so many geniuses who have small time in this world, I think she had her warning and accepted it and did her work even if we all would like to have had her stay on forever and do more.

It is all very well for those who are left to console themselves. She said what she had to say. I'm pretty certain that her work was finished. We shouldn't mourn for her but for ourselves and our loves.

After all, I saw her just twice — memory has counted it three — for the second time was a day-long affair at a Conference and a party given by Flannery's mother in the evening. And I want to tell you something I think is amusing because Flannery lived in such an old-fashioned southern village very celebrated in southern history on account of what took place during the War. But in the lovely, old, aerie, tall country house and the life of a young girl living with her mother in a country town so that there was almost no way for her knowing the difficulties of human beings and her general knowledge of this was really very impressive because she was so very young and you wondered where — how — she had learned all that. But

[*]Reprinted, by permission, from *Esprit*, 8 (1964), 50–58.

this is a question that everybody always asks himself about genius. I want to just tell something to illustrate the southern custom.

Ladies in Society there — in that particular society, I mean — were nearly always known, no matter if they were married once or twice, they were known to their dying day by their maiden names. They were called "Miss Mary" or whoever it was. And so, Flannery's mother, too; her maiden name was Regina Cline and so she was still known as "Miss Regina Cline" and one evening at a party when I was there after the Conference, someone mentioned Flannery's name and another — a neighbor, mind you, who had probably been around there all her life — said, "Who is Flannery O'Connor? I keep hearing about her." The other one said, "Oh, you know! Why, that's Regina Cline's daughter: that little girl who writes." And that was the atmosphere in which her genius developed and her life was lived and her work was done. I myself think it was a very healthy, good atmosphere because nobody got in her way, nobody tried to interfere with her or direct her and she lived easily and simply and in her own atmosphere and her own way of thinking. I believe this is the best possible way for a genius to live. I think that they're too often tortured by this world and when people discover that someone has a gift, they all come with their claws out, trying to snatch something of it, trying to share some thing they have no right even to touch. And she was safe from that: she had a mother who really took care of her. And I just think that's something we ought to mention, ought to speak of.

She managed to mix, somehow, two very different kinds of chickens and produced a bird hitherto unseen in this world. I asked her if she were going to send it to the County Fair. "I might, but first I must find a name for it. You name it!" she said. I thought of it many times but no fitting name for that creature ever occurred to me. And no fitting word now occurs to me to describe her stories, her particular style, her view of life, but I know its greatness and I see it — and see that it was one of the great gifts of our times.

I want to speak a little of her religious life though it was very sacred and quiet. She was as reserved about it as any saint. When I first met her, she and her mother were about to go for a seventeen day trip to Lourdes. I said, "Oh, I wish I could go with you!" She said, "I wish you could. But I'll write you a letter." She never wrote that letter. She just sent a post card and she wrote: "The sight of Faith and affliction joined in prayer — very impressive." That was all.

In some newspaper notice of her death mention of her self-portrait with her favorite peacock was made. It spoke of her plain features. She had unusual features but they were anything but plain. I saw that portrait in her home and she had not flattered herself. The portrait does have her features, in a way, but here's something else. She had a young softness and gentleness of face and expression. The look — something in the depth of the eyes and the fixed mouth; the whole pose fiercely intent gives an uncompromising glimpse of her character. Something you might not see on first or even second glance in that tenderly fresh-colored, young, smiling face; something she saw in herself, knew about herself, that she was trying to tell us in a way less personal, yet more vivid than words.

That portrait, I'm trying to say, looked like the girl who wrote those blood-curdling stories about human evil — NOT the living Flannery, whistling to her peacocks, showing off her delightfully freakish breed of chickens.

I want to thank you for giving me the opportunity to tell you about the Flannery O'Connor I know. I loved and valued her dearly, her work and her strange unworldly radiance of spirit in a human being so intelligent and so undeceived by the appearance of things. I would feel too badly if I did not honor myself by saying a word in her honor: it is a great loss.

[Platitudes and Protestants]   Allen Tate*

I never knew Flannery O'Connor well, having met her only twice; first at the University of Iowa, I believe in 1947, where she was a student in the Writers' Workshop, and I was the visiting writer whose job was to "criticize" the work of the young writers in the week I was there; and second, I saw her again in 1949 or 1950 in Connecticut, where she was staying at the country house of Robert and Sally Fitzgerald. The Fitzgeralds had made her a member of the family, and the role of niece or younger sister suited her very well. At that time I was not well acquainted with her work: I knew only a few short stories, and the fragment of *Wise Blood* that I had read at Iowa in 1947.

And how irrelevant my remarks on *Wise Blood* must have seemed to her! I hadn't the vaguest idea of what she was up to; I offered to correct her grammar; I even told her that her style was dull, the sentences being flat and simple declaratives. No doubt what I said was true; but it was irrelevant. The flat style, the cranky grammar, the monotonous sentence-structure were necessary vehicles of her vision of man. It was a narrow vision, but deep; unworldly, but aware of human depravity as only a good Jansenist can be (by "good Jansenist" I mean only that Flannery took a gloomy view of the human condition and that all her characters, like Mauriac's, are possibly damned. Her characters resist grace, there is no free will, etc. She was not doctrinally but temperamentally a Jansenist. — Again, by "good" I mean *thorough*.); yet compassionate towards all the maimed souls she put into her stories. I didn't know these things when I saw her in Iowa. I only read "Good Country People," the first story of hers

*Reprinted, by permission, from *Esprit*, 8 (1964), 48–49.

that I remember reading. Hulga, the girl with a wooden leg, is also spiritually maimed but she is still capable of love, even if, at the moment she thinks she is being seduced by the Bible salesman, she can see no further than physical love. The Bible salesman himself—who represents for Hulga's mother "good country people"—is a moral monster without human motivation even towards evil: he *is* evil. I would guess that all Miss O'Connor's stories are set in motion by such persons; for although the surface action is naturalistic, it is not possible to determine *why* the action starts, unless one posits a non-rational (not-rational) principle of supernatural disorder underlying the movement towards the destruction of the central characters. Her stories exhibit, either in the title or in the situation out of which the action begins, a *moral platitude*: Hulga's mother receives the Bible salesman because he is a good country boy trying to get ahead by means of the pious work of selling Bibles: the climax of the story explodes the platitude. The characters speak nothing but platitudes, and when evil has done its work with the platitudes the result is a powerful irony which, though crudely violent, is inherent in the situation, not laid on as commentary by the author.

I have frequently wondered what sort of writer Flannery would have been had she lived all her life in a Catholic community. In Milledgeville, Georgia, one would surmise, the population is about one percent Catholic. She was a Catholic necessarily writing about Protestants—and they all are decadent Protestants. Are there any Protestants at all in J. F. Powers' stories? I can't remember any. The unusual combination of Southern gentry with Roman Catholicism gave Flannery O'Connor a unique point of view. This, with her inexplicable genius, produced a writer whose like probably will not appear again in the United States.

Flannery O'Connor: A Prose Elegy
Thomas Merton*

Now Flannery is dead and I will write her name with honor, with love for the great slashing innocence of that dry-eyed irony that could keep looking the South in the face without bleeding or even sobbing. Her South was deeper than mine, crazier than Kentucky, but wild with no other madness than the crafty paranoia that is all over the place, including the North! Only madder, craftier, hung up in wilder and more absurd legends, more inventive of more outrageous lies! And solemn! Taking seriously the need to be respectable when one is an obsolescent and very agile fury.

The key word to Flannery's stories probably is "respect." She never

*From Thomas Merton, *Raids on the Unspeakable*. © 1964 by The Abbey of Gethsemani, Inc. Reprinted by permission of New Directions Publishing Corporation.

gave up examining its ambiguities and its decay. In this bitter dialectic of half-truths that have become endemic to our system, she probed our very life — its conflicts, its falsities, its obsessions, its vanities. Have we become an enormous complex organization of spurious reverences? Respect is continually advertised, and we are still convinced that we respect "everything good" — when we know too well that we have lost the most elementary respect even for ourselves. Flannery saw this and saw, better than others, what it implied.

She wrote in and out of the anatomy of a word that became genteel, then self-conscious, then obsessive, finally dying of contempt, but kept calling itself "respect." Contempt for the child, for the stranger, for the woman, for the Negro, for the animal, for the white man, for the farmer, for the country, for the preacher, for the city, for the world, for reality itself. Contempt, contempt, so that in the end the gestures of respect they kept making to themselves and to each other and to God became desperately obscene.

But respect had to be maintained. Flannery maintained it ironically and relentlessly with a kind of innocent passion long after it had died of contempt — as if she were the only one left who took this thing seriously. One would think (if one put a Catholic chip on his shoulder and decided to make a problem of her) that she could not look so steadily, so drily and so long at so much false respect without herself dying of despair. She never made any funny faces. She never said: "Here is a terrible thing!" She just looked and said what they said and how they said it. It was not she that invented their despair, and perhaps her only way out of despair herself was to respect the way they announced the gospel of contempt. She patiently recorded all they had got themselves into. Their world was a big, fantastic, crawling, exploding junk pile of despair. I will write her name with honor for seeing it so clearly and looking straight at it without remorse. Perhaps her way of irony was the only possible catharsis for a madness so cruel and so endemic. Perhaps a dry honesty like hers can save the South more simply than the North can ever be saved.

Flannery's people were two kinds of very advanced primitives: the city kind, exhausted, disillusioned, tired of imagining, perhaps still given to a grim willfulness in the service of doubt, still driving on in fury and ill will, or scientifically expert in nastiness; and the rural kind: furious, slow, cunning, inexhaustible, living sweetly on the verge of the unbelievable, more inclined to prefer the abyss to solid ground, but keeping contact with the world of contempt by raw insensate poetry and religious mirth: the mirth of a god who himself, they suspected, was the craftiest and most powerful deceiver of all. Flannery saw the contempt of primitives who admitted that they would hate to be saved, and the greater contempt of those other primitives whose salvation was an elaborately contrived possibility, always being brought back into question. Take the sweet idiot deceit of the fury grandmother in "A Good Man Is Hard to Find" whose respectable and catastrophic fantasy easily destroyed her urban son with all his plans, his last shred of trust in reason, and his insolent children.

The way Flannery O'Connor made a story: she would put together all these elements of unreason and let them fly slowly and inexorably at one another. Then sometimes the urban madness, less powerful, would fall weakly prey to the rural madness and be inexorably devoured by a superior and more primitive absurdity. Or the rural madness would fail and fall short of the required malice and urban deceit would compass its destruction, with all possible contempt, cursing, superior violence and fully implemented disbelief. For it would usually be wholesome faith that left the rural primitive unarmed. So you would watch, fascinated, almost in despair, knowing that in the end the very worst thing, the least reasonable, the least desirable, was what would have to happen. Not because Flannery wanted it so, but because it turned out to *be* so in a realm where the advertised satisfaction is compounded of so many lies and of so much contempt for the customer. She had seen too clearly all that is sinister in our commercial paradise, and in its rural roots.

Flannery's people were two kinds of trash, able to mix inanity with poetry, with exuberant nonsense, and with the most profound and systematic contempt for reality. Her people knew how to be trash to the limit, unabashed, on purpose, out of self-contempt that has finally won out over every other feeling and turned into a parody of freedom in the spirit. What spirit? A spirit of ungodly stateliness and parody—the pomp and glee of arbitrary sports, freaks not of nature but of blighted and social willfulness, rich in the creation of respectable and three-eyed monsters. Her beings are always raising the question of *worth*. Who is a good man? Where is he? He is "hard to find." Meanwhile you will have to make out with a bad one who is so respectable that he is horrible, so horrible that he is funny, so funny that he is pathetic, but so pathetic that it would be gruesome to pity him. So funny that you do not dare to laugh too loud for fear of demons.

And that is how Flannery finally solved the problem of respect: having peeled the whole onion of respect layer by layer, having taken it all apart with admirable patience, showing clearly that each layer was only another kind of contempt, she ended up by seeing clearly that it was funny, but not merely funny in a way that you could laugh at. Humorous, yes, but also uncanny, inexplicable, demonic, so you could never laugh at it as if you understood. Because if you pretended to understand, you, too, would find yourself among her demons practicing contempt. She respected all her people by searching for some sense in them, searching for truth, searching to the end and then suspending judgment. To have condemned them on moral grounds would have been to connive with their own crafty arts and their own demonic imagination. It would have meant getting tangled up with them in the same machinery of unreality and of contempt. The only way to be saved was to stay out of it, not to think, not to speak, just to record the slow, sweet, ridiculous verbalizing of Southern furies, working their way through their charming lazy hell.

That is why when I read Flannery I don't think of Hemingway, or Katherine Anne Porter, or Sartre, but rather of someone like Sophocles. What more can be said of a writer? I write her name with honor, for all the truth and all the craft with which she shows man's fall and his dishonor.

Beyond the Peacock: The Reconstruction of Flannery O'Connor

Alice Walker*

It was after a poetry reading I gave at a recently desegregated college in Georgia that someone mentioned that in 1952 Flannery O'Connor and I had lived within minutes of each other on the same Eatonton-to-Milledgeville road. I was eight years old in 1952 (she would have been 28) and we moved away from Milledgeville after less than a year. Still, since I have loved her work for many years, the coincidence of our having lived near each other intrigued me, and started me thinking of her again.

As a college student in the sixties I read her books endlessly, scarcely conscious of the difference between her racial and economic background and my own, but put them away in anger when I discovered that, while I was reading O'Connor — Southern, Catholic, and white — there were other women writers — some Southern, some religious, all black — I had not been allowed to know. For several years, while I searched for, found, and studied black women writers, I deliberately shut O'Connor out, feeling almost ashamed that she had reached me first. And yet, even when I no longer read her, I missed her, and realized that though the rest of America might not mind, having endured it so long, I would never be satisfied with a segregated literature. I would have to read Zora Hurston *and* Flannery O'Connor, Nella Larsen *and* Carson McCullers, Jean Toomer *and* William Faulkner, before I could begin to feel *well* read at all.

I thought it might be worthwhile, in 1974, to visit the two houses, Flannery O'Connor's and mine, to see what could be learned twenty-two years after we moved away and ten years after her death. It seemed right to go to my old house first — to set the priorities of vision, so to speak — and then to her house, to see, at the very least, whether her peacocks would still be around. To this bit of nostalgic exploration I invited my mother, who, curious about peacocks and abandoned houses, if not about literature and writers, accepted.

*© 1975 by Alice Walker. Abridged and reprinted from her volume *In Search of Our Mothers' Gardens* by permission of Harcourt Brace Jovanovich, Inc.

In her shiny new car, which at sixty-one she has learned to drive, we cruised down the wooded Georgia highway to revisit our past.

At the turnoff leading to our former house, we face a fence, a gate, a NO TRESPASSING sign. The car will not fit through the gate and beyond the gate is muddy pasture. It shocks me to remember that when we lived here we lived, literally, in a pasture. It is a memory I had repressed. Now, for a moment, it frightens me.

"Do you think we should enter?" I ask.

But my mother has already opened the gate. To her, life has no fences, except, perhaps, religious ones, and these we have decided not to discuss. We walk through pines rich with vines, fluttering birds, and an occasional wild azalea showing flashes of orange. The day is bright with spring, the sky cloudless, the road rough and clean.

"I would like to see old man Jenkins [who was our landlord] come bothering me about some trespassing," she says, her head extremely up. "He never did pay us for the crop we made for him in fifty-two."

After five minutes of leisurely walking, we are again confronted with a fence, fastened gate, POSTED signs. Again my mother ignores all three, unfastens the gate, walks through.

"He never gave me my half of the calves I raised that year either," she says. And I chuckle at her memory and her style.

Now we are facing a large green rise. To our left calves are grazing; beyond them there are woods. To our right there is the barn we used, looking exactly as it did twenty-two years ago. It is high and weathered silver and from it comes the sweet scent of peanut hay. In front of it, a grove of pecans. Directly in front of us over the rise is what is left of the house.

"Well," says my mother, "it's still standing. And," she adds with wonder, "just look at my daffodils!"

In twenty-two years they have multiplied and are now blooming from one side of the yard to the other. It is a typical abandoned sharefarmer shack. Of the four-room house only two rooms are left; the others have rotted away. These two are filled with hay.

Considering the sad state of the house it is amazing how beautiful its setting is. There is not another house in sight. There are hills, green pastures, a ring of bright trees, and a family of rabbits hopping out of our way. My mother and I stand in the yard remembering. I remember only misery: going to a shabby segregated school that was once the state prison and that had, on the second floor, the large circular print of the electric chair that had stood there; almost stepping on a water moccasin on my way home from carrying water to my family in the fields; losing Phoebe, my cat, because we left this place hurriedly and she could not be found in time.

"Well, old house," my mother says, smiling in such a way that I almost see her rising, physically, above it, "one good thing you gave us. It was right here that I got my first washing machine!"

In fact, the only pleasant thing I recall from that year was a field we used to pass on our way into the town of Milledgeville. It was like a painting by someone who loved tranquillity. In the foreground near the road the green field was used as pasture for black-and-white cows that never seemed to move. Then, farther away, there was a steep hill partly covered with kudzu — dark and lush and creeping up to cover and change fantastically the shapes of the trees. . . . When we drive past it now, it looks the same. Even the cows could be the same cows — though now I see that they *do* move, though not very fast and never very far.

What I liked about this field as a child was that in my life of nightmares about electrocutions, lost cats, and the surprise appearance of snakes, it represented beauty and unchanging peace.

"Of course," I say to myself, as we turn off the main road two miles from my old house, "that's Flannery's field." The instructions I've been given place her house on the hill just beyond it.

There is a garish new Holiday Inn directly across Highway 441 from Flannery O'Connor's house, and, before going up to the house, my mother and I decide to have something to eat there. Twelve years ago I could not have bought lunch for us at such a place in Georgia, and I feel a weary delight as I help my mother off with her sweater and hold out a chair by the window for her. The white people eating lunch all around us — staring though trying hard not to — form a blurred backdrop against which my mother's face is especially sharp. *This* is the proper perspective, I think, biting into a corn muffin; no doubt about it.

As we sip iced tea we discuss O'Connor, integration, the inferiority of the corn muffins we are nibbling, and the care and raising of peacocks.

"Those things will sure eat up your flowers," my mother says, explaining why she never raised any.

"Yes," I say, "but they're a lot prettier than they'd be if somebody human had made them, which is why this lady liked them." This idea has only just occurred to me, but having said it, I believe it is true. I sit wondering why I called Flannery O'Connor a lady. It is a word I rarely use and usually by mistake, since the whole notion of ladyhood is repugnant to me. I can imagine O'Connor at a Southern social affair, looking very polite and being very bored, making mental notes of the absurdities of the evening. Being white she would automatically have been eligible for ladyhood, but I cannot believe she would ever really have joined.

"She must have been a Christian person then," says my mother. "She believed He made everything." She pauses, looks at me with tolerance but also as if daring me to object: "And she was *right*, too."

"She was a Catholic," I say, "which must not have been comfortable in the Primitive Baptist South, and more than any other writer she believed in everything, including things she couldn't see."

"Is that why you like her?" she asks.

"I like her because she could *write*," I say. . . .

"When you make these trips back south," says my mother, as I give the smiling waitress my credit card, "just what is it exactly that you're looking for?"

"A wholeness," I reply.

"You look whole enough to me," she says.

"No, I answer, "because everything around me is split up, deliberately split up. History split up, literature split up, and people are split up too. It makes people do ignorant things. For example, one day I was invited to speak at a gathering of Mississippi librarians and before I could get started, one of the authorities on Mississippi history and literature got up and said she really *did* think Southerners wrote so well because 'we' lost the war. She was white, of course, but half the librarians in the room were black."

"I bet she was real old," says my mother. "They're the only ones still worrying over that war."

"So I got up and said no, 'we' didn't lose the war. '*You* all' lost the war. And you all's loss was our gain."

"Those old ones will just have to die out," says my mother.

"Well," I say, "I believe that the truth about any subject only comes when all the sides of the story are put together, and all their different meanings make one new one. Each writer writes the missing parts to the other writer's story. And the whole story is what I'm after."

"Well, I doubt if you can ever get the *true* missing parts of anything away from the white folks," my mother says softly, so as not to offend the waitress who is mopping up a nearby table; "they've sat on the truth so long by now they've mashed the life out of it."

"O'Connor wrote a story once called 'Everything That Rises Must Converge.' "

"What?"

"Everything that goes up comes together, meets, becomes one thing. Briefly, the story is this: an old white woman in her fifties—"

"That's not old! I'm older than that, and I'm not old!"

"Sorry. This middle-aged woman gets on a bus with her son, who likes to think he is a Southern liberal . . . he looks for a black person to sit next to. This horrifies his mother, who, though not old, has old ways. She is wearing a very hideous, very expensive hat, which is purple and green."

"Purple and *green*?"

"Very expensive. *Smart*. Bought at the best store in town. She says, 'With a hat like this, I won't meet myself coming and going.' But in fact,

soon a large black woman, whom O'Connor describes as looking something like a gorilla, gets on the bus with a little boy, and she is wearing this
same green-and-purple hat. Well, our not-so-young white lady is horri-
fied, out*done*."

"I *bet* she was. Black folks have money to buy foolish things with too,
now."

"O'Connor's point exactly! Everything that rises, must converge."

"Well, the green-and-purple-hats people will have to converge without me."

"O'Connor thought that the South, as it became more 'progressive,'
would become just like the North. Culturally bland, physically ravished,
and, where the people are concerned, well, you wouldn't be able to tell
one racial group from another. Everybody would want the same things,
like the same things, and everybody would be reduced to wearing,
symbolically, the same green-and-purple hats."

"And do you think this is happening?"

"I do. But that is not the whole point of the story. The white woman,
in an attempt to save her pride, chooses to treat the incident of the
identical hats as a case of monkey-see, monkey-do. She assumes she is not
the monkey, of course. She ignores the idiotic-looking black woman and
begins instead to flirt with the woman's son, who is small and black and
cute. She fails to notice that the black woman is glowering at her. When
they all get off the bus she offers the little boy a 'bright new penny.' And
the child's mother knocks the hell out of her with her pocketbook."

"I bet she carried a large one."

"Large, and full of hard objects."

"Then what happened? Didn't you say the white woman's son was
with her?"

"He had tried to warn his mother. 'These new Negroes are not like the
old,' he told her. But she never listened. He thought he hated his mother
until he saw her on the ground, then he felt sorry for her. But when he
tried to help her, she didn't know him. She'd retreated in her mind to a
historical time more congenial to her desires. 'Tell Grandpa to come get
me,' she says. Then she totters off, alone, into the night."[1]

"Poor *thing*," my mother says sympathetically of this horrid woman,
in a total identification that is *so* Southern and *so* black.

"That's what her son felt, too, and *that* is how you know it is a
Flannery O'Connor story. The son has been changed by his mother's
experience. He understands that, though she is a silly woman who has
tried to live in the past, she is also a pathetic creature and so is he. But it is
too late to tell her about this because she is stone crazy."

"What did the black woman do after she knocked the white woman
down and walked away?"

"O'Connor chose not to say, and that is why, although this is a good
story, it is, to me, only half a story. *You* might know the other half. . . ."

"Well, I'm not a writer, but there *was* an old white woman I once wanted to strike . . ." she begins.

"Exactly," I say.

I discovered O'Connor when I was in college in the North and took a course in Southern writers and the South. The perfection of her writing was so dazzling I never noticed that no black Southern writers were taught. The other writers we studied—Faulkner, McCullers, Welty— seemed obsessed with a racial past that would not let them go. They seemed to beg the question of their characters' humanity on every page. O'Connor's characters—whose humanity if not their sanity is taken for granted, and who are miserable, ugly, narrow-minded, atheistic, and of intense racial smugness and arrogance, with not a graceful, pretty one anywhere who is not, at the same time, a joke—shocked and delighted me.

It was for her description of Southern white women that I appreciated her work at first, because when she set her pen to them not a whiff of magnolia hovered in the air (and the tree itself might never have been planted), and yes, I could say, yes, these white folks without the magnolia (who are indifferent to the tree's existence), and these black folks without melons and superior racial patience, these are like Southerners that I know.

She was for me the first great modern writer from the South, and was, in any case, the only one I had read who wrote such sly, demythifying sentences about white women as: "The woman would be more or less pretty—yellow hair, fat ankles, muddy-colored eyes."

Her white male characters do not fare any better—all of them misfits, thieves, deformed madmen, idiot children, illiterates, and murderers, and her black characters, male and female, appear equally shallow, demented, and absurd. That she retained a certain distance (only, however, in her later, mature work) from the inner workings of her black characters seems to me all to her credit, since, by deliberately limiting her treatment of them to cover their observable demeanor and actions, she leaves them free, in the reader's imagination, to inhabit another landscape, another life, than the one she creates for them. This is a kind of grace many writers do not have when dealing with representatives of an oppressed people within a story, and their insistence on knowing everything, on being God, in fact, has burdened us with more stereotypes than we can ever hope to shed.

In her life, O'Connor was more casual. In a letter to her friend Robert Fitzgerald in the mid-fifties she wrote, "as the niggers say, I have the misery." He found nothing offensive, apparently, in including this unflattering (to O'Connor) statement in his Introduction to one of her books. O'Connor was then certain she was dying, and was in pain; one assumes she made this comment in an attempt at levity. Even so, I do not find it funny. In another letter she wrote shortly before she died she said: "Justice is justice and should not be appealed to along racial lines. The problem is not abstract for the Southerner, it's concrete: he sees it in terms of persons, not races — which way of seeing does away with easy answers." Of course this observation, though grand, does not apply to the racist treatment of blacks by whites in the South, and O'Connor should have added that she spoke only for herself.

But *essential* O'Connor is not about race at all, which is why it is so refreshing, coming, as it does, out of such a *racial* culture. If it can be said to be "about" anything, then it is "about" prophets and prophecy, "about" revelation, and "about" the impact of supernatural grace on human beings who don't have a chance of spiritual growth without it.

An indication that *she* believed in justice for the individual (if only in the corrected portrayal of a character she invented) is shown by her endless reworking of "The Geranium," the first story she published (in 1946), when she was twenty-one. She revised the story several times, renamed it at least twice, until, nearly twenty years after she'd originally published it (and significantly, I think, after the beginning of the Civil Rights Movement), it became a different tale. Her two main black characters, a man and a woman, underwent complete metamorphosis.

In the original story, Old Dudley, a senile racist from the South, lives with his daughter in a New York City building that has "niggers" living in it too. The black characters are described as being passive, self-effacing people. The black woman sits quietly, hands folded, in her apartment; the man, her husband, helps Old Dudley up the stairs when the old man is out of breath, and chats with him kindly, if condescendingly, about guns and hunting. But in the final version of the story, the woman walks around Old Dudley (now called Tanner) as if he's an open bag of garbage, scowls whenever she sees him, and "didn't look like any kind of woman, black or white, he had ever seen." Her husband, whom Old Dudley persists in calling "Preacher" (under the misguided assumption that to all black men it is a courtesy title), twice knocks the old man down. At the end of the story he stuffs Old Dudley's head, arms, and legs through the banisters of the stairway "as if in a stockade," and leaves him to die. The story's final title is "Judgement Day."

The quality added is rage, and, in this instance, O'Connor waited until she saw it *exhibited* by black people before she recorded it.

She was an artist who thought she might die young, and who then knew for certain she would. Her view of her characters pierces right through to the skull. Whatever her characters' color or social position she saw them as she saw herself, in the light of imminent mortality. Some of her stories, "The Enduring Chill" and "The Comforts of Home" especially, seem to be written out of the despair that must, on occasion, have come from this bleak vision, but it is for her humor that she is most enjoyed and remembered. My favorites are these:

> Everywhere I go I'm asked if I think the universities stifle writers. My opinion is that they don't stifle enough of them. There's many a best-seller that could have been prevented by a good teacher.
>
> — MYSTERY AND MANNERS

> "She would of been a good woman, if it had been somebody there to shoot her every minute of her life."
>
> — "The Misfit," A GOOD MAN IS HARD TO FIND

> There are certain cases in which, if you can only learn to write poorly enough, you can make a great deal of money.
>
> — MYSTERY AND MANNERS

> It is the business of fiction to embody mystery through manners, and mystery is a great embarrassment to the modern mind.
>
> — MYSTERY AND MANNERS

It mattered to her that she was a Catholic. This comes as a surprise to those who first read her work as that of an atheist. She believed in all the mysteries of her faith. And yet, she was incapable of writing dogmatic or formulaic stories. No religious tracts, nothing haloed softly in celestial light, not even any happy endings. It has puzzled some of her readers and annoyed the Catholic church that in her stories not only does good not triumph, it is not usually present. Seldom are there choices, and God never intervenes to help anyone win. To O'Connor, in fact, Jesus was God, and he won only by losing. She perceived that not much has been learned by his death by crucifixion, and that it is only by his continual, repeated dying — touching one's own life in a direct, searing way — that the meaning of that original loss is pressed into the heart of the individual.

In "The Displaced Person," a story published in 1954, a refugee from Poland is hired to work on a woman's dairy farm. Although he speaks in apparent gibberish, he is a perfect worker. He works so assiduously the woman begins to prosper beyond her greatest hopes. Still, because his ways are not her own (the Displaced Person attempts to get one of the black dairy workers to marry his cousin by "buying" her out of a Polish concentration camp), the woman allows a runaway tractor to roll over and kill him.

"As far as I'm concerned," she tells the priest, "Christ was just another D.P." He just didn't fit in. After the death of the Polish refugee, however, she understands her complicity in a modern crucifixion, and recognizes the enormity of her responsibility for other human beings. The impact of this new awareness debilitates her; she loses her health, her farm, even her ability to speak.

This moment of revelation, when the individual comes face to face with her own limitations and comprehends "the true frontiers of her own inner country," is classic O'Connor, and always arrives in times of extreme crisis and loss.

There is a resistance by some to read O'Connor because she is "too difficult," or because they do not share her religious "persuasion." A young man who studied O'Connor under the direction of Eudora Welty some years ago amused me with the following story, which may or may not be true:

"I don't think Welty and O'Connor understood each *other*," he said, when I asked if he thought O'Connor would have liked or understood Welty's more conventional art. "For Welty's part, wherever we reached a particularly dense and symbolic section of one of O'Connor's stories she would sigh and ask, 'Is there a Catholic in the class?' "

Whether one "understands" her stories or not, one knows her characters are new and wondrous creations in the world and that not one of her stories — not even the earliest ones in which her consciousness of racial matters had not evolved sufficiently to be interesting or to differ much from the insulting and ignorant racial stereotyping that preceded it — could have been written by anyone else. As one can tell a Bearden from a Keene or a Picasso from a Hallmark card, one can tell an O'Connor story from any story laid next to it. Her Catholicism did not in any way limit (by defining it) her art. After her great stories of sin, damnation, prophecy, and revelation, the stories one reads casually in the average magazine seem to be about love and roast beef.

Andalusia is a large white house at the top of a hill with a view of a lake from its screened-in front porch. It is neatly kept, and there are, indeed, peacocks strutting about in the sun. Behind it there is an unpainted house where black people must have lived. It was, then, the typical middle-to-upper-class arrangement: white folks up front, the "help," in a far shabbier house, within calling distance from the back door. Although an acquaintance of O'Connor's has told me no one lives there now — but that a caretaker looks after things — I go up to the porch and knock. It is not an entirely empty or symbolic gesture. I have come to this vacant house to learn something about myself in relation to Flannery O'Connor, and will learn it whether anyone is home or not.

What I feel at the moment of knocking is fury that someone is paid to take care of her house, though no one lives in it, and that her house still, in fact, stands, while mine — which of course we never owned anyway — is slowly rotting into dust. Her house becomes — in an instant — the symbol of my own disinheritance, and for that instant I hate her guts. All that she has meant to me is diminished, though her diminishment within me is against my will.

In Faulkner's backyard there is also an unpainted shack and a black caretaker still lives there, a quiet, somber man who, when asked about Faulkner's legendary "sense of humor" replied that, as far as he knew, "Mr. Bill never joked." For years, while reading Faulkner, this image of the quiet man in the backyard shack stretched itself across the page.

Standing there knocking on Flannery O'Connor's door, I do not think of her illness, her magnificent work in spite of it; I think: it all comes back to houses. To how people live. There are rich people who own houses to live in and poor people who do not. And this is wrong. Literary separatism, fashionable now among blacks as it has always been among whites, is easier to practice than to change a fact like this. I think: I would level this country with the sweep of my hand, if I could.

"Nobody can change the past," says my mother.

"Which is why revolutions exist," I reply.

My bitterness comes from a deeper source than my knowledge of the difference, historically, race has made in the lives of white and black artists. The fact that in Mississippi no one even remembers where Richard Wright lived, while Faulkner's house is maintained by a black caretaker is painful, but not unbearable. What comes close to being unbearable is that I know how damaging to my own psyche such injustice is. In an unjust society the soul of the sensitive person is in danger of deformity from just such weights as this. For a long time I will feel Faulkner's house, O'Connor's house, crushing me. To fight back will require a certain amount of energy, energy better used doing something else.

My mother has been busy reasoning that, since Flannery O'Connor died young of a lingering and painful illness, the hand of God has shown itself. Then she sighs. "Well, you know," she says, "it is true, as they say, that the grass is always greener on the other side. That is, until you find yourself over there."

In a just society, of course, clichés like this could not survive.

"But grass *can* be greener on the other side and not be just an illusion," I say. "Grass on the other side of the fence might have good fertilizer, while grass on your side might have to grow, if it grows at all, in sand."

We walk about quietly, listening to the soft sweep of the peacocks' tails as they move across the yard. I notice how completely O'Connor, in her fiction, has described just this view of the rounded hills, the tree line, black against the sky, the dirt road that runs from the front yard down to the highway. I remind myself of her courage and of how much — in her art — she has helped me to see. She destroyed the last vestiges of sentimentality in white Southern writing; she caused white women to look ridiculous on pedestals, and she approached her black characters — as a mature artist — with unusual humility and restraint. She also cast spells and worked magic with the written word. The magic, the wit, and the mystery of Flannery O'Connor I know I will always love, I also know the meaning of the expression "Take what you can use and let the rest rot." If ever there was an expression designed to protect the health of the spirit, this is it.

As we leave O'Connor's yard the peacocks — who she said would have the last word — lift their splendid tails for our edification. One peacock is so involved in the presentation of his masterpiece he does not allow us to move the car until he finishes with his show.

"Peacocks are inspiring," I say to my mother, who does not seem at all in awe of them and actually frowns when she sees them strut, "but they sure don't stop to consider they might be standing in your way."

And she says, "Yes, and they'll eat up every bloom you have, if you don't watch out."

Note

1. Or, rather, the son totters numbly off. [Ed.]

ESSAYS

The Outside and the Inside:
Flannery O'Connor's
The Violent Bear It Away
Sumner J. Ferris*

Flannery O'Connor's new novel, *The Violent Bear It Away*, has a number of immediately striking resemblances, in its religious theme, its Southern setting, its frequently violent or macabre action, and its spiritually tortured characters, both to her short stories, especially those collected in *A Good Man Is Hard to Find* (1955), and to her first and only other novel, *Wise Blood* (1952).

The novel's chief character is a fourteen-year-old Southern orphan boy, Francis Marion Tarwater (usually just "Tarwater"), who was in infancy first baptized and later kidnapped by his great-uncle, who fancied himself a religious prophet. Raised to follow the old man's "calling," Tarwater nevertheless rebels; for when the great-uncle dies, the boy refuses to give him Christian burial and instead gets drunk and sets fire to the cabin where he thinks the corpse is (a Negro has meanwhile removed and buried it). Tarwater goes to the city, to his uncle, a schoolteacher called Rayber whom his great-uncle had likewise baptized and briefly kidnapped but who, at fourteen, had rejected religion; and from whom Tarwater had been kidnapped. Rayber has an unbaptized idiot son, called Bishop, whom of course the old man had tried to baptize and to kidnap and whom Tarwater is under injunction to baptize.[1] Tarwater rejects Rayber's clumsy attempts at befriending and educating him. Indeed, Rayber unintentionally keeps impressing the old man's lessons in on him, and Tarwater eventually half-accidentally drowns and half-unwittingly baptizes Bishop. He flees back to the cabin at Powderhead where he had lived with his great-uncle. On the way he is drugged and sexually assaulted while asleep by a man who gave him a ride; and on awakening he sets fire to the clearing where he is left. At home he finds that his uncle's body had been buried after all; and in violent resignation he sets fire to the woods here too, feels the call of prophecy, and returns to the city to convert the unbelieving.

Disregarding both the more and less obvious matters for the time

*Reprinted from *Critique*, 3, No. 2 (1960), 11–19, by permission of *Critique* and Sumner J. Ferris.

being, there are several parallels between this and some of Miss O'Connor's other works. Haze Motes in *Wise Blood*, like Tarwater here, was obsessed first with denying and then with accepting Christ. Harry-Bevel in "The River" was drowned in "the water of life," as is Bishop. The relation between the boy and his great-uncle, especially in the flashback recounting a visit by the two to the city, reminds one of "The Artificial Nigger." The fires Tarwater lights are like the one in "Circle of the Fire," in both provocation and significance. Rayber as a rationalist is like Asbury in "The Enduring Chill." Miss O'Connor still uses half-whimsical symbolic names: "Bishop" and "Tarwater," the latter with its implications of dirt and of a panacea, fit neatly into a novel about baptism.[2] Humor is less obtrusive here than in some of her other works (especially *Wise Blood* and Haze's unforgettable and triumphant "What do I need with Jesus? I got Leora Watts") but this novel has its moments, too; and as usual with Miss O'Connor, comic incongruities rather add to than detract from her seriousness: the great-uncle's monomania for kidnapping and baptizing his infant male relatives is particularly funny. And lastly, some of Miss O'Connor's favorite symbols, sometimes laid on a little thick in other works, reappear here too, and as before they tend to carry two or more opposing meanings simultaneously. Thus, water brings life and death; fire destroys and purifies; eyes reveal and impose purpose; and a physical infirmity (Rayber is deaf) mirrors a spiritual one.

By and large, then, Miss O'Connor's writings are strikingly alike in topic, theme, and technique. Consequently, her admirers as well as her detractors must realize that she has restricted herself to a particular locale, a particular society, and a particular kind of theme; and it is unlikely that she will surprise her readers in any of these respects for some time. It follows that it is just as unlikely that her popularity will grow, that her increasing mastery of both the craft and the art of fiction will be much noticed, that her greater and greater spiritual vision will be taken for anything but a preoccupation with the same subjects, and, in short, that she will be considered anything but a Southern woman novelist.[3] (It is ominous that the publisher of this book is different from that of her two earlier books.)

But such observations do not give the novel itself the attention and the praise it deserves. For, first of all, *The Violent Bear It Away* is an excellently constructed novel. Although *Wise Blood* had a beginning, a middle, and an end, the connections of its parts with one another were often obscure. But the three parts of this novel are both distinct from and dependent on one another, and the individual chapters (except the sometimes awkward flashback of Chapter II, a price paid for the immediacy of Chapter I) are not merely episodes in themselves, such as a short-story writer might be expected to produce, but cumulative and effective insofar as they are parts of the whole novel.

All writers of imaginative literature are between two horns: either underlining their meaning through repetition and recurring symbolism or trusting that their slightest hint will be — or ought to be — picked up by the hawk-eyed reader. But Miss O'Connor, as a writer on a religious subject with a religious theme (*Elmer Gantry* has a religious subject; *The Elder Statesman* has a religious theme), escapes the dilemma neatly: references to Habbakuk, Jonas, and Elias and Elisha; profanity that, in context, takes on an air of blasphemy (Rayber never says "God damn" or "Jesus Christ" but the reader feels its significance); and the very subject matter of the book not only are dramatically appropriate to her story but also underline her meaning and serve as leitmotifs to unify it.

But another, and for some readers perhaps a better, kind of unity and emphasis is provided by the structure of the novel itself. At the end of the first chapter, Tarwater, after burning the cabin, has hitched a ride with a traveling salesman:

> "Look," Tarwater said suddenly, sitting forward, his face close to the windshield, "we're headed in the wrong direction. We're going back where we came from. There's the fire again. There's the fire we left!"
>
> Ahead of them in the sky there was a faint glow, steady, and not made by lightning. "That's the same fire we came from!" the boy said in a high voice.
>
> "Boy, you must be nuts," the salesman said. "That's the glow from the city lights. I reckon this is your first trip anywhere."
>
> "You're turned around," the child said; "it's the same fire." (51–52)

In the last chapter, Tarwater, after hearing his call to prophecy, walks away from Powderhead:

> The moon, riding low above the field beside him, appeared and disappeared, diamond-bright, between patches of darkness. Intermittently the boy's jagged shadow slanted across the road ahead of him as if it cleared a rough path towards his goal. His singed eyes, black in their deep sockets, seemed already to envision the fate that awakened him but he moved steadily on, his face set toward the dark city, where the children of God lay sleeping. (243)

And if only these two passages were offered in evidence, Miss O'Connor's prose style could be called brilliant. The uniformly staccato rhythms of *Wise Blood* have been developed into smoother and more flexible ones. Consider just the pauses and the emphases of "a faint glow, steady, and not made by lightning" or the subtle but certainly intentional effect produced by the omission of the comma in the last sentence of the second long passage, where the lack of the anticipated rhetorical pause signals also how Tarwater's destiny is now beyond his control. Or the dialogue, all the more horrible for being matter-of-fact and blatantly colloquial. Or the way in which description is merged with narration and both are charged with symbolic meaning. Or the compassionate moving-in of the first passage, from "Tarwater" to "the boy" to "the child";

matched and contrasted beautifully in the second by a moving-away, from "the boy's" to "the children of God" — of whom, we realize, Tarwater is not one any more. Or the unobtrusive way — any teacher of writing knows it can't be taught — that the author's description alternates and merges insensibly with Tarwater's observations in the second passage. But to talk of Miss O'Connor's style in general would be gratuitous. It is never idiosyncratic; and, like that of all artists, it bears and rewards the closest attention.

II

The theme of *The Violent Bear It Away* is announced by means of an epigraph on the title pages: "From the days of John the Baptist until now, the kingdom of heaven suffereth violence, and the violent bear it away" (Matthew 11:12 in the Douai-Challoner Version; the King James Version is not appreciably different). This passage is taken by various Catholic exegetes (*v. A Catholic Commentary on the Holy Scriptures*) to have two different meanings: either that, with Christ's ministry begun, the faithful may at last attain the kingdom of heaven or (less commonly, parenthetically anticipating verses 16–19 of the same chapter) that the Pharisees, despite John's prophecy and Christ's ministry, still remain unbelievers and try to deny the faithful their reward. Much of the power of this novel comes from Miss O'Connor's rendering in her characters of the two attitudes represented by these two interpretations, that of the believer and that of the unbeliever, the violent and the passive, the saved and the damned.

This novel has already been praised for its "psychological realism." The comment was misdirected; for insofar as these characters are significant and interesting, it is not because of their personalities but because of their souls. Rayber, for example, seems at first to be the merest pasteboard figure: his school's expert on psychological testing, who sheltered his uncle — Tarwater's great-uncle — for four months only to observe him and, in an article in a "schoolteachers' magazine," describe him as a "nearly extinct type," that is, the religious fanatic. Rayber was shot in the ear with buckshot many years before when he tried to retrieve Tarwater from the old man; and the hearing aid he now wears, and can turn on and off at will, is an obvious, if amusing, device to characterize him as a modern rationalist who has ears to hear and hears not. "Do you think in the box," Tarwater asks him about the hearing aid, "or do you think in your head?"

But Rayber has not simply had a symbolic role thrust on him by the author. His condition, the condition of the Pharisee, is the result of an act of will; for he had, at Tarwater's age (the age of apprenticeship and of confirmation), willingly chosen the way of rationalism and thereafter avoided the extremes of religion, which, he tells Tarwater, "are for violent people." Tarwater shrewdly observes, though, that "the seed fell in" onto

Rayber through baptism. "It fell on bad ground," he goes on, "but it fell in deep"; and Rayber has had to devote his life to keeping it from growing; that is, to maintaining his rational equilibrium and rejecting grace, which is God's Love. Consequently, having rejected Love, he tries to resist the love for his own son that threatens to overwhelm him: "It was love without reason, love for something futureless, love that appeared to exist only to be itself, imperious and all demanding, the kind that would cause him to make a fool of himself in an instant." Yet he cannot completely resist it; and although he once tried to drown Bishop, his love for the child prevented him from doing so. And one night, chasing Tarwater through the streets to a revivalists' meeting, Rayber hears a child preaching on the love of Christ for his world — and frantically tries to turn off his hearing aid when the child points to him and asks him if he is saved.

But when Tarwater disturbs Rayber's peace, Rayber decides to reject the boy to regain it. And lying on a cot in a motel, while Tarwater and Bishop are out on the pond in a boat, he temporarily does regain it, through absolute denial: "He told himself that he was indifferent even to his dissolution. It seemed to him that this indifference was the most that human dignity could achieve. . . . To feel nothing was peace." But when he hears screams from the pond, he knows immediately that Bishop has been drowned; and he realizes that he has created a hell for himself through his denial, a hell of vacuity, the awful state of the spiritual trimmer deprived equally of torment and of grace. The last scene in which he appears, at the end of Part II, shows him standing at a window, overlooking the dark pond:

> He stood waiting for the raging pain, the intolerable hurt that was
> his due, to begin, so that he could ignore it, but he continued to feel
> nothing. He stood light-headed at the window and it was not until he
> realized there would be no pain that he collapsed. (203)

Tarwater's rejection of God is more violent and less pharisaical than Rayber's. But Tarwater has an important task to perform. "Himself baptized by his great-uncle into the death of Christ," he must in turn bring spiritual life through baptism to his cousin Bishop: "Precious in the sight of the Lord even an idiot," his great-uncle has told him. But he goes to the city not to do this but to see whether what he had been taught about the history of the world was true; that is, for knowledge rather than grace. But grace pursues him. Rayber can not only teach him nothing but even keeps impressing, although unintentionally, his mission on him; and Bishop, whom he wants to ignore or hate, is drawn to Tarwater almost as though he knew why he had come.

Yet the long middle section of the novel, which treats the period between Tarwater's coming to the city and Bishop's death, does not often investigate the workings of Tarwater's mind; for it would be a mistake to suppose, as Rayber does, that the boy is simply responding to his great-uncle's psychological indoctrination. Rather, for all the old man's fanaticism, it is clear that for Miss O'Connor the baptism of Bishop is the most important action Tarwater could perform; and that he is being forced to do it by a concatenation of circumstances beyond his control and different from the merely psychological — which, to the Christian, is another way of saying by Providence. Twice in the novel Bishop tries to jump into a fountain; the second time he is illuminated by a sudden bright shaft of sunlight as by a nimbus. And even when Tarwater has decided, as a final act of rejection, to drown his cousin (for, he thinks, "In dealing with the dead [that is, his great-uncle] you have to act. There's no mere word sufficient to say NO"), Bishop himself stands up in the boat, climbs onto Tarwater's back like the Christ child onto St. Christopher's and falls into the water with him. That is, Bishop, having been refused salvation through baptism by his own father, forces Tarwater to give it to him, although it is the moment of Tarwater's most violent rejection of God and although it is at the cost of his own physical death.

Both Rayber and Tarwater, then, are described in different ways by the title. Rayber's passivity has done violence to Bishop's soul; Tarwater's violence, though it involved Bishop's death, has at least thrust him into the kingdom of heaven. And although a certain pathos undoubtedly attaches to Rayber, Tarwater's action must be, in the world Miss O'Connor depicts, for the greater glory of God.

This is not to say, however, that Tarwater himself is saved; for he may be an instrument of God's providence without being of His company. (One reason, it seems, why Rayber could not drown Bishop was that he could not baptize him at the same time.) Early in the novel, after the old man has died, a "stranger," whom Tarwater soon comes to think of as just his "friend," begins to talk to the boy in his mind, to sow doubts in his mind about the religious teaching he has received, and to urge him not to give the corpse Christian burial (and thus, in orthodox theology, the hope of resurrection at the Last Judgment). Tarwater, of course, follows the stranger's suggestions, recoiling from his uncle's vision of the final reward of the just, "The Lord Jesus Himself, the bread of life":

> The boy would have a hideous vision of himself, sitting forever with his great-uncle on a green bank, full and sick, staring at a broken fish and a multiplied loaf. (62)

This image is not picked up immediately, but it becomes crucial to the interpretation of Tarwater's end. In the city the boy becomes dissatisfied with the unfamiliar food his uncle gives him; and, when they reach the resort together, he finds himself increasingly unable to eat. In the last section of the novel, after Tarwater has assisted in his cousin's drowning, and he himself has come to identify his physical hunger with a spiritual hunger, he is unable to eat the half of a chicken sandwich a truckdriver has given him and is refused a bottle of pop by a store-owner who has heard of his intended desecration of his great-uncle's corpse. It is hardly extreme to equate the sandwich and the pop with the sacramental bread and wine, which in turn become the body and blood of Christ and nourish the faithful; and so Tarwater's proud rejection of God has excommunicated him from the society of the faithful. The brutal assault he suffers is therefore an image of what he has done to himself, an awful reflection of the perverted love of man without God; for he has refused the bread of life.

The call that Tarwater hears and obeys at the end of the novel, after he discovers that his great-uncle had after all been buried, is thus a specious one, a capitulation to circumstances rather than to God; for although he has fulfilled God's will, he has rejected God's ways. It is with the passion of fanaticism and despair, not of religion, that, hellfire behind him and darkness before him, he begins to walk back to the city.

Miss O'Connor's world is a violent one, but the violence is ultimately spiritual, inflicted by the characters on themselves. Her theology is, furthermore, Catholic (although none of her characters in the novel are). God neither saves nor damns any of the characters who have free will; although He provides that the helpless Bishop be baptized and thus saved, He does no more than give Rayber and Tarwater the opportunity to work out their own salvation or damnation. And it is this characteristic that makes *The Violent Bear It Away* not only a subtle and profound and disturbing study of spiritual states but a great religious novel. Miss O'Connor has shown that a Christian tragedy can be written; for in her novel fate and doom do not conspire against man. Either struggling against grace or opening his arms to accept it, his choice is his own.

Notes

1. As originally published in *New World Writing* 8 (1955), with the title of "You Can't Be Any Poorer Than Dead," the memorable first chapter did not show the old man as a self-appointed prophet nor, more important, Rayber's son as an idiot. Did Miss O'Connor change an originally picaresque conception of the novel to a theological one?

2. One far-fetched but attractive observation may be made about these two names, that although Bishop Berkeley was a famous empirical philosopher, he nevertheless attributed almost magic powers to tarwater.

3. I shall not compare Miss O'Connor with the so-called Southern school not only because — for good reasons — she eschews membership in such a school (see her essay in Granville Hicks's *The Living Novel*), but because insofar as she does treat concerns that other Southern authors do, her treatment, in both theme and technique, is as different from theirs as theirs are from one another and because such vogue words as "decadent" and "Gothic" are so vague as to be almost meaningless. Nevertheless, Bishop has a resemblance in some particulars to Benjy in *The Sound and the Fury*; and so has Lucette Carmody's sermon to "Rev'un Shegog's" in the same novel. (Perhaps Miss O'Connor's method of treating introspection, especially on matters of "doom" or "fate" — words she uses sparingly, however — may owe something to Faulkner, too.) But the resemblances are only superficial; and a great novel by a Nobel-Prizewinner can hardly be called just a "Southern novel."

Flannery O'Connor's Devil   John Hawkes*

Eventually students of literature may come to think of Flannery O'Connor not only in terms of coldness, detachment and "black" humor, but also in terms of an older or more familiar tradition. In a letter not long ago she said, "I think I would admit to writing what Hawthorne called 'romances'. . . . I feel more of a kinship with Hawthorne than with any other American writer. . . ." Surely such an expression of kinship is a sober one, coming as it does from a comic writer whose humor was described as "slam-bang" and whose style was called "as balefully direct as a death sentence" by *Time Magazine*. But of course this comic writer is a serious writer — say, in her moral preoccupations, her poetic turn of mind and incredible uses of paradox — and her remark about her affinity with Hawthorne deserves juxtaposition, it seems to me, with a statement such as this one from Edwin Honig's book on allegory: "Melville's problem, like Hawthorne's, was to find a method whereby a vigorous moral and aesthetic authority could be recreated in fiction. For him, as for his predecessors, the challenge was to map out the relation of the unknown country of allegory to the known countries and conditions of contemporary actuality."[1]

That this statement is more appropriate to Flannery O'Connor than to most other contemporary American writers; that the problem and challenge it describes are curiously hers; that the authority it describes is precisely what lies behind her "brutal" laughter; that "unknown country" and "actuality" are precisely what her fiction combines in a mercilessly pleasurable tension — all this is reason enough for making the juxtaposition above. And also reason enough for raising and perhaps evading the final question of the extent to which Flannery O'Connor's work should be considered allegorical. But here I must mention my faith in the occult nature of minor coincidence since it was Melville's granddaughter, a lady I was once privileged to know in Cambridge, Massachusetts, who first urged me to read the fiction of Flannery O'Connor, and — further — since this experience occurred just at the time I had discovered the short novels of Nathanael West.

At that time — about ten years ago — the sudden confluence of West and Flannery O'Connor to me suggested twin guffawing peals of thunder (the figure is borrowed from "The Life You Save May Be Your Own") above a dead landscape quite ready for new humor, new vision, new and more meaningful comic treatments of violence. Though he died in 1940, West is the one writer who, along with Flannery O'Connor, deserves singular attention as a rare American satirist. I would propose that West

*Reprinted from *Sewanee Review*, 70 (1962), 395–407, by permission of *Sewanee Review* and John Hawkes.

and Flannery O'Connor are very nearly alone today in their pure creation of "aesthetic authority," and would also propose, of course, that they are very nearly alone in their employment of the devil's voice as vehicle for their satire or for what we may call their true (or accurate) vision of our godless actuality. Their visions are different. And yet, as we might expect, these two comic writers are unique in sharing a kind of inverted attraction for the reality of our absurd condition.

We may think of satire as "centralizing a dominant ideal by means of irony and analogy,"[2] and also as a form which "demolishes man's image of himself as a rational creature."[3] It may be that most generally in West's satiric fictions the "dominant ideal," never more than implied, is merely the serenity of dissolution, or release from the pains of sexual struggle and from the dead-end of an impossible striving toward God, all of this brought to "pitch" (to use Faulkner's word) by the comedy of the sexual struggle itself. Though Flannery O'Connor's "dominant ideal" is likely to be as difficult to discover as West's, it is nonetheless an absolute of which she is perfectly aware. She writes: "I don't think you should write something as long as a novel around anything that is not of the gravest concern to you and everybody else and for me this is always the conflict between an attraction for the Holy and the disbelief in it that we breathe in with the air of the times." Obviously West would never have made such a statement, and the polarity of the religious positions of these two writers is borne out in their novels.

West's preoccupation with the "Christ business" begins as joke in *The Dream Life of Balso Snell*, reaches a partly confused and sentimental climax in *Miss Lonelyhearts*, and in *The Day of the Locust* finally dwindles to sporadic and surface satires on the freak Hollywood church as bad answer. Whereas Flannery O'Connor's first novel, *Wise Blood*, concerns a circuit preacher's grandson who is so violently opposed to Christ that in the end, after an immolation that involves self-blinding (among other things), he is last seen by his worldly landlady as "going backwards to Bethlehem"; and *The Violent Bear It Away*, her recent and more ambitious novel, describes the metamorphosis of a similar young Fundamentalist into a prophet who accepts his burden and turns "toward the dark city, where the children of God lay sleeping."

But if West wrote less effectively whenever he attempted to take into account the presence or absence of God, while Flannery O'Connor would not write at all without what she calls the "attraction for the Holy"; or if it appears that Flannery O'Connor is writing about the spirit (the absurdity of disbelief), while Nathanael West was writing about the dream (the painful absurdity of sexual desire), at least I would say that the "pitch" of their comic fictions is very nearly the same. Both writers are demolishing "man's image of himself as a rational creature" (Flannery O'Connor, for instance, in her wonderfully unsympathetic portrait of the ridiculous school teacher, Rayber, in *The Violent Bear It Away*, and West in his creation of total and hapless dementia in *The Day of the Locust*). And both writers are reversing their artistic sympathies, West committing himself to the creative pleasures of a destructive sexuality, Flannery O'Connor committing herself creatively to the antics of soulless characters who leer, or bicker, or stare at obscenities on walls, or maim each other on a brilliant but barren earth. And finally both writers—one a Roman Catholic, the other a man of no particular religious drive—are remarkably similar in their exploitation of the "demolishing" syntax of the devil. But then a good many readers would mistake Flannery O'Connor's belief in the Holy for its opposite, in the same way that many readers might be misled into thinking of Nathanael West as a Christian *manqué*. The point is that in the most vigorously moral of writers the actual creation of fiction seems often to depend on immoral impulse.

It is obvious that West's distortions (his incorrigible giving way to joke, or his use of cathected patterns of physical detail in the place of conventional plotting) are constructed for the sake of psychological truth as well as from the sheer necessity for liberation from a constraining realism. Furthermore, it is obvious that his distortions depend in no way on an outside "framed" body of orthodoxy for their "authority." Once imagined, his comic vision *is* in fact its own authority. However, it needs to be said that Flannery O'Connor's work is just as great a violation of probability and of anticipated, familiar "reality" as West's. In *Wise Blood* two policemen turn out to be sadistic versions of Tweedledum and Tweedledee; in *The Violent Bear It Away* the devil himself quite literally appears, wearing a cream-colored hat and lavender suit and carrying a whiskey bottle filled with blood in the glove compartment of his enormous car; or, in this same novel, there is the comic fanaticism of the old great-uncle who continues to sit for a whole morning bolt upright at the breakfast table where he "died before he got the first spoonful to his mouth." And it also needs to be said that such fictive distortions of Flannery O'Connor are just as independent as those of Nathanael West.

Surely if the elements of Flannery O'Connor's fiction could be referred point for point to the established principles of a known orthodoxy, then many of the imaginative beauties and tensions of her fiction would disappear. But this is not the case. The very revivalist or circuit-preacher Protestant world of her fiction, with its improbable combination of religious faith and eccentricity, accounts in large part for the way in which "unknown country" and "actuality" are held in severe balance in her work. And then there is the creative impulse itself, so unflagging and so unpredictable as to become, in a sense, "immoral." Hovering behind the fiction this impulse has about it the energy and unassailable paradox of the grandfather in *Wise Blood*, who was "a waspish old man who had ridden over three counties with Jesus hidden in his head like a stinger." Within her almost luridly bright pastoral world—usually created as meaningless or indifferent or corrupted—the characters of Flannery O'Connor are *judged*, victimized, made to appear only as absurd entities of the flesh. Or, sometimes, they are allowed to experience their moments of mystery. But the mysterious baptismal drowning of an idiot child (to take one central example from *The Violent Bear It Away*) is in certain ways quite similar to the call — "full of melancholy and weariness, yet marvelously sweet" — of a trapped quail about to be cut apart with a pair of tin shears and fried in a skillet (*The Day of the Locust*). In other words, and thinking of artistic commitment in conflict with "dominant ideal," the improbable yet fictionally true Hollywood landscape of West is very like the improbable yet fictionally true "Free Thinking" evangelistic landscape of Flannery O'Connor. There is no security, no answer, to be found in either of these horrifying and brightly imagined worlds.

I have spoken of the devil's voice as vehicle for satire, and of the devil's "demolishing" syntax; and have suggested that there is a relationship to be found between fictive "authority" and "immoral" author-impulse in the comic works of West and Flannery O'Connor. To me it is important to stress these generalities because both West and Flannery O'Connor write *about* the devil, or at least about diabolical figures (most obviously Shrike in *Miss Lonelyhearts* and Tarwater's Friend — who is a literal *heard* version of the devil — in *The Violent Bear It Away*), but seem also to reflect the verbal mannerisms and explosively reductive attitudes of such figures in their own "black" authorial stances. When I suggested to Flannery O'Connor some time ago that as writer she was on the devil's side she responded at once — and of course to disagree.

Despite the comparison made above between the baptismal drowning of the idiot child and the "marvelously sweet" call of the trapped quail, it is clear that there is, actually, a considerable difference between the experiences of mystery as created by West and by Flannery O'Connor. No matter his preoccupation with the darkness of life, West could never have taken seriously an idea of the devil (as he could not an idea of the Holy), while on the other hand Flannery O'Connor has phrased this aspect of her concern with typical and shocking clarity: "I want to be certain that the devil gets identified as the devil and not simply taken for this or that psychological tendency." A statement as matter-of-fact as this one, with its explicit acceptance of the devil's existence and explicit renunciation of all his works, does little to help my argument concerning her "true" fictional allegiance — the more so since Flannery O'Connor herself has pointed out the difference between her devil (Lucifer, a fallen angel) and the authorial-devil I have been speaking of (to her no more than a subjective creation and rather alien to her thinking). But there is an interesting distance between the directness of her statement and profundity of belief, and the shifting, even deceptive substance of what Flannery O'Connor, with disarming humor and understatement, has called her "one-cylinder syntax." My own feeling is that just as the creative process threatens the Holy throughout Flannery O'Connor's fiction by generating a paradoxical fusion of improbability and passion out of the Protestant "do-it-yourself" evangelism of the South, and thereby raises the pitch of apocalyptic experience when it finally appears; so too, throughout this fiction, the creative process transforms the writer's objective Catholic knowledge of the devil into an authorial attitude in itself in some measure diabolical. This is to say that in Flannery O'Connor's most familiar stories and novels the "disbelief . . . that we breathe in with the air of the times" emerges fully as two-sided or complex as "attraction for the Holy."

Two passages from *The Violent Bear It Away* will illustrate the shifting substance of Flannery O'Connor's language and authorial attitude. The action of this novel is centered about a legacy of two obligations left to the young protagonist, Tarwater, by the old man (and Prophet) who is his great-uncle and who is also the medium through which the course of Tarwater's life is determined. One obligation is to bury the old man when he dies (which Tarwater fails to do because of the persuasive voice of his new Friend, the devil), and another is to baptize little Bishop, the idiot child (which Tarwater does manage to do, but against his will, and then only by drowning the "dim-witted boy"). The first passage below appears early in the novel and concerns the argument between Tarwater and his Friend over the burial; the second appears toward the end of the novel and concerns the lake in which the baptism finally occurs (the dialogue in both passages occurs in Tarwater's head, hence the absence of quotation marks; italicizing is mine):

> Oh I see, the stranger said. It ain't the Day of Judgment for him [the old Prophet] you're worried about. It's the Day of Judgment for you.
> That's my bidnis, Tarwater said.
> I ain't buttin into your bidnis, the stranger said. It don't mean a thing to me. *You're left by yourself in this empty place. Forever by yourself in this empty place with just as much light as that dwarf sun wants to let in. You don't mean a thing to a soul as far as I can see.*

> The first sight that met his eyes when he [Tarwater] got out of the car at the Cherokee Lodge was the little lake. It lay there, glass-like, still, reflecting a crown of trees and an infinite overarching sky. *It looked so unused that it might only the moment before have been set down by four strapping angels for him to baptize the child in.* A weakness working itself up from his knees, reached his stomach and came upward and forced a tremor in his jaw. *Steady, his friend said, everywhere you go you'll find water. It wasn't invented yesterday.*

The Violent Bear It Away actualizes the truth of the devil's sentiments — Tarwater does not, in fact, "mean a thing to a soul" and lives only in the stalwart nausea of his resistance to the Prophet's calling and in the ultimate grim pleasure of his acceptance of that call. By the end of the novel we know that Tarwater will be destroyed by "the children of God," or destroyed by our godless actuality.

But surely in giving voice to his dry country-cadenced nihilism and in laying out the pure deflated truth of mere existence ("Forever by yourself in this empty place"), the devil is speaking not only for himself but for the author. Of course the devil is attempting to persuade Tarwater that he is exactly like everybody else in "this empty place," and is attempting to persuade Tarwater to *be* himself and to *do* what he wants, since given the fact of mere existence there is nothing else to be or do. While of course the author is dramatizing the opposite, that Tarwater is *not* like everybody else and that he is destined to suffer the extremities of the pain involved in the conflict between the "mean" earth and symbolic waters. However, the devil takes obvious pleasure in going about his own "bidnis" and the author takes a similar obvious pleasure in going about hers. And there are numerous examples to indicate that the author's view of "everybody else" is exactly the same as her devil's view. (There is the young mother "whose face was as broad and innocent as a cabbage" in "A Good Man Is Hard to Find"; there is the old woman who "was about the size of a cedar fence post" in "The Life You Save May Be Your Own"; or the mother who has two little boys who stand with faces "like pans set on either side to catch the grins that overflowed from her" in *Wise Blood*.)

In these last examples the creation of flat personality—each instance is a kind of small muffled explosion—depends on the extreme absurdity of juxtaposing the human and the inanimate, and I think that the fact of the reductive or diabolical value judgment is clear, though to be sure there are degrees of judgment and degrees of sympathy too in the range of Flannery O'Connor's wonderfully merciless creations of the human type. But even more clear perhaps, or at least more important, is the basic principle or association that fills out the devil's nihilism and defines the diabolical attitude that lies behind the reversal of artistic sympathy—that is, the "meanness"-pleasure principle. When Tarwater discovers what he takes to be his freedom—for him it is the license to do whatever he wants, and it comes to him while he is trying to dig his great-uncle's grave—his first thought is simply, "Could kill off all those chickens if I had a mind to. . . ." And Flannery O'Connor appears to reveal her own understanding of earthly (and, I would say, artistic) pleasure when she writes that "Haze [the protagonist of *Wise Blood*] knows what the choice is and the Misfit [the extraordinary convict in 'A Good Man Is Hard to Find'] knows what the choice is—either throw away everything and follow Him or enjoy yourself by doing some meanness to somebody, and in the end there's no real pleasure in life, not even in meanness." I suspect that for many readers today such a principle or such a cold paradox of stringent alternatives would prove merely accurate or baffling or offensive. Yet here, I think, is the core of traditional satiric impulse, or the core of what we may call contemporary "anti-realistic" impulse.

However, to return to the italicized portions of the two passages quoted above from *The Violent Bear It Away*, and noticing the similarity between the devil's country-cadences or constructions and the author's, we might well ask how a reader baffled by the purity of the devil's attitude and intention is to react to an author capable of tilting our expectations *negatively* toward the apocalyptic by confronting us suddenly with the incongruous vision of "four strapping angels." Certainly this second passage about the lake is lovely and shocking both. We admire it essentially for the extreme compression within which the writer modulates through three distinct "voices." That is, we are taken abruptly but skillfully from the direct and unbiased allusion to spirituality (the "*crown* of trees" and "infinite overarching sky") to the dispersive ambiguity of "unused" (the word has the disturbing connotations of "unused" in the earthly pragmatic sense—say, unused for boating—and hence extends this comically "realistic" view of life into the other world—"unused" for baptism) to the thoroughly double-purposed "angels" and Tarwater's sickness of recoil and anticipation, and finally to the ultimate reduction of the devil's own absurdly pragmatic (and at the same time pathetic) view of "invented" water. Here the shifting voices and attitudes alone produce considerable tension. And even the devil's comic relief—at once poised on the edge of incredibility but also actualizing simultaneously the range of our possible "resistance" and the sheer fact of the impossibility of resistance (even the devil knows the implication of "everywhere you go you'll find water")—is in a sense an unwanted comic relief. However, the center of the tension for the reader, himself ensnared in the meanness-pleasure paradox, still lies in the metaphor of the "four strapping angels." If we consider what the passage might have been like had "four" and "strapping" been omitted ("It looked so unused that it might only the moment before have been set down by angels for him to baptize the child in") we have become aware, first of the enormous loss that would have resulted from such omission, and second that the basis for the figure as it stands is a *literalness* which in its faithfulness to rationality is at once appropriate and absurd. Since literalness is also the basis of Fundamentalism, we may say that the figure returns us to the two components (improbability and "attraction for the Holy") originally seen as constituting the apocalyptic half of Flannery O'Connor's fiction. Or we may say that through her exploitation of satiric and sympathetic impulses she is attempting to maintain the balance of that conflict grounded in the fictional possibility of redemption. But my own feeling is that the comic humanizing of the giant "strapping" angels cannot be explained away in this fashion, and that it actually represents those creative impulses of the writer which point toward the other side of her imagination—the demonic.

I would not say that Flannery O'Connor's uses of image and symbol are inconsistent, but rather—to pursue the lines of this argument—that they are mildly perverse. If the writer commits herself at least creatively to the voice and attitude of her imagined devil, or if her imagined devil is at least a partial heightening of her own creative voice and attitude, then we have only to compare "that dwarf sun" with the "crown of trees" in order to interpret the very strength of her authority as being in a way perverse. In Flannery O'Connor's fiction personified nature is often minimized (the devil's view of the sun, or this corresponding author-description from "The Life You Save May Be Your Own": "A fat yellow moon appeared in the branches of the fig tree as if it were going to roost there with the chickens"). Or it is made to assume a baldly leering attitude toward the jocular evil antics of the men in its midst (the "guffawing peal of thunder" from the same story). And if Bishop, the little idiot child, is intended to establish an innocence that points toward the apocalyptic, old Singleton, an insane comic figure in "The Partridge Festival," is intended to be exactly the opposite — crazy and lecherous and pointing toward the demonic. The danger inherent in any over-simplified effort to discover consistent patterns or systems of traditional symbolic materials in this fiction is obvious (thinking of idiocy or insanity as traditionally sanctified conditions) when all at once the windshield wipers of an automobile make "a great clatter like two idiots clapping in church" (*Wise Blood*).

Certainly Flannery O'Connor reveals what can only be called brilliant creative perversity when she brings to life a denuded *actuality* and writes about a "cat-faced baby" or a confidence man with "an honest look that fitted into his face like a set of false teeth" or an automobile horn that makes "a sound like a goat's laugh cut off with a buzz saw." This much, I should think, is happily on the side of the devil.

Since I have mentioned that Flannery O'Connor does not agree with my notion of her central fictional allegiance, it is only right to say that our disagreement may not be so extensive after all, and that she has written that, "Those moments (involving awareness of the Holy) are prepared for — by me anyway — by the intensity of the evil circumstances." She also writes, "I suppose the devil teaches most of the lessons that lead to self-knowledge." And further that "her" devil is the one who goes about "piercing pretensions, not the devil who goes about seeking whom he may devour." If Flannery O'Connor were asked where she would locate the center of her creative impulse, she might reply, "in the indication of Grace." But then again she might not. And I suspect that she would not reply at all to such a question. It may be, too, that I have been giving undue stress to the darker side of her imaginative constructions, and that the devil I have been speaking of is only a metaphor, a way of referring to a temperament strong enough and sympathetic enough to sustain the work of piercing pretension. To think so, of course, takes much of the pleasure out of the piercing.

I shall continue to evade the final question of whether Flannery O'Connor is a writer of allegories, and whether she is to be associated with

Hawthorne because he wrote "romances" or because he had his own indebtedness to evil principle. Very likely the principle and the form are inseparable. At any rate, and though the landscape is not as dead or mirthless as it was ten years ago, Flannery O'Connor's writing stands out against all those immediate fictions which are precious or flatulent or tending to retreat into the security of a constraining realism. The voice of her devil speaks with a new and essential shrewdness about what Nathanael West called "the truly monstrous."

Notes

1. Edwin Honig, *Dark Conceit: The Making of Allegory* (Evanston: Northwestern Univ. Press, 1959), pp. 102–103.
2. Honig, p. 158.
3. Honig, p. 163.

The Audacity of Flannery O'Connor

Michel Gresset*

"In fiction two and two is always more than four."
— Flannery O'Connor

Once more, mostly through the agency of Maurice-Edgar Coindreau, the French public can now read virtually the whole of Flannery O'Connor's prose work: two novels and thirty or so short stories.[1] A small oeuvre, indeed. And yet few literary careers so small hide so many magnificent punches from the reader, or have, for the critic, so many difficulties in interpretation. Certain of her stories are of a near geometrical perfection: for instance, "Everything That Rises Must Converge." The two longest stories, "The Displaced Person" and "The Lame Shall Enter First," shock by both their severity and their emotional intrusiveness. As for the two novels, *Wise Blood* and *The Violent Bear It Away*, their value derives from being unique in a genre that the author virtually invented: not tragicomedy but a narrative whose tone is located at once beyond that of comedy, in farce, and outside that of tragedy, in a spiritual drama. Last and most important, Flannery O'Connor's work draws its power from a remarkable gift for *audacity*.

By audacity, I don't mean the sort of quantitative license in which a writer like Updike has squandered his gifts and which will always appeal

*This essay was translated for this volume by T. G. Bernard-West and is published here with the permission of Michel Gresset. The French version originally appeared in *La Nouvelle Revue Française*, No. 216 (December 1970), 61-71.

to publishers and writers of American best-sellers.[2] This is, rather, a kind of *permissiveness*, the largest common denominator of a commercial calculation, an intellectual slovenliness and a moral abdication. (It sometimes passes for tolerance but this sort of tolerance resembles the last, besieged refuge of "liberal" philosophy.)

Nor do I mean the sort of audacity Rex Warner once spoke of, defining it as "the perfection of the unexpected."[3] It is that quality which urged Melville, in *Moby-Dick*, to open with his cheeky gambit, "Call me Ishmael," and Conrad with his masterful introduction to *Lord Jim*: "He was an inch, perhaps two, under six feet, powerfully built. . . ." This kind of audacity raises questions of style and form whilst the former is concerned more with sociology.

Flannery O'Connor's audacity might be defined as the perfection of repetition in spite of differences. One might think of this as a *line* (in the sense of an "ideological line"): it is all at once a continuity of invention, an unshakable faithfulness to one central aim, an imperturbable and resolute will to demonstrate, and a quality of total intransigence and supreme reticence that nothing can alter, not even indecency — nowhere better illustrated than in the last, superb part of *The Violent Bear It Away*.

Tarwater, the great-nephew of an aging and solitary madman whose fanatical religious obsessions have tempered like steel the still mobile mind of the child he has reared, draws to the end of a long journey of initiation after murdering a retarded boy, whose death forms part of a ritual profoundly determined by Tarwater's bizarre upbringing. He returns to the heart of the forest where he lived with his great-uncle. On the way, he is given a lift by a stranger singularly reminiscent of Popeye in *Sanctuary*:

> Then he turned and looked at the man and an unpleasant sensation that he could not place came over him. The person who had picked him up was a pale, lean, old-looking young man with deep hollows under his cheekbones. He had on a lavender shirt and a thin black suit and a panama hat. His lips were as white as the cigaret that hung limply from one side of his mouth. His eyes were the same color as his shirt and were ringed with heavy black lashes.[4]

On the way, the anonymous man makes Tarwater drink liquor. Then he stops and carries off the numbed boy into the woods.

> Nothing passed on the dirt road and the sun continued to move with a brilliant blandness on its way. The woods were silent except for an occasional trill or caw. The air itself might have been drugged. Now and then a large silent floating bird would glide into the treetops and after a moment rise again.
>
> In about an hour, the stranger emerged alone and looked furtively about him. He was carrying the boy's hat for a souvenir and also the corkscrew-bottleopener. His delicate skin had acquired a faint pink tint as if he had refreshed himself on blood. He got quickly into his car and sped away.

> When Tarwater woke up, the sun was directly overhead, very small and silver, sifting down light that seemed to spend itself before it reached him. He saw first his thin white legs stretching in front of him. He was propped up against a log that lay across a small open space between two very tall trees. His hands were loosely tied with a lavender handkerchief which his friend had thought of as an exchange for the hat. His clothes were neatly piled by his side. Only his shoes were on him. He perceived that his hat was gone. (*TVBIA*, 231–32)

Nothing is said. But this rape, dissimulated by finely calculated writing, must surely be without equal in literature. Each paragraph, taken as a number of motifs or as the sum of those motifs (shirt, lavender handkerchief — pink skin — blood — white legs; silence — birds — drugged air; the fetishist symbolism of clothing, and in particular the play of hat / shoes), is arranged in a singular manner, the motifs repeated like an echo that gathers volume; the motifs disseminate obliquely an unambiguous meaning in the narration, for what happens in the scene is unmistakable. Moreover, it is impossible not to grasp, even if confusedly, that this scene crowns Tarwater's education symbolically, and marks as well the immediate revenge of the retarded boy, and that something (grace perhaps, Flannery O'Connor's own message that is buried and preserved in the irony?) insinuates itself between these two readings. At whatever depth this message is to be found on the scale that begins with innocence and ends with cynicism, the reader is *aware* of a creeping malaise, here impossible to overlook. This is not an incidental but an essential part of O'Connor's art ("Fiction writing is very seldom a matter of saying things; it is a matter of showing things"),[5] which in this sense emulates Conrad, who already in 1897, in the preface to *The Nigger of the Narcissus*, wrote:

> My task which I am trying to achieve is, by the power of the written word, to make you hear, to make you feel — it is, before all, to make you *see*. That — and no more, and it is everything. If I succeed, you shall find there, according to your deserts, encouragement, consolation, fear, charm, all you demand — and, perhaps, also that glimpse of truth for which you have forgotten to ask. (quoted in *MM*, 80)

In Flannery O'Connor as in Conrad and all the great Anglo-Saxon symbolists, without ever leaving the sensual world we are in a world of pure fiction: nothing she writes depends in any way whatsoever on verisimilitude or on statistical probability. This is where, it seems to me, the whole mistaken, absurd debate about her art has taken place, between herself and a number of her American critics (often Northerners).

> Of course, I have found that anything that comes out of the South is going to be called grotesque by the Northern reader, unless it is grotesque, in which case it is going to be called realistic. (*MM*, 40)

You cannot parry such a repartee, just as you cannot parry her work, because it is like a gun that stalks a moving target; and its trajectory is just as linear as that of a bullet. But what is the target, the goal?

The name of the target, to my mind, is quite simply complacency. One has perhaps a tendency to forget that O'Connor's work is on one level a pitiless satire that, like that of Faulkner, echoes in three kinds of space — Southern, American and universal. Occasionally, of course, one of these reverberations is wanting: for example, in the short stories where the action begins with the arrival of a new employee on a farm run by a woman ("The Life You Save May Be Your Own" and "The Displaced Person"), we move directly from the tableau of typically Southern and rural manners to universal meanings (often underscored in fact by the titles of the short stories). On the other hand, in the stories that have more the feel of comedy ("A Stroke of Good Fortune," "A Temple of the Holy Ghost," "Parker's Back," and "Judgement Day"), some aspect of American rather than Southern culture is the target of the satire.

The satire is always aimed, like a spurt of vitriol, at woman folk. Flannery O'Connor's work unveils an unequalled gallery of ladies in green hats, some fat, vulgar and pretentious, and others skinny, mean and envious. The mother of Julian belongs to the former category:

> She was almost ready to go, standing before the hall mirror, putting on her hat, while he, his hands behind him, appeared pinned to the door frame, waiting like Saint Sebastian for the arrows to begin piercing him. The hat was new and had cost her seven dollars and a half. She kept saying, "Maybe I shouldn't have paid that for it. No, I shouldn't have. I'll take it off and return it tomorrow. I shouldn't have bought it."
>
> Julian raised his eyes to heaven. "Yes, you should have bought it," he said. "Put it on and let's go." It was a hideous hat. A purple velvet flap came down on one side of it and stood up on the other; the rest of it was green and looked like a cushion with the stuffing out. He decided it was less comical than jaunty and pathetic. Everything that gave her pleasure was small and depressed him.[6]

In a good third of the short stories we read of sons rebelling against their mothers or against a mother figure. In "The River," for instance, little Harry alias Bevel's suicide, by drowning in the river used for baptism, seems to be a commentary on the "absence" of his mother, who is ill, and on the indifference of his father, who has a neighbor take his son for walks. The fact that he assumes immediately the name of the preacher indicates what is missing and what the substitution for this must be.

In general, however, it is the mother who pays, often with her life, for her total incomprehension of the inner life of her child. This is the case in several of the short stories that make up *Everything That Rises Must Converge*, the author's last book, in which death, at the time close to her personally, hovers above like a true promise, an absolute certainty of the body (and not like an obsession). The same hierarchy applies moreover to the relationship between mother and daughter in the frequently recurring moments when the latter is as unfeminine as the former is excessively maternal.

In these stories a clear conscience is always the prerogative of mothers who are also widows and who do not cease to express their blind satisfaction: the worst has not befallen them (this includes the loss of their husbands); they have displayed their valor in overcoming the loss; and their lukewarm if scrupulous respect of prevailing religious practices no doubt reflects both circumstance and good fortune. One can simply cite their own testimony, in a grotesque and odious monologue of self-contentment that recalls that of Cora Tull in *As I Lay Dying*, or the testimony of their neighbors, who naturally lend an attentive if also undiscriminating ear, or indeed the testimony of their children, who experience anger.

This anger thus is often the first level of suspense in Flannery O'Connor's stories. She dramatizes how innocence is deceit, how ignorance of evil is sin. The second level presents (and causes) the antagonism of the couple, mother-child. It is remarkable that almost always the latter is male (or even a bull). It is always he who brings on one of two dénouements that are, in reality, but two aspects of one dénouement, the one toward which the author's *line* unavoidably leads: death or revelation.

This is the essential quality of the art and the audacity of Flannery O'Connor, whose dramatic structure brings with it as much meaning, if not more, than her symbols—i.e., that there is no true life outside this choice: death or revelation. To this one must add that revelation never descends without imparting the painful feeling that the future is fully compromised. From this fact follows the relative unimportance of knowing, at the end of stories like "Everything That Rises Must Converge" and "The Enduring Chill," whether death has occurred or is simply a probability. This fact also conditions our response to the story entitled precisely "Revelation," which could also be taken for the name of the heroine, and which ends with a vision that is so consuming as to cancel out virtually any future. From all this comes, in fine, the most rewarding discovery that a rereading of Flannery O'Connor brings: death, in her work, is strictly a metaphor. Death is, for almost all protagonists, the only possible form of revelation. The author restricts the good fortune of another kind of death to a small number of her characters, the fortune of revelation without death. As the irrefragable kernel of O'Connor's fiction, revelation occurs as two metaphors: one, dramatic, is death; the other, symbolic, is fire—solar fire or some other.

This gives rise to a question that is difficult to resolve without making an a priori judgment in one direction or the other: how is art indebted to faith? One knows that Flannery O'Connor was a fervent Catholic (in a

Protestant country). An attempt to dissociate art and faith in her work has already been made.[7] But, after what has been said, it would seem that the answer is bound to the problem posed thus: what is the content of Flannery O'Connor's revelations?

Such a question is best served by looking at a passage where the narrative explicitly displays (something that is rare) the precise phenomenon of a vision. This occurs at the end of "Revelation." In the waiting room of a country doctor, Mrs. Turpin, who is accompanying her husband, Claud ("florid and bald and sturdy, somewhat shorter than Mrs. Turpin, but he sat down as if he were accustomed to doing what she told him to" [*ETRMC*, 192]), after an extraordinary dialogue made up of displays of self-contentment and shared opinions with a neighbor, has been literally attacked by a pimply student from Wellesley, an ugly girl whose name happens to be Mary Grace and who has hurled at her, along with her book entitled *Human Development*, this insult: "Go back to hell where you came from, you old wart hog" (*ETRMC*, 207). After going home in a traumatic state, Mrs. Turpin meditates on her pigsty, the pigs suffused with a red glow and seeming "to pant with a secret life"; she lifts her head and

> There was only a purple streak in the sky, cutting through a field of crimson and leading, like an extension of the highway, into the descending dusk. She raised her hands from the side of the pen in a gesture hieratic and profound. A visionary light settled in her eyes. She saw the streak as a vast swinging bridge extending upward from the earth through a field of living fire. Upon it a vast horde of souls were rumbling toward heaven. There were whole companies of white-trash, clean for the first time in their lives, and bands of black niggers in white robes, and battalions of freaks and lunatics shouting and clapping and leaping like frogs. And bringing up the end of the procession was a tribe of people whom she recognized at once as those who, like herself and Claud, had always had a little of everything and the God-given wit to use it right. She leaned forward to observe them closer. They were marching behind the others with great dignity, accountable as they had always been for good order and common sense and respectable behavior. They alone were on key. Yet she could see by their shocked and altered faces that even their virtues were being burned away. She lowered her hands and gripped the rail of the hog pen, her eyes small but fixed unblinkingly on what lay ahead. (*ETRMC*, 217–18)

Just like a parody of baptism, a veritable sacrilege where the child's buttocks, turned up, serve as forehead, Flannery O'Connor's audacity consists in never hesitating to make use of mockery to reach for theology, or of sexuality to speak of religion. To the contrary: she rushes headlong into the first of these, as in "Greenleaf," where the bull excites the virility of the antagonist to the point of making him an accomplice in goring the protagonist. (If the Catholic religion had been able to incorporate sexuality, I would have become a Catholic, said in substance another important symbolist, John Cowper Powys.) Here, revelation begins with fertilization in a highly sexualized setting, and ends in a vision whose light the protagonist finds unbearable. To borrow the expression Robert Frost uses in describing a poem — "It begins in delight and ends in wisdom" — one can say that, with Flannery O'Connor, revelation (and the art that is its vessel) begins with pain and ends with knowledge.

But revelation belongs to fable: it is shown, not told; insofar as it refers back to itself at the end of the story, that is, back to what provokes it and justifies it, the revelation has a reflexive or self-conscious quality. It suffices (but it is also necessary) that good people arrive at this point. The revelation takes care of the message. It is up to the reader to reread. In other words, truth lies beyond questions, not beyond answers. Moreover, there is no "beyond" to the answer Flannery O'Connor imagines. An artist, she shows the path to the ineffable instead of trying to say it.

Not only do Flannery O'Connor's works refuse to give the answer, they are not written with a view to such a goal. The task is not to impart a message, even less to preach it — especially since the message was quite unlikely to be appreciated in a largely Protestant and even Baptist area and in a period when faith is hardly a universal reality. One clearly grasps all that separates Flannery O'Connor from Thomas Merton or Gilbert Cesbron, not to mention François Mauriac. It is rather in Bernanos that one might look for an analogy.

However, if there are few works less moralizing than those of Flannery O'Connor, there are few authors less equivocal on the relationship between art and religion. She has devoted several essays to the subject. In one, she writes:

> I see from the standpoint of Christian orthodoxy. This means that for me the meaning of life is centered in our Redemption by Christ and what I see in the world I see in its relation to that. I don't think that this is a position that can be taken halfway or one that is particularly easy in these times to make transparent in fiction. (*MM*, 32)

One can therefore say that if, as I hope to have shown, revelation in one form or another is the *center* of the work, then faith, outside this, is in some manner its *motor*. It is thus possible to attribute the initial ferocity of Flannery O'Connor's vision to her faith as it is challenged by a puny world of tepidness, self-importance, foolishness, compromise, mediocrity: a demanding kind of faith, intransigent, demythifying, pure and remedial as a flame and marked — let us not forget (as with no doubt the greatest of Catholic or simply Christian writers) — by a ferocious will to reconcile the scandal of suffering with a vision of the world. (We know that Flannery O'Connor, born in 1925, began already in 1951 to suffer from systemic lupus and had to use crutches from 1955 on, and that the writing of *Everything That Rises Must Converge*, finished in 1964, represents a miracle of willpower. She died after an operation on August 3, 1964, and the collection appeared a year later.)

In "Novelist and Believer," whose title is itself symbolic (she does not say "believing novelist"), Flannery O'Connor challenges the modern temptation to conceive "religion broadly as an expression of man's ultimate concern rather than identify it with institutional Judaism or Christianity or with 'going to church' " (*MM*, 154). She calls this phenomenon the "vaporization" of religion, which, she says, began in 1832 when Emerson refused to take communion *sub specie* (*MM*, 161).

Then, she says, "When Conrad said that his aim as an artist was to render the highest possible justice to the visible universe, he was speaking with the novelist's surest instinct" (*MM*, 157). Because the problem of the novelist is "to make everything, even an ultimate concern, as solid, as concrete, as specific as possible" (*MM*, 155). However, "When the physical fact is separated from the spiritual reality, the dissolution of belief is eventually inevitable" (*MM*, 161–62). This brings us back to her conviction, expressed several years earlier, that "fiction is so very much an incarnational art" (*MM*, 68), a certainty that explains why she should choose to see herself, a novelist and a Catholic, in a special situation whose meaning she felt it her duty to elaborate. In other words, "The novelist and the believer, when they are not the same man, yet have many traits in common — a distrust of the abstract, a respect for boundaries, a desire to penetrate the surface of reality and to find in each thing the spirit which makes it itself and holds the world together" (*MM*, 168). It is this coherence of vision, as offensive weapon or as defensive shield, which allows for Flannery O'Connor's audacity.

Yet here is perhaps the most illuminating statement by the writer:

> When I write a novel in which the central action is a baptism, I am very well aware that for a majority of my readers, baptism is a meaningless rite, and so in my novel I have to see that this baptism carries enough awe and mystery to jar the reader into some kind of emotional recognition of its significance. To this end I have to bend the whole novel — its language, its structure, its action. I have to make the reader feel, in his bones if nowhere else, that something is going on here that counts. Distortion in this case is an instrument; exaggeration has a purpose, and the whole structure of the story or novel has been made what it is because of belief. This is not the kind of distortion that destroys; it is the kind that reveals, or should reveal. (*MM*, 162)

The art of Flannery O'Connor owes the very essence of its ferocious audacity to the faith of the author; but, insofar as it always takes risks by obliging one to search out some message, art ends in some way at the threshold of her faith. For this reason, one may say that the author's faith is not implicated in her art — what would be perhaps the second level of audacity: the rare intelligence of the author confronted by her own faith. It is revelation, not grace, that concerns Flannery O'Connor. The novelistic structure can recall just as well the relationship an atheist holds with his doubt (which refuses the possibility of irrationality) as that of the believer with his faith (which accepts mystery). But, in this sense, all Western literature tends to imitate the Incarnation, possibly the key myth of our "Judeo-Christian" civilization. In this way the audacity most comparable to that of Flannery O'Connor is perhaps that of a writer for whom the absence of faith tends to create an image as distinct, with edges as clear-cut or as aflame, as that of revelation in Flannery O'Connor — I am thinking of Samuel Beckett. One need, in the passage just quoted, only replace the word "baptism" with the idea of living without God, to see the depth of this relation.[8]

Notes

1. This article appeared in *La Nouvelle Revue Française* soon after the publication of the French translation of Flannery O'Connor's second collection of stories, *Everything That Rises Must Converge*. After the publication of *The Complete Stories*, a third collection, with seven hitherto untranslated stories, was published, along with a translation of *Mystery and Manners* (both in 1975).

2. The French translation of *Couples* had been published the year before.

3. Rex Warner, "Audace," trans. Michel Gresset, *Les Lettres Nouvelles*, No. 41 (December 1963–January 1964), pp. 5–14.

4. *The Violent Bear It Away* (New York: Farrar, Straus & Cudahy, 1960), p. 227. Further citations to this edition will be given in the text, preceded by *TVBIA*.

5. *Mystery and Manners: Occasional Prose*, selected and edited by Sally and Robert Fitzgerald (New York: Farrar, Straus & Giroux, 1969), p. 93. Further citations to this edition will be given in the text, preceded by *MM*.

6. *Everything That Rises Must Converge* (New York: Farrar, Straus & Giroux, 1965), pp. 3–4. Further citations to this edition will be given in the text, preceded by *ETRMC*.

7. See André Bleikasten, "Théologie et dérision chez Flannery O'Connor," *Les Langues Modernes*, March–April 1970, pp. 124–34.

8. See my "Le Petit Monde de Flannery O'Connor," *Le Mercure de France*, No. 1203 (January 1964), pp. 141–43.

Flannery O'Connor: The Catholic Writer as Baptist
Albert Sonnenfeld*

> Mais selon un baptême
> Illuminée au même
> Principe qui m'élut
> Penche un salut.
> — Stéphane Mallarmé[1]

*Reprinted from *Contemporary Literature*, 13 (1972), 445–57, by permission of *Contemporary Literature* and Albert Sonnenfeld.

An epigraph is an author's apostolic blessing to his creation as it goes forth to meet the infidel. And when that epigraph becomes eponymous, it reveals itself an emblem of the meaning of that creation. The famous *regnum coelorum vim patitur, et violenti rapiunt illud* of Matthew XI, 12 has generally been considered one of the most polyvalent passages in the Gospels: "We cannot be sure of its meaning. If the context were certain, interpretation would be easier," says *The Interpreter's Bible.*[2] "Passage énigmatique," admit the monks of Maredsous.[3] The *King James Bible* translates "the kingdom of heaven suffereth violence, and the violent take it by force;"[4] the *Revised Standard Version* agrees, but in modernized terms: "the kingdom of heaven has suffered violence, and men of violence take it by force," with the alternative "has been coming violently."[5] *The Jerusalem Bible* also concludes: "the violent are taking it by storm."[6] These are all restrictive rather than qualitative interpretations, though the monks of Maredsous seem truly in harmony with Flannery O'Connor's epigraph. They write: "le royaume des cieux est emporté de force et ce sont les violents qui le conquièrent."[7] This seems much more positive and even prescriptive, as indeed would seem to be the intent of Flannery O'Connor's interpretation: "the kingdom of heaven suffereth violence, and the violent bear it away."[8] In other words, the kingdom of heaven does not suffer from violence: it authorizes it — and to the violent belongs the kingdom; they bear away the prize of salvation after the struggle.

There are two orders of baptism in the *Gospel According to St. Matthew*, John the Baptist's and Christ's own, and in the narration the two coexist in parallel from III, 1 through XI, 13. John's repentance was a formula for violent exorcism: "every tree which bringeth not forth good fruit is hewn down, and cast into the fire" (III, 10);[9] his prophecy of Christ's order of baptism speaks of the Holy Ghost and of fire (III, 11).[10] But in the chapter from which Flannery O'Connor derived her epigraph, this prophecy was belied by Jesus himself; for his way is the new way of rest: "I am meek and lowly in heart, and ye shall find rest unto your souls. For my yoke is easy, and my burden is light" (XI, 28–30).[11] John's denunciation of the vipers' generation of Pharisees and Sadducees (III, 7)[12] does indeed anticipate Christ's "Woe unto thee, Chorazin! woe unto thee, Bethsaida" (XI, 21),[13] but in chapter 11 of Matthew we have come to an historical transition from the intemperate old order of fire and action to the new code of instruction through parable and example. Jesus takes the measure of John and finds him wanting: "he that is least in the kingdom of heaven is greater than he. And from the days of John the Baptist until now the kingdom of heaven suffereth violence . . ." (XI, 11–12).[14]

This brief exegesis may help us assess the violence of salvation in Flannery O'Connor's vision. It is no accident that the Christian denomination of the South is Baptist and that religious extremists in that region are "fundamentalists," for Flannery O'Connor sees the essential strategy of salvation as a return to the stormy principles of the prophet in the wilderness. We are not now ready for the kingdom of heaven to be taken by the suave yoke and lightened burden of Christ's love; our juncture of spiritual history is that of John the Baptist and of violent conquest of the kingdom (*A diebus autem Joannis Baptistae usque nunc*). "I'm as good, Mr. Motes, not believing in Jesus as many a one that does," the Pharisee landlady, Mrs. Flood, tells the hero of *Wise Blood* (*T*, p. 120). His is the violent order of hewing down the tree which does not bring forth good fruit and casting it in the fire. In the tradition of the desert fathers, he has mutilated himself by striking the mote or beam from his seeing eyes with quicklime, by filling his shoes with broken glass and stones, by wrapping three strands of barbed wire around his chest (*T*, pp. 114, 121, 122): " 'It's easier to bleed than sweat, Mr. Motes,' she said in the voice of High Sarcasm. 'You must believe in Jesus or you wouldn't do these foolish things. You must have been lying to me when you named your fine church [Church without Christ]. I wouldn't be surprised if you weren't some kind of an agent of the pope or got some connection with something funny' " (*T*, p. 122). Like the prophet vagabond, the blind Hazel Motes ventures forth into the wilderness. Two policemen, summoned by Mrs. Flood, find him in a drainage ditch two days later. He dies in the police car after being clubbed, but in death Hazel Motes marks the transition from the era of the Baptist to that of Christ, as he becomes a pinpoint of light in the darkness of the Pharisee's soul (*T*, p. 126). The violence of the self-inflicted mutilations has yielded to the passivity of Christ the victim, as Mrs. Flood gazes into "the deep burned eye sockets . . . into the tunnel where he had disappeared" (*T*, p. 126) and toward the far away point of light.

Flannery O'Connor's obsession with the regression to the fundamentalist strategy of exorcism is, of course, most convincingly dramatized in *The Violent Bear It Away*, for Francis Marion Tarwater is John the Baptist reincarnate. One can say of him, as Jesus says of John in Matthew XI, 18: "For John came neither eating nor drinking, and they say, He hath a devil."[15] The oft-noted sun imagery in this novel is the very emblem of the Baptist's name day. Little wonder then that the devil proclaims, "There's your sign" (*T*, p. 401), when the blinding brightness strikes the fountain as the holy idiot Bishop moves toward it:"Then the light, falling more gently, rested like a hand on the child's white head. His face might have been a mirror where the sun had stopped to watch its reflection" (*T*, p. 401). The tonality struck by the epigraph finds echoes throughout the novel, making it an archetypal new version of Matthew's narration of John's mission. Like the Baptist (Matthew III, 1–2),[16] Tarwater comes from the wilderness to the city to baptize and to prophesy. He is an emissary of God, of someone who said he was his great-uncle (*T*, p. 305) but is referred to constantly as "the old man," a spectral voice urging Tarwater to baptize Christ in the person of the innocent child, Bishop: "And the Lord, the old man said, had preserved the one child he [Rayber] had got out of her from being corrupted by such parents . . . in the only possible way: the child was dim-witted" (*T*, p. 308). Late in the novel, Tarwater remembers his first meeting with Bishop: "He had saved himself forever from the fate he had envisioned when, standing in the schoolteacher's hall and looking into the eyes of the dim-witted child, he had seen himself trudging off into the distance in the bleeding stinking mad shadow of Jesus, lost forever to his own inclinations" (*T*, pp. 434–35). In that initial encounter, the mysterious presence of the patriachal God, the old man, had been transferred to Bishop: "[he] looked like the old man grown backwards to the lowest form of innocence" (*T*, p. 371). This son of God is instinctively drawn to water, almost like Jesus soliciting baptism from John (Matthew III, 13ff.);[17] twice he tempts Tarwater by wandering into a fountain. Finally, heeding his demonic voice and the signal from the sun, Tarwater resolves to drown the boy, to murder God as he had thought to incinerate his great-uncle's remains. But in the very act, meaning only to drown, he murmurs the sacramental formula, "they were just some words that ran out of my mouth and spilled in the water" (*T*, p. 428). The Pentecostal banner in the slum tabernacle had borne the words "*Unless ye be born again ye shall not have everlasting life*" (*T*, p. 370). Tarwater will be reborn into everlasting life as a reincarnation of Jesus. He had hoped to burn "the old man's fancies out of him," but the fire in the woods had been the fulfillment of John's prophecy of baptism through fire; he had tried to murder, had instinctively baptized Bishop into everlasting life. Now returning to old Tarwater's woods, he meets a new devil, "a pale, lean, old-looking young man" (*T*, p. 438), who tempts him with tobacco and whiskey ("It's better than the Bread of Life!" Tarwater proclaims drunkenly; *T*, p. 440), and following the perverse communion, the stranger rapes him: "his delicate skin had acquired a faint pink tint as if he had refreshed himself on blood" (*T*, p. 441). Tarwater has become a Christlike victim; he will be reborn a prophet. He puts fire to the woodland setting of the violation as though to purify himself: "His scorched eyes no longer looked hollow or as if they were meant only to guide him forward. They looked as if, touched with a coal like the lips of the prophet, they would never be used for ordinary sights again" (*T*, p. 442). Flannery O'Connor compares Tarwater's progress homeward to Moses' return to the promised land (*T*, p. 443). If the devil's voice tempts Tarwater once more (*T*, p. 444), his answer is still fire, "the fire that had encircled Daniel, that had raised Elijah from the earth, that had spoken to Moses and would in the instant speak to him" (*T*, p. 447). Tarwater's final gesture is to pick up a handful of dirt from the simple grave that the Negro Buford had made for the old man and to smear it on his forehead. The ashes of repentance become one with the earth of regeneration. The old man's command, "*Go warn the children of God of the terrible speed of mercy*," is likened to seeds opening one at a time in his blood (*T*, p. 447). Like John the Baptist, Tarwater had gone into the city as a prophet of violence; like Christ himself he will now go toward "the dark city, where the children of God lay sleeping" (*T*, p. 447), as a prophet of mercy.

That Mason Tarwater's violence was the necessary final station of the old order of John the Baptist is confirmed by the story of Bishop's biological father, the schoolteacher Rayber. Just before Bishop wanders to the fountain, Rayber cautions Tarwater: " 'The old man used to enrage me until I learned better. He wasn't worth my hate and he's not worth yours. He's only worth our pity. . . . You want to avoid extremes. They are for violent people and you don't want . . .' he broke off abruptly as Bishop let loose his hand and galloped away" (*T*, p. 390). This advocate of moderation had himself been tempted to drown Bishop, but his nerve had failed: "You didn't have the guts," Tarwater taunts him. "He always told me you couldn't do nothing, couldn't act" (*T*, p. 403). At first glance, Rayber seems to be exactly what the critics have said, the lukewarm Pharisee. His father had been an insurance salesman who would sell a policy against any contingency, including danger to the soul. He called himself a prophet of life insurance (*T*, p. 338) and we all know what the Catholic novelists, those advocates of risk, think of "insurance." With his interest in aptitude tests, his popular psychology magazine article analyzing the fanaticism of Old Tarwater, and his marriage to the "welfare woman," Rayber would join the ranks of countless caricatured intellectuals and believers in progress that populate the works, say, of a Bernanos. Rayber remembers the day he was informed of Bishop's condition and was told to be grateful his son's health at least was good; he had asked the classic question of an Ivan Karamazov: "How can I be grateful, when one—just one—is born with a heart outside" (*T*, p. 386). *Grateful* takes on full etymological force here.

Yet Rayber *is* the father of the holy fool Bishop. He is more than a caricature of a Pharisee; his function in *The Violent Bear It Away* is to be a double, a mirror, of young Tarwater. He is a Tarwater who has rejected violence and by this abdication failed. As he looks at Tarwater, Rayber "realizes with an intense stab of joy that his nephew looked enough like him to be his son" (*T*, p. 363). Like Tarwater, Rayber had been borne away by the old man, kidnapped literally, and baptized. For a time he had been an extreme fundamentalist himself. He seems to have become disillusioned, but we learn that he has merely repressed or distorted his vocation:

> The affliction was in the family. It lay hidden in the line of blood that touched them, flowing from some ancient source, some desert prophet or polesitter, until, its power unabated, it appeared in the old man and him and, he surmised, in the boy. . . . He had kept it from gaining control over him by what amounted to a rigid ascetic discipline. . . . He slept in a narrow iron bed, worked sitting in a

straight-backed chair, ate frugally, spoke little. . . . He knew that he
was the stuff of which fanatics and madmen are made. (*T*, pp. 372–73)

As, Christlike, he walks barefoot through the streets of the city in pursuit
of Tarwater, a chorus of small boys sings: "Hi yo Silverwear, Tonto's lost his
underwear" (*T*, p. 377). Tarwater is a Lone Ranger, and his companion
with the name of *madman* finds him at a pentecostal meeting. A child is
preaching (*revelasti ea parvulis*, Matthew XI, 25):[18] "The Word of God is a
burning Word, to burn you clean" (*T*, p. 384). With the taste of his own
childhood on his tongue "like a bitter wafer" (*T*, p. 382), Rayber looks in
through the window, an outsider. He had made his barefoot calvary only
to receive from a child the revelation of his fall: " 'Listen you people,' she
shrieked, 'I see a damned soul before my eye! I see a dead man Jesus hasn't
raised. His head is in the window, but his ear is deaf to the Holy Word!' "
(*T*, p. 385). Rayber's only escape is to turn off his hearing aid, to
acknowledge his deafness. He had lost his hearing when he had gone to the
old man to reclaim his kidnapped nephew and had been shot at. Rayber
had no gun with which to counterattack; he once again rejected violence,
and his hearing aid represents the barrier modern scientific man has
erected against the violent, gunshot sound of salvation. Despite his
vocation for violence and blasphemy, those two essential itineraries of
salvation (Rayber sprinkles water over his nephew's bottom, remarking,
"Now Jesus has a claim on both ends"; *T*, p. 347), Rayber had indeed
become a moderate and a realist. When Tarwater stops before a bakery
window containing a single loaf of bread, the schoolteacher's only thought
is "If he had eaten his dinner, he wouldn't be hungry" (*T*, p. 378). We
recall Rayber's father's words at his son's baptism, "One bath more or less
won't hurt the bugger" (*T*, p. 381); and, of course, Flannery O'Connor's
own preface to *Wise Blood*: "That belief in Christ is to some a matter of
life and death has been a stumbling block for readers who would prefer to
think it a matter of no great consequence" (*T*, p. 8). The schoolteacher
would be one of those readers; he is a John the Baptist who has turned a
deaf ear to the *vocatus*. "He's full of nothing," the old man had said of his
nephew. After Bishop's death, Rayber collapses upon the realization that
there would be no pain, no hurt, no feeling (*T*, p. 423). His emptiness is
the fulfillment of his own prophecy for Tarwater: "This one is going to be
brought up to live in the real world. . . . He's going to be his own saviour.
He's going to be free" (*T*, p. 345).

Flannery O'Connor's comments on violence in her own work have
been oft quoted, much discussed, but only partially understood. In the
light of our reading of the epigraph to *The Violent Bear It Away* as the
culmination of the Johannine mission before the advent of the gentle yoke
of Jesus, I believe that her mission as a writer stands more clearly revealed.
She wrote in "The Fiction Writer & His Country":

The novelist with Christian concerns will find in modern life distortions which are repugnant to him, and his problem will be to make these appear as distortions to an audience which is used to seeing them as natural; and he may well be forced to take ever more violent means to get his vision across to this hostile audience. When you can assume that your audience holds the same beliefs you do, you can relax a little and use more normal means of talking to it; when you have to assume that it does not, then you have to make your vision apparent by shock — to the hard of hearing you shout, and for the almost-blind you draw large and startling figures. (*M*, pp. 33–34)

The analogy immediately brings to mind the deaf schoolteacher Rayber and the mote in the eye of the hero of *Wise Blood*. In her introductory remarks to a reading of "A Good Man is Hard to Find" at Hollins College, the author elaborates, after citing Baudelaire's theory that the devil's greatest wile is to convince us that he does not exist:

We hear many complaints about the prevalence of violence in modern fiction, and it is always assumed that this violence is a bad thing and meant to be an end in itself. With the serious writer, violence is never an end in itself. It is the *extreme situation* that best reveals what we are essentially, and I believe these are times when writers are more interested in what we are essentially than in the tenor of our daily lives. Violence is a force which can be used for good or evil, and among other things taken by it is the kingdom of heaven. But regardless of what can be taken by it, the man in the violent situation reveals those qualities least dispensable in his personality, those qualities which are all he will have to take into eternity with him. . . . (*M*, pp. 113–14; italics mine)

If I read these important lines correctly, they mean that the author's relation to her work is identical to John the Baptist's incendiary assault on the kingdom of heaven. Her fiction marks the culmination of John's way ("the last of the Old Testament prophets," the *Jerusalem Bible* calls him) in anticipation of the hoped for, eventual transition to the way of Jesus, the way of the victim. Flannery O'Connor and the prophet in the wilderness both want to hew down the unfruitful tree and cast it into the fire (Matthew III, 10)[19] and to burn up the chaff of the wheat with unquenchable fire (Matthew III, 12).[20] Moreover, the author's relation to her material must be likened to the reaction of old Tarwater and his nephew to the normal lives of the lukewarm. What the novelist does by means of violent plots and language, the characters do in their actions. "I am more and more impressed with the amount of Catholicism that fundamentalist Protestants have been able to retain. Theologically our differences with them are on the nature of the Church, not on the nature of God or our obligations to Him."[21] This letter from O'Connor to Sister Mariella Gable seems almost a reworking of Christ's assessment of John's mission in Matthew XI. Flannery O'Connor may have been a Roman Catholic, but she is, quite literally, a *Baptist*.

In contrast to John's reliance on threats of direct action and punishment, Christ's method in Matthew XI is instruction through parables, exemplary maxims, or miracles. Here, too, Flannery O'Connor reveals herself a Baptist. Tarwater said after drowning Bishop: "There are them that can act and them that can't, and them that are hungry and them that ain't. That's all. I can act. And I ain't hungry" (*T*, p. 428). The intellectual Rayber "couldn't do nothing, couldn't act," his nephew tells him after he admitted his failure of nerve with Bishop (*T*, p. 403). Rayber believes in "questions that meant more than one thing, planting traps around the house watching him fall into them" (*T*, p. 305). One could, of course, prepare a statistical study of the number of murders, suicides, rapes, and insults in Flannery O'Connor's work to prove her commitment to violent action as a means of dispelling the cloud of nonbeing of the Pharisees. "I'll make it happen. I can act," Tarwater had said to a traveling salesman (*T*, p. 351). But O'Connor's strategy is more complex. What in parable had been figurative, even ambiguous, she removes from the realm of language: she *makes it happen.* This is especially true of her prophet figures' messages and the hortatory signs of the fundamentalists. "*Woe to the Blasphemer and Whoremonger! Will Hell Swallow You Up?*" (*T*, pp. 44–45) Hazel Motes reads on a roadside sign. *These words become action*: he goes to the whore, Leora Watts; he becomes a preacher of blasphemy in the Church without Christ. If his very name contains the figurative "mote" in the eye (Matthew VII, 3–5),[22] Hazel Motes makes his blindness total and literal. Unlike the false blindman, Asa Hawks, the Evangelist whose nerve failed at the last moment (the same words were applied to Rayber and the drowning), Motes's blindness allows him to shut out the false light of Lucifer and to see the purest light (*T*, pp. 65, 126). If the epigraph from Matthew tells us "the violent bear it away," this too becomes direct action: Old Tarwater *kidnaps* both Rayber and Francis Marion to baptize them. When an evangelist echoes Christ's words that "wisdom comes out of the mouth of babes" (*T*, p. 379), a child commences to preach. Her own words also move from the figurative to literal enactment. The man whose "head is in the window but his ear is deaf to the Holy Word" (*T*, p. 385) is actually looking in through the window and shuts off his hearing aid. Her message to Tarwater was: "The Word of God is a burning Word to burn you clean" (*T*, p. 384). He turns the Word to flame by setting fire to the woods.

The same pattern is maintained in the most violent of the short stories. Mrs. Greenleaf exorcises evil by clipping news stories of rapes, divorces, and plane crashes and burying the documents in a hole in the woods (*E*, p. 30). The Pharisee Mrs. May, who "thought the word, 'Jesus,' should be kept inside the church building like other words inside the bedroom" (*E*, p. 31), comes upon the prayer healer writhing on the ground covering her clippings and groaning, "Jesus! Jesus! Stab me in the heart!" For Mrs. May (her very name indicates latent potential), "the sound was so piercing that she felt as if some violent unleashed force had broken out of the ground and was charging toward her" (*E*, pp. 30–31). At the end of the story, the bull which had strayed from the Greenleaf farm sinks his horn into her heart "like a wild tormented lover," while his victim takes on the look "of a person whose sight has been suddenly restored but who finds the light unbearable" (*E*, p. 52). The words of the prayer have become action. In "The Lame Shall Enter First," a reworking of Tarwater's story, Norton longs for his dead mother. When the fundamentalist Rufus Johnson, one of Flannery O'Connor's many Dostoevskian holy criminals, tells the boy that she is "on high" because she believed in Jesus and that you have to be dead to get there (*E*, p. 165), Norton begins looking for her through a telescope. His social worker father had taught him about space travel; now Norton launches his flight into space by hanging himself. Mr. Sheppard ("He thinks he's Jesus Christ," the ungrateful Rufus says; *E*, p. 161) tells the fundamentalist who is reading the Bible at the dinner table that he is too intelligent to believe literally in the Word; whereupon Johnson (the son of John, after all) rips out a page and swallows it whole (*E*, p. 185). The whorish Sarah Ham, in "The Comforts of Home," laughingly asks Thomas as he drives recklessly: "Jesus, where's the fire" (*E*, p. 125). The fire is both in hell and in his loins, as he shoots his mother who had thrown herself in front of the whore, his intended victim: "Thomas fired. The blast was like a sound meant to bring an end to evil in the world. Thomas heard it as a sound that would shatter the laughter of sluts until all shrieks were stilled and nothing was left to disturb the peace of perfect order" (*E*, p. 141). The police mistakenly think that he plotted with the girl to kill the mother, and yet for once they are right: the firing of the gun *was* a sexual act. But suddenly that literal enactment of the answer to the question "Where's the fire?" becomes figurative or symbolic once more. The fire becomes the image of hell.

It is this movement from the literal to the symbolic which marks the cadence or harmony in Flannery O'Connor's violent world of action. By this I mean that a prosaic word or gesture suddenly flows back into the great mainstream of consecrated Christian symbolism. Hazel Motes's words to the truckdriver, "Take your hand off me. I'm reading the sign" (*T*, p. 45), become the *noli mi tangere* of Jesus. "I'm Fahther Finn — from Purrgatory," a hearty priest announces to identify his home parish (*E*, p. 105). Mrs. May's casual and empty expletive, "I thank God for that!" is answered by Mr. Greenleaf's "I thank Gawd for everthang" (*E*, p. 41). When Tarwater smears dirt from his great-uncle's grave on his forehead, he is reenacting a symbolic gesture that has marked the Ash Wednesday penitents since the founding of the Church. This technique, one which Flannery O'Connor shares with other Catholic novelists who resort to Christological patterns, could be illustrated further.

The essential violence of salvation in the works of Flannery O'Connor can, however, best be characterized as a combination of these techniques, as a movement from the figurative to the literal and back to a renewed and heightened figuration. This is, of course, the very progression of poetry, which takes the words of the tribe, originally liturgical and incantatory, and reendows them with symbolic power. "The only way to the truth is through blasphemy," Hazel Motes preaches (*T*, p. 81) — familiar words to readers of De Maistre and Baudelaire. Blasphemy begins as a satanic *non serviam* or negative faith, then becomes meaningless expletive or absent faith. "Jesus, Jesus," Motes says in panic to the sleeping-car porter closing the curtain of his berth around him. "Jesus been a long time gone," the porter answers in "a sour triumphant voice" (*T*, p. 19). An empty oath is abruptly made literal and then takes on renewed symbolic or figurative power. The most striking example, though countless others could be adduced, can be found in the rightly admired used-car-lot scene in *Wise Blood*. The young apprentice car salesman's relentless swearing is likened to a hacking cough. To Motes's query, "How much is it?" he answers vacuously, "Jesus on the cross. Christ nailed" (*T*, p. 41). "Why don't he shut up?" Motes mutters angrily. For Hazel Motes, blasphemy is a serious business, not a verbal tic, and is the central article of negative faith in his Church without Christ. But the contradiction of his naive belief in swearing as a means of denying Jesus soon becomes apparent. During one of his proselytizing homilies to a young garage attendant, he explains his new awareness "that you couldn't even believe in that [blasphemy] because then you were believing in something to blaspheme" (*T*, p. 112). As he says this, Motes begins to act out his own spiritual discovery, cursing "in a quiet intense way but with such conviction that the boy paused from his work to listen" (*T*, p. 112). The very purchase of the run-down old Essex was intended as an act of blasphemy: "Nobody with a good car needs to be justified" (*T*, p. 64). Instead, it leads Motes toward the stations of redemption. He drives from the lot onto the highway lined with Fundamentalist signs; and there he stops in the middle of the roadway, reading the sign: "*Woe to the Blasphemer and Whoremonger! Will Hell Swallow You Up?*" And in smaller letters, at the bottom of the sign: "Jesus Saves" (*T*, pp. 44–45).

For Flannery O'Connor, the Word always leads to the Act; and this, not what one benighted regionalist critic has called "gratuitous grotesque,"[23] is the origin and justification for her obsession with violence. When Mrs. Turpin hears herself assaulted by an hysterical Wellesley student named Mary Grace ("Go back to hell where you came from, you old wart hog"; *E*, p. 207), she goes to the hogpen and receives confirmation of that *Revelation*. In "The Fiction Writer & His Country," we read: "The anguish that most of us have observed for some time now has been caused not by the fact that the South is alienated from the rest of the country, but by the fact that it is not alienated enough, that every day we are getting more and more like the rest of the country, that we are being forced out not only of our many sins, but of our few virtues" (*M*, pp. 28–29). Rufus

Johnson's literal belief in hell, in the incontrovertible teratology of Satan's world (*E*, p. 150) is manifested physically in his monstrously swollen foot; the willfully good Mr. Sheppard, with his modern theories of social rehabilitation, tries to camouflage that physical incarnation of evil with a new specially therapeutic shoe. In her insistence on the violent plot, Flannery O'Connor sharpens the barrier between herself and "the rest of the country." She leads away from intention and back to action: melodrama is by definition bloody, but there is in blood both wisdom and redemption. One may be disgusted by blood, one may be morbidly attracted, one cannot remain neutral and impassive. And in *passion*, that word at once literal and figurative, there is instinctive sex, suffering, and the redemptive agony of Christ. To those who would protest this salvation through violence, she might well have cited Blake's *Everlasting Gospel:*

1   The Vision of Christ that thou dost see
     Is my vision's greatest enemy.

----

7   Thine loves the same world that mine hates;
     Thy Heaven doors are my hell gates.

----

24   Thunder and lightnings broke around,
     And Jesus' Voice in Thunders' sound:
     "Thus I seize the spiritual prey.
     Ye smiters with disease, make way.
     I come your King and God to seize,
     Is God a smiter with disease?"

----

32   He bound old Satan in His Chain,
     And, bursting forth, His furious Ire
     Became a Chariot of Fire.[24]

Notes

1. *Oeuvres Complètes* (Paris: Gallimard, 1945), p. 49.

2. Ed. G. Buttrick (New York: Abingdon Press, 1951), VII, 382.

3. *La Sainte Bible* (Namur, Belgium: n. p., 1949), p. 13.

4. (London: Oxford Univ. Press, 1904), VI, 19.

5. (New York: Nelson, 1952), II, 12.

6. *Readers' Edition* (New York: Doubleday, 1971), II, 18.

7. *La Sainte Bible*, p. 14.

8. *The Violent Bear It Away* in *Three by Flannery O'Connor* (including *Wise Blood* and *A Good Man Is Hard to Find* [New York: Signet, 1964]), p. 302; hereafter referred to parenthetically as *T*. Other O'Connor works and their respective abbreviations are as follows: *E* — *Everything that Rises Must Converge* (New York: Noonday Press, 1966); *M* — *Mystery and Manners* (New York: Farrar, 1969).

9. *King James Version*, VI, 6.

10. *Ibid.*

11. *Ibid.*, p. 20.

12. *Ibid.*, p. 6.

13. *Ibid.*, p. 19.

14. *Ibid.*

15. *Ibid.*

16. *Ibid.*, p. 6.

17. *Ibid.*

18. *Ibid.*, p. 20.

19. *Ibid.*, p. 6.

20. *Ibid.*

21. Quoted by C. W. Martin, *The True Country* (Nashville: Vanderbilt Univ. Press, 1969), p. 20. See also Thelma J. Shinn, "Flannery O'Connor and the Violence of Grace," *Contemporary Literature*, 9 (Winter 1968), 58–73.

22. *King James Version*, VI, 12.

23. William Esty, quoted by S. E. Hyman in *Flannery O'Connor*, American Writers Series No. 54 (Minneapolis: Univ. of Minnesota Press, 1966), p. 44.

24. *Poetical Works* (London: Oxford, 1914), pp. 146–48.

Flannery O'Connor's Rage of Vision

Claire Kahane*

In discussing the writer in America, A. Alvarez has noted that the ubiquitous violence which threatens to devour us in this age has been internalized by the artist who works out in the microcosm of his self the destructive potentiality of the time.[1] Certainly the times have provided spectacular metaphors for the darkest side of the mind; the violence of Dachau, Hiroshima, Mississippi too easily supports our most primitive fears. But the writer does more than assimilate the outer world to his purposes; he also projects his own corresponding impulses onto the macrocosm, shaping through his fictions a world which reflects his specific inner vision. For the writer, the inner and outer worlds merge in an imaginatively extended country, and in the fiction of Flannery O'Connor that country is dominated by a sense of imminent destruction. From the moment the reader enters O'Connor's backwoods, he is poised on the edge of a pervasive violence. Characters barely contain their rage; images reflect a hostile nature; and even the Christ to whom the characters are ultimately driven is a threatening figure, "a stinking, mad shadow" full of the apocalyptic wrath of the Old Testament.

O'Connor's conscious purpose is evident enough, and has been

*Reprinted, by permission, from *American Literature*, 46, No. 1, 54–67. © 1974 by Duke University Press, Durham, N.C. Also by permission of Claire Kahane.

abundantly observed by her critics: to reveal the need for grace in a world grotesque without a transcendent context. "I have found that my subject in fiction is the action of grace in territory largely held by the devil," she wrote,[2] and she was not vague about what that devil is: "an evil intelligence determined on its own supremacy." It would seem that for O'Connor, given the fact of Original Sin, any intelligence determined on its own supremacy was intrinsically evil. For in each work, it is the impulse toward secular autonomy, the smug confidence that human nature is perfectible by its own efforts, that she sets out to destroy, through an act of violence so intense that the character is rendered helpless, a passive victim of a superior power. Again and again she creates a fiction in which a character attempts to live autonomously, to define himself and his values, only to be jarred back to what she calls "reality" — the recognition of helplessness in the face of contingency, and the need for absolute submission to the power of Christ.

Since O'Connor had identified her theme as Christian, it is no surprise to find critics discussing this prototypical pattern in religious terms: the protagonist is humiliated in order to recognize his state of sin, and is thus open to grace and redemption. Characters are classified analogically, Christian symbols and biblical references noted, and what emerges from these studies is the portrait of a writer tracing a timeless moral schema instead of engaging imaginatively with her felt experience.[3] Yet one might wonder at the readiness with which O'Connor's anagogic intent is critically accepted as definitive. For although she remarked that "violence is strangely capable of returning my characters to reality and preparing them for their moment of grace" (p. 112), she unleashes a whirlwind of destructive forces more profound than her Christian theme would seem to justify — murder, rape, mutilation — for ostensibly religious purposes. Tarwater in *The Violent Bear It Away* must be anally raped to accept his religious mission; the unappealing family in "A Good Man Is Hard To Find" must be methodically killed in turn to strip away the grandmother's petty selfishness; Sheppard's son in "The Lame Shall Enter First" must hang himself for Sheppard to recognize his egoism. This violence, however, is conventionally justified as a rhetoric necessitated by the modern secular temper, by the insentience of a society whose plastic surface has smoothed over and accommodated the most grotesque characteristics.[4] O'Connor herself had stated, "The novelist with Christian concerns will find in modern life distortions which are repugnant to him, and his problem will be to make these appear as distortions to an audience which is used to seeing them as natural; and he may well be forced to take ever more violent means to get his vision across to this hostile audience" (pp. 33–34).

While most of her critics seem determined not to question this line of reasoning[5] — and certainly it is a coherent argument — obviously violence is not just a rhetoric demanded by a secularized audience; it expresses the way O'Connor sees. "To some extent the writer can choose his subject," she once remarked, "but he can never choose what he is able to make live" (*Esprit*, VIII [Winter, 1964], p. 23). Yet the conventional readings ignore the deeply private nature of O'Connor's vision, the inner necessities which dominate her fictional world. Her peculiar insistence on absolute power-lessness as a condition of salvation so that any assertion of autonomy elicits violence with a vengeance, the fact that she locates the means of grace repeatedly in the sexually perverse as in Tarwater's rape, or in the literally murderous rage of characters like the Misfit, suggest that at the center of her work is a psychological demand which overshadows her religious intent, shaping plot, image and character as well as her distinctive narrative voice. As Preston M. Browning, Jr., so aptly stated before he unfortunately backed away from his own insight, "If it was Christian orthodoxy to which she subscribed, her work is manifest proof that it was orthodoxy with a difference. For her persistent habit of finding the human reality in the extreme, the perverse, and the violent calls for a closer examination."[6]

Perhaps nowhere is her use of violence more sophisticated than in her narrative voice. For O'Connor as narrator plays the role of scourge. Using the weapon of wit, she derides the pretensions of personality in icily-wrought metaphors. Enoch in *Wise Blood* "looked like a friendly hound dog with light mange" (p. 27). Ruby in "A Stroke of Good Fortune" appears carrying her groceries, her "head like a big florid vegetable at the top of the sack" (p. 95). Mrs. Freeman in "Good Country People," "besides the neutral expression that she wore when she was alone . . . had two others, forward and reverse, that she used for all her human dealings" (p. 271). One might surmise that O'Connor was a cartoonist, for here her eye is the eye of the caricaturist who, with an economy of aggressive strokes, degrades by unmasking ugliness or weakness, penetrates character in order to ridicule. Interestingly, such "penetration" is precisely the kind of violation against which her characters struggle. Tarwater feels his privacy imperilled by the drill-like eyes of Rayber, and is actually penetrated by the traveling homosexual; Old Mason Tarwater resists his nephew's tests, his "crawling into my soul through the back door"; Mrs. May is penetrated by a bull's horns in "Greenleaf"; General Sash, in "A Late Encounter with the Enemy," feels music penetrating his head, "probing various spots" until he has his fatal, albeit revelatory, stroke. Ultimately the literal or figura-tive penetration of characters reveals their destiny to them, just as O'Connor reveals them to us by aggressive delineation.

There is, then, a sadistic quality to the narrator, who acts as an archaic superego, a primitive internalized image of the parent forcing the characters through the triadic ritual of sin, humiliation and redemption by wit as well as by plot structure. Significantly, this identifies the narrator with the Christ of her imagination, not Christ the Lamb, but "Jesus hidden in [her] head like a stinger" (*Wise Blood*, p. 15). Using her stinger, exercising the scorn characteristic of the superego, she imposes on the characters a humiliation so intense that they are forced to acknowledge their impotence. Redemption becomes equated with accepting the position of child-like dependence on the power of Christ, the ultimate superego figure. Potency is the Lord's—or the narrator's.

O'Connor's narrative identification with the superego binds her to her characters in an unusually ambivalent relationship. For as superego she can allow herself to express precisely those demonic impulses which she must punish in them. This is why John Hawkes, in comparing Nathanael West and O'Connor, finds "they both not only write about diabolical figures, but seem also to reflect the verbal mannerisms . . . and explosively reductive attitudes of such figures in their own 'black' authorial stance."[7] The sadism of the narrator exorcises the sadism of the characters, but both participate in the sadistic impulse. Indeed, narrator and protagonist are two aspects of one dynamic: the author's psyche, split into the punishing parent and the rebellious child. Thus most of her protagonists, even when they are adults, seem fixed as children, acting out a drama of infantile conflict in a context strangely isolated from social realities. Her work is "literal in the same sense that a child's drawing is literal," she said; that is, the fantasies are on the surface, the landscape more subjective than objective. Although O'Connor conceived of art as an adjustment of inner and outer worlds, the inner world predominates. Paradoxically, it is because the narrator functions as punishing parent that she can distance herself from the protagonist and express the fantasies and forbidden impulses of the rebellious child, punishing him simultaneously by both the resolution of plot and her acidic wit.

This authorial ambivalence causes the reader to respond to her work on two levels. The reader identifies with the narrator, enjoying the wit and the sadistic impulses behind it. What one critic finds problematic—"no one identifies with O'Connor's people"[8]—is actually the *function* of her narrative irony. In the opening section of *Wise Blood*, for example,

> Hazel Motes sat at a forward angle on the green plush train seat, looking one minute at the window as if he might want to jump out of it, and the next down the aisle at the other end of the car. . . . Mrs. Wally Bee Hitchcock, who was facing Motes in the section, said that she thought the early evening like this was the prettiest time of day and she asked him if he didn't think so too. She was a fat woman with pink collars and cuffs and pear-shaped legs that slanted off the train seat and didn't reach the floor. (p. 9)

Not only are the characters reductively delineated by a few strokes, but the use of indirect discourse intensifies the pettiness of cliché communication, distancing the reader from sympathy and forcing him to regard the characters as puppets. This perspective is made explicit almost immediately: "Haze got up and hung there a few seconds. He looked as if he were held by a rope caught in the middle of his back and attached to the train ceiling" (p. 11).

But the reader also identifies with the protagonist to the extent that the violent confrontations arouse dread and anxiety even under the surveillance of wit. Indeed, wit itself originates in what was once feared but is now mastered; and security from danger, both internal and external, is a precondition of comic enjoyment. Yet O'Connor undermines the reader's sense of security, undermines comic elements by making the familiar world strange, by weakening our sense of reality through the distorting lens of an imagery that evokes archaic fears. A construction machine seems a "big disembodied gullet" which gorges itself on clay and then, "with the sound of a deep sustained nausea and a slow mechanical revulsion," turns and spits it up. The smile of a prostitute becomes a "mouth split into a wide gull grin that showed her teeth. They were small and pointed and speckled with green and there was a wide space between each one." A cloud "shaped like a turnip" descends "over the sun, and another, worse looking, crouched behind the car." Trees "pierce out of the ground" or stand "in a pool of red light that gushed from the almost hidden sun setting behind them." Aggressive verbs make the landscape threatening: "the fields stretched sodden on either side until they hit the scrub pines"; "trains passing appeared to emerge from a tunnel of trees and, hit for a second by the cold sky, vanish terrified into the woods again." Sun, sky and woods constantly engage in violent interactions: the sun "was swollen and flame-colored and hung in a net of ragged cloud as if it might burn through any second and fall into the woods"; "the blank sky looked as if it were pushing against the fortress wall [of trees], trying to break through." This is an animistic world, fraught with images of infantile fears — of devouring, of penetration, of castration — in which the distinctions between physical and psychical reality blur. The comic vision has yielded to reveal its fearsome, uncanny origins.

Traditionally, it is this admixture of the uncanny and the comic which comprises the grotesque.[9] While "grotesque" has been the word used to label O'Connor's world, it has not been used to explain it. In his essay "The Uncanny," Freud has provided a key to understanding the essential aspect of the grotesque. The uncanny exists "when repressed infantile complexes have been revived by some impression, or when the primitive beliefs we have surmounted seem once more to be confirmed."[10] As elements which compose the uncanny, he lists the castration complex, womb fantasies, the idea of the double, the animistic conception of the universe, the omnipotence of thoughts, and the primitive fear of the dead — all concepts of very early mental life which, when they emerge in the context of ordinary adult reality, have the effect of weakening our ego faculty. These elements, skillfully integrated into the imagery of O'Connor's fiction, are responsible for its disturbingly grotesque quality.

Even when an image is not itself objectively threatening, O'Connor can make it so by a vividness of inconsequential detail which in its special intensity suggests a deflection of focus from something frightening to something reassuringly innocuous. For example, in *Wise Blood*, O'Connor's seemingly gratuitous description of the ash on a cigarette about an inch long creates the impression of displaced attention, and thus contributes to the sense of apprehension in the novel. An instant before Guizac is crushed by a tractor in "The Displaced Person," Mrs. McIntyre sees "his feet and legs and trunk sticking impudently out from the side of the tractor. He had on rubber boots that were cracked and splashed with mud. He raised one knee and then lowered it and turned himself slightly" (p. 234). Perhaps the most brilliant use of this prolonged focus on inconsequential detail is the succession of irrelevant description ending with an almost parenthetical but climactic image in this passage from "A Good Man Is Hard To Find":

> [The car] came to a stop just over them and for some minutes, the driver looked down with a steady expressionless gaze to where they were sitting, and didn't speak. Then he turned his head and muttered something to the other two and they got out. One was a fat boy in black trousers and a red sweat shirt with a silver stallion embossed on the front of it. . . . The other had on khaki pants and a blue striped coat and a gray hat pulled down very low, hiding most of his face. . . .
>
> The driver got out of the car and stood by the side of it, looking down at them. He was an older man than the other two. His hair was just beginning to gray and he wore silver-rimmed spectacles that gave him a scholarly look. He had a long creased face and didn't have on any shirt or undershirt. He had on blue jeans that were too tight for him and was holding a black hat *and a gun*. The two boys *also had guns*. (p. 126 [italics mine])

In extremely frightening experiences, psychoanalyst Phyllis Greenacre notes, "inconsequential details of the scene . . . stick in the mind as inexplicably vivid, although the central horror of the experience is not missing."[11] With the psychological acumen of the artist, O'Connor characteristically focuses on such details to intensify horror.

The source of imaginative power in O'Connor's fiction, then, lies in her ability to evoke fearful primitive fantasies, fantasies made especially vivid by her use of uncanny imagery but countered both by a defensive wit which barely assuages the terror of her vision and by resolutions of plot which mitigate the provoked anxiety. In O'Connor's world the environment becomes a projection of sadistic impulses and fears so strong that the dissolution of the ego's power, ultimately death, is the only path to safety. Paradoxically, to be destroyed is to be saved.

To understand the psychoanalytic dynamics of this paradox, it is helpful to recall that initially a child conceives of himself as essentially omnipotent, the external world, including the parent, an extension of himself. As reality collapses that fantasy, every frustration is reacted to with a rage of destructive fantasies directed at the source of frustration, typically the mother. But the child's helplessness and his fears of retaliation cause him to project his aggressive wishes onto the environment. Edmund Bergler, for example, points out the existence of a "septet of baby fears" which are projections of the child's thwarted aggression: fears of being starved, devoured, poisoned, choked, drained and castrated.[12] Significantly, the fates of O'Connor characters parallel these childhood fantasies. They are drowned ("The River"), engulfed by the rottenness of the world ("The Life You Save May Be Your Own"), raped or otherwise destructively penetrated (*The Violent Bear It Away*), blinded or otherwise symbolically castrated (*Wise Blood*). Since, according to the talion principle of the unconscious, "any deed [or wish] may be undone (or must be punished) by a similar deed inflicted on the original doer,"[13] the fates of her characters would seem to mirror their own undispelled hostility. To act itself becomes potentially murderous, and self-annihilation, through merger with a more powerful being, becomes a saving grace.

This regressive fantasy dominates O'Connor's fiction, appearing repeatedly in the situation of a rebellious child confronting a parent who exerts some form of control. In each case, the child perceives that control as violation of his integrity; but, although he angrily insists on his self-reliance, violence forces him into submission. In *Wise Blood*, Hazel Motes rejects the faith of his dead mother and grandfather in an attempt to deny their control over him. His Church Without Christ repudiates the influence of the past on the present and the power of the parent through whom the past is transmitted. But the compulsive actions he takes to prove his autonomy result only in his seeing mirror images of what he denies, until he blinds himself and by this sacrifice of aggressive power is allowed to become one with Christ, the son who is also part of the all-powerful father.

Similarly, Tarwater thinks he can free himself from his great-uncle's injunction to be a prophet. When Mason dies, Tarwater tries to reject that destiny and determine his own future. From his first defiant act, his refusal to bury Mason's body, the boy moves through a series of confrontations attempting to separate his identity from his uncle's. To the probing questions of Rayber, another parent-figure, he responds, "I'm free. . . . I'm outside your head." But the novel shows he is not free; old Tarwater has taken a place in his head, and, although the boy insists on his inviolability, his rape proves him wrong.

The first sentence of the novel tells the reader that Tarwater's initial gesture of independence, his burning of the house which he thinks contains Mason's body, has been futile:

> Francis Marion Tarwater's uncle had been dead for only half a day when the boy got too drunk to finish digging his grave and a Negro named Buford Munson, who had come to get a jug filled, had to finish it and drag the body from the breakfast table where it was still sitting and

bury it in a decent and Christian way, with the sign of its Saviour at the head of the grave and enough dirt on top to keep the dogs from digging it up. (p. 305)

Thus from the very beginning the reader has the knowledge that Tarwater must wait for until the end — that his uncle's wishes have been carried out. The circle of completed action has closed on Tarwater from the start. In a sense, this is a metaphor for the state of being of all O'Connor's characters, precluding free choice. Although critics have called *The Violent Bear It Away* an exploration of freedom, they ignore the novel's structure, the inevitability of Tarwater's destiny. O'Connor dramatizes a psychic determinism more profound even than Freud's and constructs a literary form that allows no escape from the infantile determinations of personality. Like *Wise Blood*, *The Violent Bear It Away* shows us that the more Tarwater thinks he is going forward in time, the more he is carried backward to the point where he began.

The short stories also deal repeatedly with a child's desire for autonomy. Joy Hopewell in "Good Country People" challenges her mother, who "still thought of her as a child though she was thirty-two years old and highly educated," by insisting on her own ugliness, even changes her given name to Hulga in order to create herself in her own image. But robbed of her wooden leg, which she sees as a symbol of unique power, she becomes pitifully dependent. Mrs. Cope's daughter in "A Circle in the Fire," expressing the resentment of all O'Connor's children, screams at her mother, "Leave me be. I ain't you." Yet at the end of the story, she and her mother merge in an identity of misery and helplessness before the destructive teenagers who set fire to their land. Indeed, as this story implies, when O'Connor's children are "let be," when their independent will is not checked, the parent is destroyed.

The equation between independence and anarchic aggression is complicated by the child's unresolved relation to the father. Actual fathers rarely appear in O'Connor's fiction; when they do, they are usually sadistic figures, their aggressiveness associated with the sexual role of the male as penetrator. The child can identify with this role and with the father's power, as Thomas does in "The Comforts of Home"; but this story shows the awful consequences of that identification. Thomas shoots his mother; and, although the act is apparently accidental, the Sheriff's misconstruction of the crime as intentional is supported by O'Connor's textual ambiguities: she implies that Thomas's assumption of his father's role is responsible for his mother's death.

Or the child can choose to be the object of this aggression, equating it masochistically with love. Mary Fortune, in "A View of the Woods," about to be beaten by her father, "followed him, almost ran after him," eager to accept the beating as an act of love. But because of the guilt evoked by this forbidden gratification, with its incestuous overtones, she ritually denies that her father beats her. Challenged by her grandfather on this very issue, she defensively identifies with her father—"I'm pure Pitts"—and attacks her grandfather, whipping him in a vicious repudiation of her passive role. To act, O'Connor implies, is to assume the male role and the power associated with the father.

Perhaps because power is associated with the male role, O'Connor is peculiarly harsh toward women who try to succeed by their own efforts. As Robert Drake noted, O'Connor's women "constitute some of her more villainous characters, almost as though she believed in some spiritual double standard."[14] Typically widows determined to make circumstances fit their needs, they are repeatedly revealed to lack the power they think they have. Like Mrs. May in "Greenleaf," their iron fists are unmasked as little hands dangling "like the head of a broken lily." O'Connor supports this image of impotence by portraying the actual disadvantages these women labor under, having to struggle far more intensely than men to be taken seriously. But the inference of actual inferiority exemplified in the image of the broken lily, and the contempt O'Connor levels against her female characters, suggest that for her the female role itself is burdened with anxiety, that being a woman in itself involves culpability. Not only the contemptuous portrayal of widows but the long line of ugly girls who populate her fiction—pimple-faced Mary Grace in "Revelation," the homely daughter of "A Circle in the Fire" dressed in overalls and gripping her pistols, the fat girl whose braces "glared like tin" in "A Temple of the Holy Ghost"—indicate a repugnance toward femaleness. Indeed, all these girls explode with rage at the very idea of being female and restricted to the behavior of "ladies" and either reject the female role or emphasize their ugliness in a negative assertion of power.

The exhibition of ugliness as a magical exercise of power, psychoanalytic theory infers, can have multiple significance. As Annie Reich explains, "exhibition of devaluated parts of the body, of defects . . . serves via projection . . . to unmask rivals."[15] When ugliness is unconsciously related to castration fantasies, the exhibition can be a type of revenge, an attack meaning "I show you how ugly (how castrated) you ought to be." Certainly Mary Grace's ugliness, both in appearance and word, serves to reduce to impotence the formidable Mrs. Turpin. Yet this aggressive unmasking, linked to exposure of her ugliness, her defects, makes Mary Grace as helpless as a child, overwhelmed by impotence.

O'Connor's portrayal of women, dominated by a need to expose their weakness, seems dynamically related to castration fantasies. According to Karen Horney, the need to expose castration derives from a masochistic fantasy of having suffered castration through a love relation with the father. To show that a woman is castrated is to prove the reality of that relation.[16] Perhaps in part to deny this fantasy, O'Connor's women, like Mary Fortune, usually try to assume the male role, a solution which coincides with the real disadvantages of being a woman in a patriarchal culture. Yet in the end the underlying masochistic fantasy of submission breaks through, as when the self-sufficient Mrs. May, in what is perhaps the only erotic scene in O'Connor's fiction, is gored by a bull, a phallic god who "buried his head in her lap, like a wild tormented lover"; this is her moment of truth, O'Connor implies, in which she discovers her real identity.

Second only to the contempt O'Connor levels at women is her ridicule of intellectuals. Reason and speech are usually associated with potency, but O'Connor denies potency to her intellectuals. "That's the trouble with you innerleckchuls, you don't never have nothing to show for what you're saying," Hoover Shoats, one of her least sympathetic Southerners, says. But O'Connor supports this accusation by making intellectuals the butts of irony. Rayber in "The Barber," his namesake in *The Violent Bear It Away*, Sheppard in "The Lame Shall Enter First," Asbury Fox in "The Enduring Chill," all are characters whose belief in the power of reason is made to seem ridiculous. Holding before themselves the ideal of the enlightened mind, indeed, hiding behind it, they discover that it crumbles to dust at the first confrontation with the intractable world. Rayber, for example, in "The Barber," carefully prepares a speech to persuade his townsmen in the barber shop of the superiority of his progressive political candidate. Although he believes "he could make everything in that shop squirm if he put his mind to it" (p. 21), the only response he evokes is indulgent laughter. In impotent fury, he knocks down the barber, simultaneously knocking down his own belief in the sweet reasonableness of men. Not only is the power of reason shown up as a sham, but words themselves, when they are tools of the intellect and not magical incantations, are presented as worse than meaningless, a preparation for action never taken, a symbol of naïveté if not cowardice.

If we look at the characters O'Connor chooses to pillory — children who rebel against parental control, women, intellectuals — what becomes startlingly clear is that she addresses rage and contempt to characters who at least partially represent herself. She was a woman, an intellectual, a writer with meticulous concern for words, a child forced by illness to depend on her mother. Yet her fiction turns her world upside down, and these aspects of herself become the objects of her hatred. "To know oneself is, above all, to know what one lacks" (*Mystery and Manners*, p. 35), she suggestively remarked; and that idea resonates through her fiction. That is the knowledge she forces upon the reader, upon her characters and, through her relation to them, upon herself, with a violence that strips away all pretension to power.

What makes Flannery O'Connor's fiction so compelling to the contemporary imagination is that her personal conflict precisely reflects a major twentieth-century dilemma. The central struggle between parent and child, defined by the child's relative helplessness and anger, by his fear of engulfment by omnipotent figures, is paradigmatic. It parallels our subsequent struggle to assert the magnitude of the individual against the engulfing enormity of a technological society which fragments social roles, shatters community, and splits off those qualities of warmth, intimacy and mutual dependence which nourish a sense of identity. The violence in American life which punctuates and relieves the tension of that struggle is like a mirror projection of the violence with which O'Connor's characters respond to frustration. Searching for an identity in an isolating context, her characters bring to bear on that search all the psychological components of the desire to create oneself, of the impulse in the American character to become one's own parent, to break away from the limits of the past. But in O'Connor these moral impulses become confused with a literal conflict with the parent; her fiction must satisfy the unconscious level of conflict as well as the moral dilemma. O'Connor's Christian theme provides that double solution: by submitting themselves to Christ, her characters acknowledge their powerlessness, yet share in the power of the parent-God.

But the obsessive nature of her concerns imposed limitations on her work, limitations which critics with a theological perspective seem not to recognize. Haunted by the encounter between parent and child, she could not deal with adult relations; torn by a desire for independence but by fear of the essential estrangement it involves, she could not portray the responsibilities of the autonomous personality in a social context. She was compelled to undercut the power of reason, making her intellectuals a limited, infantile lot; to deny to the secular world either dignity or value or the possibility of nourishing human involvement. Instead, she presents us a closed universe, fixed by infantile conflict — irrational, destructive, grotesque — in which adult interrelations do not — can not — exist. Yet her fiction draws us into the agonizing world of childhood anxiety. The violence she depicts allows us to experience the gratification of raging against the limits imposed on us, raging with all the fury of our common childhood fantasies, while she forces us to submit to those limits, to turn the rage back on ourselves. Because of her extraordinary fictional talent, she could so shape and project her inner vision that, against our rational, progressive wills, we identify with freaks, equate human with grotesque, and renounce our humanistic heritage and the desire to grow up.

Notes

1. A. Alvarez, "The Problem of the Artist," *Under Pressure* (Baltimore: Penguin, 1965), p. 178.

2. Flannery O'Connor, *Mystery and Manners*, ed. Sally and Robert Fitzgerald (New York: Noonday, 1976), p. 118. Unless otherwise noted, O'Connor's remarks on her own work are from this edition. Quotations from her fiction are taken from the following: *Flannery O'Connor: The Complete Stories* (New York: Farrar, Straus, and Giroux, 1971); *Wise Blood*

and *The Violent Bear It Away*, rpt. in *Three by Flannery O'Connor* (New York: New American Library, 1964).

3. For book-length religious interpretations, see Carter W. Martin, *The True Country* (Nashville: Vanderbilt Univ. Press, 1969); Leon V. Driskell and Joan T. Brittain, *The Eternal Crossroads* (Lexington: Univ. Press of Kentucky, 1971); Sister Kathleen Feeley, *Flannery O'Connor: Voice of the Peacock* (New Brunswick: Rutgers Univ. Press, 1972).

4. See especially Nathan A. Scott, Jr., "Flannery O'Connor's Testimony: The Pressure of Glory," and Frederick J. Hoffman, "The Search for Redemption," in *The Added Dimension*, ed. Melvin J. Friedman and Lewis A. Lawson (New York: Fordham Univ. Press, 1966), pp. 149–50, 42, respectively; Louise Y. Gossett, *Violence in Recent Southern Fiction* (Durham: Duke Univ. Press, 1965), p. 97.

5. Several critics do suggest a discontinuity between O'Connor's artistic commitment and her religious one. See Irving Malin, "Flannery O'Connor and the Grotesque," *The Added Dimension*; John Hawkes, "Flannery O'Connor's Devil," *Sewanee Review*, LXX (Summer 1962), 395–407; Josephine Hendin, *The World of Flannery O'Connor* (Bloomington: Indiana Univ. Press, 1970).

6. "Flannery O'Connor and the Grotesque Recovery of the Holy," in *Adversity and Grace*, ed. Nathan A. Scott, Jr. (Chicago: Univ. of Chicago Press, 1968), p. 159. Browning concludes that certain spiritual attainments are impossible without insanity and crime, a view characteristic of conventional O'Connor criticism.

7. Hawkes, p. 397.

8. Walter Sullivan, "The Continuing Renascence: Southern Fiction in the Fifties," *South: Modern Southern Literature in its Cultural Setting*, ed. Louis D. Rubin, Jr., and Robert D. Jacobs (Garden City, N.Y.: Doubleday, 1961), p. 379.

9. See the comprehensive study of the grotesque by Wolfgang Kayser, *The Grotesque in Art and Literature*, trans. Ulrich Weisstein (Bloomington: Indiana Univ. Press, 1963). Although Kayser shows that historically the grotesque comprises both the ridiculous and the terrifying, he ultimately develops a definition which stresses the terrifying, the uncanny.

10. "The Uncanny" (1919), rpt. in *On Creativity and the Unconscious*, ed. Benjamin Nelson (New York: Harper, 1958), p. 157.

11. *Trauma, Growth and Personality* (New York: Norton, 1952), p. 191.

12. *The Basic Neurosis* (New York: Academic Press, 1949), pp. 19–21.

13. Otto Fenichel, *The Psychoanalytic Theory of Neurosis* (London, 1966), p. 44.

14. *Flannery O'Connor* (Grand Rapids, Mich.: Eerdmans, 1966), p. 26.

15. "The Structure of the Grotesque-Comic Sublimation," *Bulletin of the Menninger Clinic*, XIII (Sept. 1949), rpt. in *The Yearbook of Psychoanalysis*, VI, 202.

16. "Genesis of Castration Complex in Women," *International Journal of Psychoanalysis*, V, Part 1 (1924), 50–65, rpt. in *Female Sexuality*, ed. Harold Kelman (New York, 1967), pp. 37–53.

Flannery O'Connor in France: An Interim Report
Melvin J. Friedman*

The French have performed miracles of taste and interpretation when they have flirted with a succession of American writers from Edgar Allan Poe on.[1] Many of these writers were either Southern by birth or spent a

*Reprinted, by permission, from *Revue des Langues Vivantes*, 43 (1977), 435–42.

considerable period in the American South. The case of the Virginian Edgar Poe is legendary in the annals of literary appropriation. The French took him over, gave him (according to one critic) a "French face," and transformed him into a Symbolist poet. Baudelaire's translations of Poe strike one as superior to the originals. Mallarmé and Valéry treated him with a special awe and reverence. The hermetic words and cadences of Mallarmé's "Le Tombeau d'Edgar Poe" suggest it all. Debussy struggled for long periods, mostly in vain, trying to musicalize Poe. For the Symbolist generation Poe became a kind of *umbilicus mundi*.

The instance of William Faulkner is even more astounding — if this is possible. Interestingly enough, one of Faulkner's earliest literary gestures was to translate four of Verlaine's poems into English. At this point in his career he could not have known that he would later be taken up so vigorously and creatively by the French and even, on occasion, deemed to be an inheritor of the French Symbolists. The situation of Faulkner in France has been much studied: in a book-length work of S.D. Woodworth, *William Faulkner en France (1931–1952)*; in two skillful essays by Percy G. Adams, "The Franco-American Faulkner" and "Faulkner, French Literature, and 'Eternal Verities' "; in a chapter of Ward Miner and Thelma Smith's *Transatlantic Migration: The Contemporary American Novel in France*; and in Maurice-Edgar Coindreau's "William Faulkner in France." The last is especially interesting because it offers us the privileged glance of Faulkner's most accomplished translator. Indeed it was Coindreau who introduced Faulkner into France with a perceptive essay in the June 1931 *Nouvelle Revue Française*. He then went on to translate into French *As I Lay Dying* (1934), *Light in August* (1935), *The Sound and the Fury* (1938), *The Wild Palms* (1952), *Requiem for a Nun* (1957), and *The Reivers* (in collaboration with Raymond Girard, 1964).[2]

While Coindreau did more than anyone else to make Faulkner understood and appreciated in France before he was in his native America, it should still be remembered that André Malraux, Valery Larbaud, and Jean-Paul Sartre all wrote seminal pieces on the Mississippi novelist in the 1930s: Malraux wrote the preface to the French translation of *Sanctuary* (1933); Larbaud the preface to the French translation of *As I Lay Dying* (1934); and Sartre wrote essays on *Sartoris* and *The Sound and the Fury* in 1938 and 1939 respectively.

Two other writers of Faulkner's generation who lived for a time in the South and fared well at the hands of the French were John Dos Passos and Sherwood Anderson. Coindreau's first gesture as a translator of American fiction was to turn Dos Passos' *Manhattan Transfer* into French in 1928. Sartre wrote an important essay on Dos Passos and his *1919* in 1938, placing this novelist even above Faulkner. The first book in any language on the author of *Manhattan Transfer* was written by a Frenchman: G.A. Astre, *L'Oeuvre de John Dos Passos* (Lettres Modernes, 1956). Sherwood Anderson came to the fore somewhat later in France but he has continued

to exert an irresistible appeal. The Sorbonne professor, Roger Asselineau —
perhaps the most consistently reliable French critic of American literature — has written brilliantly on *Winesburg, Ohio*, a work which was
added to the prestigious *agrégation* list for the academic year 1975–76.

The French have continued to be drawn to writers from the American
South down to our own time. Coindreau's translations of Truman Capote
and even of the younger Southerner Reynolds Price have attracted wide
attention. But the Virginia-born William Styron offers perhaps the most
compelling case of all. His novels are all available in French translation:
two of them, *La Proie des flammes* (*Set This House on Fire*) and *Les
Confessions de Nat Turner* (*The Confessions of Nat Turner*), are the work
of Coindreau. Just as major novelists like Sartre and Malraux performed
the early job of exegesis with Faulkner so Michel Butor was to write a quite
remarkable preface to the French translation of *Set This House on Fire*. At
a time when Styron's reputation in America is at a surprisingly low ebb —
perhaps even due at this late date to the Nat Turner imbroglio — his
position is very secure in France. In fact, his *Lie Down in Darkness* was on
the agrégation list for the year 1973–74, and Styron made a tour of several
French universities, including Nantes, Paris, Rennes, and Bordeaux, in
April 1974.[3]

Which brings us to the Georgia writer Flannery O'Connor. It is again
Coindreau who led the way, this time with his 1959 translation of *Wise
Blood* (*La Sagesse dans le sang*). Coindreau's preface, which accompanies
the French text, offers a valuable brief history of American revivalism,
including sketches of Billy Sunday and Aimee Semple McPherson. It also
manages a useful appreciation of *Wise Blood* by speaking of the "monde
tragicomique de ces évangélistes" and by placing the novel in its proper
historical perspective. Coindreau rightly insists that Flannery O'Connor
was the first fiction writer who justly appraised the evangelists and offered
them an *entrée* into American literature. While this view now strikes us as
distinctly one-sided and limited, it should be remembered that Coindreau
penned his preface at a time when O'Connor criticism in America was still
rather exploratory and even primitive.

Five years later Michel Gresset, the important Faulkner scholar,
wrote a thoroughly sophisticated review of the French translation of *A
Good Man Is Hard to Find* ("Le Petit Monde de Flannery O'Connor,"
Mercure de France, January 1964). Gresset starts off by suggesting that
Southern literature stands to American literature in much the same way
that Irish literature stands to English literature. (In vitality there is
certainly a relationship between Southern literature since the first World
War and Irish literature of the Gaelic Revival.) He places Flannery
O'Connor squarely within the Southern tradition and suggests a kinship
between her work and that of Bosch, Poe, and Beckett. He finally defines
the unlikely shape of Flannery O'Connor's Catholicism as being "nu,
tragique et douloureux." In this review Gresset seems to have set the tone

for subsequent French writing on Flannery O'Connor. His observations expand and deepen in his essay in the December 1970 *Nouvelle Revue Française*, "L'Audace de Flannery O'Connor." This study reintroduces the connection with Beckett, as expressed in this revealing and eloquent sentence: "De sorte que l'audace la plus comparable avec celle de la croyante Flannery O'Connor est peut-être celle d'un écrivain chez qui l'absence de la foi tend à créer une figure aussi nette, aux bords aussi tranchés, ou brûlés, que la révélation chez Flannery O'Connor—je veux dire Samuel Beckett."

Other important French critics of Southern literature, like André Bleikasten (the author of a seminal study of Faulkner's *As I Lay Dying*), were beginning to turn their efforts to Flannery O'Connor and respond to the finer tunings of her language and the subtleties of her craft. The academic year 1975–76 was to prove crucial to her position in France: her *A Good Man Is Hard to Find* was added to the *agrégation* list, which meant that this collection of stories was required reading for all English literature *agrégatifs* along with such other fiction as Sherwood Anderson's *Winesburg, Ohio*. These two "books of the grotesque" joined the works of Poe, Faulkner, Styron, and others which had already gained a permanent place on the library shelves of advanced graduate students in France. The coupling of *A Good Man Is Hard to Find* and *Winesburg, Ohio* makes inspired good sense. When Anderson said, "They were all grotesques. All of the men and women the writer had ever known had become grotesques," he could easily have been describing a good number of O'Connor characters from *A Good Man Is Hard to Find*: The Misfit in "A Good Man Is Hard to Find," Hulga Hopewell and Manley Pointer in "Good Country People," and Mr. Shiftlet in "The Life You Save May Be Your Own."

Virtually all of Flannery O'Connor is now available in French translation. Coindreau sensitively translated both *Wise Blood* and *The Violent Bear It Away* and Henri Morisset has given us French versions of *A Good Man Is Hard to Find* and *Everything That Rises Must Converge*. *Mystery and Manners*, the collection of O'Connor's "occasional prose," is now available in André Simon's 1975 translation. The most recent addition to the French canon is a volume entitled *Pourquoi ces nations en tumulte?*, which contains translations of five of O'Connor's M.F.A. thesis stories ("The Geranium," "The Barber," "Wildcat," "The Crop," and "The Turkey") as well as "The Partridge Festival" and "Why Do the Heathen Rage?". Thus all the stories which make up *The Complete Stories of Flannery O'Connor* are available in French except for the early versions of chapters of *Wise Blood* and *The Violent Bear It Away*. So with Flannery O'Connor we have what virtually amounts to a complete *oeuvre* in French.

Pourquoi ces nations en tumulte? deserves a further look. There is no collection quite like it in English although all seven stories are available in *The Complete Stories of Flannery O'Connor*. The arrangement of the stories in *Pourquoi ces nations en tumulte?* follows the chronological ordering of *The Complete Stories* — which enables us to follow the growth of a remarkable talent from her earliest fictional gestures as a graduate student through the work of her final years. The translations seem generally accurate and faithful to the original.[4] The five early stories, those which were part of her Master's thesis at the University of Iowa, abound in regionalisms and dialectal peculiarities: these do not always make their way into the French. Thus in the earliest story, "The Geranium," the main character, Old Dudley, says at one point: " 'I say they got 'em a servant next door — a nigger — all dressed up in a Sunday suit.' " This comes over in Fleurdorge's French as " 'Je te dis qu'à côté ils ont un domestique. Un nègre. Tout endimanché.' " The latter is far more formal. One wonders whether Old Dudley could have managed a word as sophisticated as "endimanché," given his mentality and background.

Fleurdorge probably manages best with the one story in the early group which does not thrive on regional expressions or colloquial turns, "The Crop." This satirical portrait of a female story writer features a language of startling simplicity, with many repetitions. Thus this statement of her compositional habits: ". . . if Miss Willerton were going to write a story, she had to think about it first. She could usually think best sitting in front of her typewriter, but this would do for the time being. First, she had to think of a subject to write a story about. There were so many subjects to write stories about that Miss Willerton never could think of one. That was always the hardest part of writing a story, she always said. She spent more time thinking of something to write about than she did writing." Fleurdorge's French captures the monotony and gracelessness of the original: ". . . si Miss Willerton voulait écrire une histoire, il fallait d'abord qu'elle y réfléchisse. D'habitude c'était assise devant sa machine à écrire qu'elle réfléchissait le mieux, mais, pour l'instant ceci ferait l'affaire. Il fallait d'abord qu'elle réfléchisse à un sujet sur lequel écrire une histoire. Il y avait tellement de sujets sur lesquels écrire des histoires que Miss Willerton n'arrivait jamais à en trouver un. C'était toujours là le plus difficile quand on écrivait une histoire, disait-elle. Elle passait plus de temps à réfléchir à ce sur quoi elle écrirait qu'elle n'en passait à écrire."

"The Partridge Festival" is the most finished story in this French collection and indeed the one which offers the most intriguing challenges for a translator. The combined efforts of Michel Gresset and Claude Richard produced a triumph of the translator's art: their "La Fête des Azalées" reads more naturally than anything else in *Pourquoi ces nations en tumulte?*. "The Partridge Festival" records the vantage point of the young intellectual, Calhoun, who sees himself as "the rebel-artist-mystic," and hence the language is quite formal and only rarely corrupted by regionalisms. Irony serves something of the same purpose here as it served in the earlier "artist story," "The Crop" — but here it is more subtly managed. The following paragraph reveals Calhoun's sense of being removed from the "madding crowd": "He wondered if any of them might think he was here for the same reason they were. He would have liked to start, in Socratic fashion, a street discussion about where the real guilt for the six deaths lay, but as he surveyed the scene, he saw no one who looked capable of any genuine interest in meaning. Without set purpose, he entered a drugstore. The place was dark and smelled of sour vanilla." Gresset and Richard get over much of the bathetic effect of the original: "il se demanda s'il y avait dans cette foule des gens qui pouvaient penser qu'il était là pour la même raison qu'eux. Il aurait aimé inaugurer, à la manière de Socrate, une discussion publique sur le véritable responsable des six assassinats, mais, en regardant autour de lui, il ne vit personne qui fût susceptible de s'intéresser vraiment à leur signification. Il entra, sans but, dans un drugstore. La salle était obscure et sentait la vanille rance."

These few samples of the translator's craft reveal how easily O'Connor's idiom seems to adjust to the movements of the French language (even if the regionalisms do not always come across). *Pourquoi ces nations en tumulte?*, which virtually completes the canon in French, appeared in October 1975 — just in time for the start of the academic year which found *A Good Man Is Hard to Find* on the *agrégation* list. It was the first of several publishing events which made the year 1975–76 an *annus mirabilis* for Flannery O'Connor in France. The second was a special issue of a new journal, *Delta*, devoted entirely to Flannery O'Connor. Published by the "Centre d' Étude et de Recherches sur les Écrivains du Sud aux États-Unis" of the Université Paul Valéry at Montpellier, *Delta* led off with a special issue devoted to Poe, followed with the O'Connor issue in March 1976, and has announced subsequent issues on Faulkner (predictably!), Shelby Foote, and Eudora Welty.[5]

The O'Connor number of *Delta* starts off with a conversation between Gresset and Coindreau in which Coindreau confirms her preeminent gift as a story writer rather than as a novelist and accurately describes her type of humor as "pince-sans-rire." This "entretien" is followed by a group of letters which Coindreau received from Flannery O'Connor between 1958 and 1964; they mainly touch on Coindreau's translations of *Wise Blood* and *The Violent Bear It Away*. The seven essays which follow vary enormously in length, approach, and subtlety. One of these pieces is merely a reprint of the Southern novelist William Goyen's review of *Wise Blood* in the May 18, 1952 *New York Times Book Review*. Another is a two-page *aperçu* by a certain Jacques-Pierre Amette which ends with the questionable statement that O'Connor more closely resembles Poe than Faulkner. Three of the remaining essays abound in commonplace judgments and seem to make no special contribution to O'Connor criticism. The exhaustive reading Claude Fleurdorge gives "Good Country People" and Claude Richard's close and subtle examination of "A Good Man Is Hard to Find" are, however, among the most thorough and convincing treatments these two stories have ever received. This issue of *Delta* also contains an invaluable bibliography of works by and about Flannery O'Connor drawn up by Gresset and Claude Richard. The bibliography is especially useful for its listing of all French translations of O'Connor's work and of the critical writing done about her in France.

It is interesting that a center for Southern literature and a journal devoted to its study should be located in Montpellier, the heart of the Midi. The American South and Provence are really not so very different in temperament. The same sense of regional pride and of restlessness prevails in both areas. I had the feeling when I lectured on Flannery O'Connor in Montpellier in March 1976 that this was indeed O'Connor country and that enthusiasm ran especially high for her in this meridional city.

But Montpellier clearly does not have a monopoly on this enthusiasm. Students and professors in Paris, Lyon, Aix-en-Provence, Nice, and Nantes, for example, are also seriously into the study of her work. The first issue of a new journal, *Revue Française d'Études Américaines*, appeared in Paris in April 1976. André Le Vot, a professor at l'Université de Paris-III, edited this first number which has a notoriously post-modern bias — with essays on William Burroughs, Richard Brautigan, Robert Coover, Ishmael Reed, John Hawkes, and Kurt Vonnegut, Jr. Still there is a quite capable essay on O'Connor in the collection by a Toulouse professor, Maurice Lévy, who comments tellingly, among other things, on O'Connor's "monde *sub specie ironiae*."

Le Vot, who runs his own center in Paris-III, "Centre de Recherche sur la Littérature Américaine Contemporaine," brought out the first issue of his own new journal, *Tréma*, in the spring of 1976: the emphasis here is even more emphatically on the post-modern scene than it is in the *Revue Française d'Études Américaines* and so articles on Jerzy Kosinski, Brautigan, Coover, and John Barth have predictably usurped the field. Flannery O'Connor does, however, make a kind of backdoor appearance at the end of an interview with John Hawkes — in which he insists, in most compelling terms, that she is one of two contemporaries (the other is John Barth) who matters to him.[6]

Ranam (an abbreviation for "Recherches Anglaises et Américaines"), a yearbook published in Strasbourg and now in its ninth year, devoted its 1976 number to Southern literature. Half of the issue is devoted to Faulkner; the rest is given over to a variety of other Southern novelists. The article on Flannery O'Connor concentrates on what its author Christiane Beck calls "la vision schizomorphe." The basis of the argument is: "Cette alternance de styles éclaire la double face de la vision de F. O'Connor et lui permet d'intégrer le mode schizomorphe de la représentation objective à la vision globale paranoïde. C'est à la lumière du monde intérieur des personnages que le monde morcelé, disloqué se révèle être un monde dominé par la hantise de la persécution." If this strikes one as being too ridden with psychoanalytic jargon to be entirely credible, one should still acknowledge the need for this kind of inquiry in regard to Flannery O'Connor.

The outlook for the future seems bright. O'Connor criticism in France has already reached an admirable level of sophistication. French critics who have of late sharpened their structuralist tools on surfictionists[7] like Brautigan, Coover, Barth, and Vonnegut are beginning to turn their talents to the more traditional Flannery O'Connor. Her reputation in France seems firmly established only a dozen years after her death. The French seem on the way to appropriating Flannery O'Connor in the same agreeable way they once appropriated Poe and Faulkner.

Notes

1. The present essay was written while I was a Fulbright/Hays Senior Lecturer in Belgium in the spring of 1976. I am very grateful to the United States Information Service, which arranged lecture tours to the Universities of Paris, Aix-en-Provence, Montpellier, Lyon, and Nantes during my Fulbright tenure. I lectured on Flannery O'Connor to *agrégation* students in each of these universities, as well as at the University of Nice. The inspiration for the present study is profoundly indebted to these visits.

2. A valuable book which contains almost all of Coindreau's writing on Faulkner as well as a sampling of his work on other American fiction writers is *The Time of William Faulkner: A French View of Modern American Fiction*, edited and chiefly translated by George M. Reeves (Columbia, South Carolina: University of South Carolina Press, 1971). I have made considerable use of this volume in the essay which follows.

3. See the interview which came out of the Nantes visit: Ben Forkner and Gilbert Schricke, "An Interview with William Styron," *The Southern Review*, X (Fall 1974, pp. 923–34). In their introductory remarks the interviewers comment revealingly: "It should be mentioned that the French gave Styron one of the warmest receptions accorded an American writer in recent years." See also my *William Styron* (Bowling Green, Ohio: Bowling Green University Popular Press, 1974), especially chapter 2.

4. The French versions of "The Geranium," "The Barber," "Wildcat," "The Crop," "The Turkey," and "Why Do the Heathen Rage?" are the work of Claude Fleurdorge, while Michel Gresset and Claude Richard combined to translate "The Partridge Festival."

5. The Poe issue is revealingly called "Edgar Allan Poe et les textes sacrés" and the O'Connor number is entitled "Flannery O'Connor et le réalisme des lointains." The phrase "realist of distances" occurs several times in *Mystery and Manners*.

6. It should be recalled that Hawkes published a major essay on her, "Flannery O'Connor's Devil," in the Summer 1962 *Sewanee Review*. See my "John Hawkes and Flannery O'Connor: The French Background," *Boston University Journal*, XXI (Fall 1973), pp. 34–44.

7. For the use of this word see Raymond Federman's admirable collection, *Surfiction: Fiction Now . . . and Tomorrow* (Chicago: The Swallow Press, 1975).

The Heresy of Flannery O'Connor

André Bleikasten*

L'écriture est pour l'écrivain, même s'il n'est pas athée, mais
s'il est écrivain, une navigation première et sans grâce.
— Jacques Derrida

A devout Roman Catholic, Flannery O'Connor was not reluctant to acknowledge her Christian position as a novelist. A hazardous position for a writer to adopt: literature and orthodoxy — religious or otherwise — make uneasy bedfellows. He who knows, or thinks he knows, the answers even before the questions have been asked, may be sincere as a person but compromises his honesty as a writer. Literature has its own truths, elusive and modest; truths it generates in close cooperation with each individual reader outside the massive certainties and ready-made patterns of fixed beliefs. This does not mean, of course, that religious faith — especially one so pregnant with mystery and so rich in paradox as the Christian faith — cannot find its way into literary texts, but that it can only do so at the cost of temporary suspension. What has prevented Bernanos, Mauriac, T. S. Eliot, and other so-called "Christian writers" from becoming trapped in apologetics is the fact that in their best work the demands of writing clearly prevailed over their private preconceptions, impelling them, whatever their avowed goals, to use language in such ways as to make it an instrument of questioning rather than of affirmation, and to produce texts whose plural significance no amount of exegesis is likely ever to exhaust.

Flannery O'Connor's work is no exception to this rule of the literary game, although the validity of the rule has seldom been fully recognized by her critics. Admittedly, no reader can fail to discern the permanence and seriousness of her religious concerns. Fall and redemption, nature and grace, sin and innocence — every one of her stories and novels revolves around these traditional Christian themes. It is hardly surprising that O'Connor should have acknowledged close affinities with Hawthorne. Her fiction is of a coarser fabric than his, less delicately shaded in its artistry and far less muted in its effects, but it belongs without any doubt to the same tradition of American romance: characters and plots matter less than "the power of darkness" one senses behind them; symbol, allegory, and parable are never far away, and with O'Connor as with Hawthorne, the accumulated mass of allusions and connotations derives in a very large measure from the rich mythology of Christian culture. The temptation is therefore great to decipher works like theirs through the cultural and hermeneutic codes which the Christian tradition provides, and in O'Connor's case it is all the more irresistible since we have the author's blessing.

*Reprinted from *Les Américanistes* by Ira D. and Christiane Johnson, by permission of Associated Faculty Press, Inc. © 1978 by Kennikat Press, National University Publications.

Yet between intended meanings and completed work there is necessarily a gap, whatever the writer's efforts to close it. In the creative process the author's shaping mind is not alone at play, and language uses him as much as he uses language. Literature always says something more — or something else — than what it was meant to say. Its order is that of multivalence and reversibility. Ambiguity is its very life.

Not that we should feel free to discount the writer's intentions, and to discard the conscious assumptions on which his work was built as irrelevant to critical inquiry. But we can dispense with his approving nods over our shoulders while we read his books. O'Connor's public pronouncements on her art — on which most of her commentators have pounced so eagerly — are by no means the best guide to her fiction. As an interpreter, she was just as fallible as anybody else, and in point of fact there is much of what she has said or written about her work that is highly questionable. The relationship between what an author thinks, or thinks he thinks, and what he writes, is certainly worth consideration. For the critic, however, what matters most is not the extent to which O'Connor's tales and novels reflect or express her Christian faith, but rather the problematical relation between her professed ideological stance and the textual evidence of her fiction.

Seedy Satan

Ideologically·O'Connor was an eccentric. Her commitments were definitely off-center: antisecular, antiliberal, antiindividualistic, and she had as little patience with the cozy assumptions of conventional humanism as with the bland pieties and anemic virtues of its fashionable Christian variants. What counted for O'Connor was not so much man as his soul, and perhaps not so much his soul as the uncanny forces that prey on it. Hers is a world haunted by the sacred — a sacred with two faces now distinct and opposed, now enigmatically confused: the divine and the demonic. Hence, we find in most of her characters the double postulation noted by Baudelaire: one toward God, the other toward Satan.

In accordance with this dual vision, the human scene becomes in her fables the battleground where these two antagonistic powers confront each other and fight for possession of each man's soul. To judge from O'Connor's hellish chronicle, however, the chances hardly seem to be equal. To all appearances, Evil wins the day. Or rather: Satan triumphs. For in her world Evil is not just an ethical concept; it is an active force, and it has a name, personal, individual. In the middle of the twentieth century O'Connor, like Bernanos, was rash enough to believe not only in God but also in the Devil. And, like the French novelist, she had the nerve to incorporate him into her fiction. In *The Violent Bear It Away* we first hear his voice — the voice of the friendly "stranger" who accompanies young Tarwater during his tribulations; then we see him in the guise of a homosexual sporting a black suit, a lavender shirt, and a broad-rimmed panama hat. For the reader he may be little more than a *diabolus ex machina*; for the author, however, he was not just a handy device: "I want to be certain that the devil gets identified as the devil and not simply taken for this or that psychological tendency."[1]

But the Devil does not have to strut about the stage to persuade us of his existence and power. Reflected in the implacable mirror O'Connor holds up to it, the whole world becomes transfixed in a fiendish grimace: mankind has apparently nothing to offer but the grotesque spectacle of its cruel antics. At first glance, it almost looks as if all souls had already been harvested by the Demon. For, despite O'Connor's firm belief in the existence of immortal souls, her world strikes us most often as utterly soulless. There is indeed little to suggest the "depths" and "secrets" of inner life which are the usual fare of religious fiction. The ordinary condition of most of her heroes is one of extreme emotional exhaustion and spiritual numbness, and from that catatonic torpor they only emerge to succumb to the destructive forces of violence or insanity. Moreover, in their deathlike apathy as well as in their sudden convulsions, O'Connor's characters are ruthlessly stripped of any pretense to dignity. People, in her fiction, suffer and die, but pettily, just as they are pettily evil. Wrenching from the Devil the dark, handsome mask afforded him by romantic satanism, O'Connor exposes his essential banality and restores him to his favorite hunting ground: the everyday world. The color of evil, in her work, is gray rather than black—a grim grayness set off by lurid splashes of red. Its face is difficult to distinguish from that of mediocrity, and its most characteristic expression is meanness. The banality of evil is what brings it within range of mockery: insofar as it thrives on human folly and wretchedness, it becomes laughable.

Yet with O'Connor laughter is never harmless, and her savage humor seldom provides comic release. It is not an elegant way of defusing horror. Far from dissolving evil in farce, it emphasizes its demonic character, and calls attention to its terrifying power of perversion and distortion. Woven into the fabric of everydayness, evil becomes trivial, but at the same time the world of common experience is defamiliarized and made disquieting through its contagion by evil. Under Satan's sun the earth spawns monsters. O'Connor's tales drag us into a teratological nightmare, a ludicrous Inferno partaking at once of a hospital ward, a lunatic asylum, a menagerie, and a medieval *Cour des Miracles*. Like a Brueghel painting or a Buñuel film, the stories of *A Good Man Is Hard to Find* invite us to a sinister procession of freaks and invalids: a 104-year-old general, doddering and impotent ("A Late Encounter with the Enemy"), a retarded deaf-mute, a one-armed tramp ("The Life You Save May Be Your Own"), a hermaphrodite ("A Temple of the Holy Ghost"), and a thirtyish bluestocking with a weak heart and a wooden leg ("Good Country People"). Elsewhere the same obsession with infirmity is attested by the presence of

a hideous clubfoot (Rufus in "The Lame Shall Enter First"), or reverberates through the theme of blindness (Hazel Motes in *Wise Blood*) or
deafness (Rayber in *The Violent Bear It Away*). And just as evil deforms,
corrupts, and maims the body, it distills its poisons into the mind. There
are almost as many cases of mental debility in O'Connor as in Faulkner,
and there is hardly a character in her fiction whom a psychiatrist would
not identify as, at least, neurotic. Most of her stories deal with sick
individuals entrapped in sick families: they oppose domineering father
figures (grandfathers and great-uncles more often than fathers) and
possessive, ghoulish mothers to rebellious and helpless children, and they
end almost invariably in explosions of violence, if not in death.[2]

O'Connor's penchant for freaks, idiots, and cripples, her fascination
with the morbid, macabre, and monstrous, are traits she shares with many
southern writers. The same gothic vein can be found to varying degrees in
Erskine Caldwell, Eudora Welty, Carson McCullers, William Goyen, and
Truman Capote, as well as in William Faulkner. Like them, she belongs to
the manifold progeny of Poe. Yet the primal function assumed in her art
by the grotesque cannot be explained away by fashion or tradition. Nor
can one ascribe it merely to the gratuitous play of a perverse imagination.
O'Connor used the grotesque very deliberately, and if it became one of her
privileged modes, it was because she thought it fittest to express her vision
of reality. As she herself stated, its meaning in her fiction is closely linked
to her religious concerns; in her eyes, the grotesque can no more be
dissociated from the supernatural than evil can be separated from the
mysteries of faith.[3] The grotesque has the power of revelation; it manifests
the irruption of the demonic in man and brings to light the terrifying face
of a world literally *dis-figured* by evil. The derangement of minds and
deformity of bodies point to a deeper sickness, invisible but more irremedi-
ably tragic, the sickness of the soul. Gracelessness in all its forms indicates
the absence of grace in the theological sense of the term.

This, at least, is how O'Connor vindicated her heavy reliance on
grotesque effects and how she expected her readers to respond to them. Yet
her vigorous denunciation of spiritual sickness is not devoid of ambiguity,
and its ambiguity partly proceeds from the very rage with which she
fustigates man's sins and follies. Christian novelists have often been taken
to task for their self-indulgence in describing evil, and in reading them the
suspicion grows indeed time and again that they feel secretly attracted by
what they pretend to censure. In Mauriac's novels, for example, one often
senses a half-hidden complicity between the writer and his criminal
heroines. This is surely not the kind of complacency and duplicity
O'Connor could be accused of. Between her and her characters (with a
few notable exceptions) lies all the distance of contempt, disgust, and
derision, and it is the very harshness of the satire that arouses suspicion. By
dint of hunting evil, O'Connor—like most evil hunters—descries its
hideous leer at every turn. Nothing finds grace in her eyes, nothing is

spared her avenging fury. Wherever she looks, she discovers nothing but meanness and ugliness, horror and corruption. Or is it not rather her inquisitorial stare that distorts and diminishes, defaces and defiles all she sees? With O'Connor, character creation is a process comparable to the baptismal drownings described in her fiction: the very gesture that calls her creatures into life, stills them in the stark contours and absurd postures of caricature. When she describes a face, she transforms it into a cabbage,[4] gives it the expression of "a grinning mandrill,"[5] or likens it to "a big florid vegetable" ("A Stroke of Good Fortune," p. 95). Characters, in her hands, become mere puppets, and she does not even care to hide the strings: "Haze got up and hung there a few seconds. He looked as if he were held by a rope caught in the middle of his back and attached to the train ceiling" (WB, p. 12). With methodic thoroughness and almost sadistic glee, O'Connor exploits all the resources of her talent to reduce the human to the nonhuman, and all her similes and metaphors have seemingly no other purpose than to degrade it to the inanimate, the bestial, or the mechanical. Like Gogol and Dickens, she possesses a weird gift for deadening people into things while quickening things into objects with a life of their own (Hazel's rat-colored Essex in Wise Blood, the giant steam shovel in "A View of the Woods").

Hence a world both frozen and frantic, both ludicrous and threatening. O'Connor's landscapes — her fierce, fiery suns, her blank or blood-drenched skies, her ominous woods — are landscapes of nightmare. But at the same time nature shrinks to laughable proportions: clouds come to look like turnips ("The Life You Save May Be Your Own," p. 156), and raindrops like "tin-can tops" (ibid.). True, there are also fleeting glimpses of natural beauty. Yet, even though O'Connor defended her use of the grotesque as a necessary strategy of her art, one is left with the impression that in her work it eventually became the means of a savage revilement of the whole of creation.

Questions then arise on the orthodoxy of her Catholicism. For Barbey d'Aurevilly, Catholicism was, in his own phrase, an old wrought-iron balcony ideally suited for spitting upon the crowd. It would be unfair, certainly, to suggest that O'Connor used it for similar purposes. Yet one may wonder whether her Catholicism was not, to some extent, an alibi for misanthropy. And one may also wonder whether so much black derision is compatible with Christian faith, and ask what distinguishes the extreme bleakness of her vision from plain nihilism. Péguy and Bernanos were just as hostile to the secular spirit of modern times and no less vehement in their strictures, but after all Péguy also celebrated the theological virtue of hope, and Bernanos was also the novelist of Easter joy. In O'Connor, on the other hand, the most arresting feature, as in Swift, Kafka, or Beckett, is a compulsive emphasis on man's utter wretchedness, and what gives her voice its unique quality is a sustained note of dry and bitter fury.

If we are to believe the Christian moralists, one of the Devil's supreme wiles is to leave us with the shattering discovery of our nothingness and so to tempt us into the capital sin of despair. From what one knows of O'Connor's life, it seems safe to assume that this was the temptation she found most difficult to resist, and it might be argued that her writing was in many ways a rite of exorcism, a way of keeping despair at a distance by projecting it into fiction. Small wonder then that in her work the demon of literary creation, as John Hawkes so judiciously noted,[6] is inseparable from the Demon himself. When, as in *The Violent Bear It Away*, O'Connor makes the Devil speak, his sarcastic voice sounds startlingly like the author's. That her voice and vision so often verge on the diabolical should not surprise us: what better vantage point is there to observe and describe hell than Satan's, and who could know it better than he?

By God Possessed?

Yet it is not enough to say that O'Connor was of the Devil's party. Many ironies and paradoxes interact in her work, and exegetes of Christian persuasion would probably contend that in its very abjection O'Connor's world testifies to the presence of the divine, the fall from grace being the proof *a contrario* of man's supernatural destination. O'Connor's heroes live mostly in extreme isolation yet they are never truly alone. However entrenched in their smugness or embattled in their revolt, they find no safe shelter in their puny egos, and sooner or later, by degrees or — more often — abruptly, some invisible force breaks into their lives to hurl them far beyond themselves. They are *called* — called by whom? By what? How can anyone tell if the calling voice is God's or the Devil's?

A major theme in O'Connor's fiction, the enigma of *vocation*, is nowhere more fully explored than in her two novels. As most critics have pointed out, *Wise Blood* and *The Violent Bear It Away* offer very similar narrative and thematic patterns. Their heroes, Hazel Motes and Francis Marion Tarwater, are likewise obsessed by their vocation as preachers and prophets, and in both of them the obsession is significantly embodied in the figure of a despotic old man, the more formidable since he is dead: a fanatical grandfather, "with Jesus hidden in his head like a stinger" (*WB*, p. 20) for Hazel; a great-uncle no less single-minded and intolerant for young Tarwater. Both of them start by resenting the prophetic mission laid upon them as a cumbersome legacy and an intolerable violation of their free will. Hazel and Tarwater rebel alike: the former by leading a life of deliberate sin and crime, and by preaching the anti-Gospel of "the Holy Church Without Christ"; the latter by fleeing from the old prophet's wilderness to the godless city. Yet, do what they will, they equally fail in their frantic attempts to escape, and ultimately submit to their destinies as prophets.

Prophets or false prophets? The question is not easy to answer. Many of O'Connor's backwoods preachers are simply frauds, and for a sincere

Christian there is perhaps nothing more scandalous than religious impos-
ture. As J. M. G. LeClézio remarks, "The illusion-monger, the sorcerer,
tries to capitalize on something infinitely serious. He degrades. He
dishonors."[7] Satirizing southern evangelism, however, was obviously not
O'Connor's main concern. Her preachers and prophets are by no means all
vulgar charlatans. Nor are we supposed to regard them as lunatics. The
reader is of course free to dismiss characters such as Hazel Motes or the
two Tarwaters as insane, and to interpret their extravagant stories as cases
of religious mania, but it is clear that this is not how the author intended
them to be read. As a Roman Catholic, O'Connor must have had her
reservations about the fanatic intolerance and apocalyptic theology of
primitive fundamentalism. Yet, as she herself admitted on several occasions, its integrity and fervor appealed to her, for she found them
congenial to the burning intransigence of her own faith.[8] Her fascination
with the southern evangelist — whom she came to envision as a crypto-
Catholic — is not unlike the attraction Bernanos and Graham Greene felt
for the priest figure. No matter how crazy and criminal they are, Hazel
Motes and Tarwater are for her witnesses to the Spirit, and their madness
is God's madness.[9] Violent men, prone to every excess, they sin with a
vengeance, but strenuous sinners are precisely the stuff saints are made of.
As O'Connor reminds us in the title and scriptural epigraph of her second
novel, "The kingdom of heaven suffereth violence, and the violent bear it
away."

In O'Connor violence rules man's relation to the sacred, just as it
rules his relation to other men. Nothing here that suggests "spirituality":
the word is too smooth, too polished, too blandly civilized to apply to the
compulsions and convulsions of these savage souls. For Motes and Tarwater as well as for the "Misfit" of "A Good Man Is Hard to Find," God is
above all an idée fixe, and the divine is primarily experienced as an
intolerable invasion of privacy, a dispossession — or possession — of the self.
What torments O'Connor's heroes, at least at first glance, is not their
being deprived of God but rather the fact that their obsession with Him
cannot be escaped. Religious experience, as it is rendered dramatically in
her fiction, comes pretty close to Freud's definition: a variant of obses-
sional neurosis.

God is the Intruder. Therefore the first move of O'Connor's "prophet
freaks" (as she herself called them) is to resist or to flee. Hazel Motes tries
his utmost to get rid of God. Even as a child he imagines he can avoid Jesus
by avoiding sin; later, on the other hand, he blasphemes, fornicates, and
even murders to prove to himself that sin does not exist. What is more, he
sets out to preach a new church, "the church of truth without Jesus Christ
Crucified" (WB, p. 55), publicly denies the Fall and the Redemption, and
calls Jesus a liar. Each one of his words and actions becomes an open
defiance to the revealed God. With young Tarwater, the mutinous impulse

is just as radical. Hardly has his great-uncle died when he listens to the voice of the Tempter: "Jesus this and Jesus that. Ain't you in all your fourteen years of supporting his foolishness fed up and sick to the roof of your mouth with Jesus?"[10] In a sense, the old man's death is for Tarwater the equivalent of the (provisional) death of God, and if God is dead, everything is permissible: "Now I can do anything I want to. . . . Could kill off all those chickens if I had a mind to" (*TVBIA*, p. 25). Intoxicated with a sudden sense of absolute freedom, Tarwater — a lamentable latter-day Ivan Karamazov whose field of action has shrunk to a chickencoop — resolves to flout his great-uncle's last wishes. Instead of burying him decently, he gets drunk and sets fire to his house so as to destroy both the cumbrous corpse and all the past it symbolizes. He then goes to the city, not to baptize his uncle's dim-witted child, as the old man had ordered him, but intent on renouncing once and for all his prophetic mission. Yet these two gestures of denial are plainly not sufficient to rid him of Christ: "You can't just say NO . . . You got to do NO. You got to show it. You got to show you mean it by doing it. You got to show you're not going to do one thing by doing another. You got to make an end of it. One way or another" (*TVBIA*, p. 157). The break with God requires consummation by an act beyond atonement: to demonstrate his freedom, Tarwater consequently murders the child he should have baptized.

Rebellious children, O'Connor's heroes assert themselves only by willful transgression of the divine order, as if only the certainty of flouting God's will and of doing evil could give them an identity of their own. Their revolt springs essentially from a refusal to submit, to alienate their freedom and have their fate coerced into some preestablished pattern. In their stubborn striving for autonomy, they commit what Christian tradition has always considered to be the satanic sin par excellence: the sin of pride.

Yet pride is not the only obstacle to the fulfillment of their spiritual destinies. Soiled from birth by the sin of their origins, how could these fallen souls hoist themselves up to God's light? They do not know God; they experience only his burning absence. For the theologian and the philosopher God is a matter of speculation; for the mystic he may become the living object of inner experience. For O'Connor's Christomaniacs he becomes "the bleeding stinking mad shadow of Jesus" (*TVBIA*, p. 91). Their God is above all a haunting specter, a power felt and feared in its uncanny emptiness, and this ominous power they can only apprehend anthropomorphically through the incongruous phantasmagoria of their guilt-ridden imaginations. There is apprehension, but no comprehension. Their notion of the godly is not exempted from the distortions of the corrupt world in which they live, and therefore the divine gets so often confused with the demonic. In its extreme form, this rampant perversion comes to manifest itself as radical inversion. Everything, then, is turned upside down, and the religious impulse is subverted into its very opposite: desire for God is transformed into God-hatred, prayer into blasphemy, and the quest for salvation turns into a mystique of perdition.

Nothing exemplifies this inversion better than the *imitatio Christi* in reverse which O'Connor presents us in *Wise Blood*. After turning himself into the prophet of the Church Without Christ (the negative of the Church of God, the very image of the "body of sin" referred to by St. Paul), Hazel Motes ironically becomes a Christ without a church, an anonymous, solitary pseudo-Christ or anti-Christ. His disciples are morons and mountebanks, his preaching meets only with indifference, and his calvary at the close of the novel ends in a seemingly pointless death. Worn out by self-inflicted pain and privation, he is clubbed to death by two fat policemen. Motes dies like a dog, and his atrocious end reminds one strongly of the last pages of *The Trial*, when two men appear and lead Joseph K. to the outskirts of the town to kill him. The life and death of O'Connor's hero appear likewise as an absurd Passion. Or are we to assume that Motes is eventually saved? At the very end of the novel, the imagery of light and darkness, sight and blindness is manipulated in such a way as to suggest a less sinister meaning to Motes's martyrdom and death: staring into his burned-out eye sockets, Mrs. Flood, his landlady, sees him "moving farther and farther away, farther and farther into the darkness until he was the pin point of light" (*WB*, p. 232). Earlier this pinpoint of light had been identified as the star over Bethlehem (see *WB*, p. 219), and it might be taken as a hint that this "Christian *malgré lui*" (as the author called him in her note to the second edition) has been redeemed after all. The oblique reference to the birth of the Savior, however, is a little too pat, and the ultimate flicker of light, instead of lessening the horror of what precedes, simply adds a final twist to the novel's baffling ambiguity.

Christian references and Christian parallels abound in O'Connor's fiction, and more often than not they strike us as ironic. In *Wise Blood*, especially, parodic overtones are so frequent that the whole novel might almost be read as sheer burlesque. A "new jesus" appears in the guise of a shrunken museum mummy; a slop-jar cabinet becomes the tabernacle to receive him, and Sabbath Lily Hawks, a perverse little slut, cradles the mummy in her arms as if she were the Madonna. O'Connor's penchant for travesty is likewise reflected in the eccentric ritualism of many of her characters: baptismal drownings (in "The River" and *The Violent Bear It Away*), rites of exorcism (Tarwater setting fire to his great-uncle's house), purification rites (Tarwater firing the bushes where the rape occurred), initiation rites (Enoch Emery's shedding of clothes in *Wise Blood* and Tarwater's in *The Violent Bear It Away*), sacrificial rites (Motes's self-blinding), etc. In their appalling extravagance, these ritual actions are likely to shock any reader, whether Christian or not. But here again, if we are prepared to accept the premises of the author, we shall avoid mistaking them for mere fits of madness, for to her, in a desacralized world like ours, these savage and sacrilegious rites paradoxically assert the presence of the sacred through the very excess of its distortion or denial.

Yet what would we make of all these outrageous scenes had we not been told to read them in terms of Christian paradox? There are as many scenes of religious travesty in the films of Buñuel (the best-known being probably the Last Supper scene in *Viridiana*). Buñuel, however, has never made bones about his contempt for Christianity, and he has been as explicit about his atheism as O'Connor was about her Catholicism. This has not deterred well-meaning Christian critics from reclaiming him (after Baudelaire, Rimbaud, Kafka, Joyce, Camus, Beckett, and many others) as an errant son of the church. Why then, one might perversely ask, could not unbelievers pay them back in their own coin and, O'Connor's professions of faith notwithstanding, assert equal rights upon her work?

This is not to insinuate that O'Connor was an atheist *malgré elle*, but rather to suggest again the possibility of more than one reading of her fiction. O'Connor's satiric stance, her penchant for parody, her reliance on the grotesque, and her massive use of violence—the features of her art we have examined so far all contribute to the subtle interplay of tensions and ambiguities through which it comes alive, and they resist alike reduction to a single interpretative pattern. The same irreducible ambiguity also attaches to another significant trait of her fictional world: the enormous amount of suffering and humiliation which is inflicted on most of her characters, and the inevitability of their defeat and/or death. Hazel Motes's destiny probably offers the most telling example of this process: after an active career in sin and crime, all his aggressiveness is eventually turned against himself, driving him to a positive frenzy of masochism and self-destruction. He blinds himself with quicklime, exposes himself to cold and illness, walks in shoes "lined with gravel and broken glass and pieces of small stone" (*WB*, p. 221), wraps three strands of barbed wire round his chest, and when his baffled landlady protests at so much self-torture, Motes replies imperturbably: "I'm not clean," or again "I'm paying" (see *WB*, pp. 222, 224). The same compulsive concern with purity/impurity and the same need for penitential suffering bred from a deep-seated sense of guilt are also found, although to a lesser extent, in *The Violent Bear It Away*. With Tarwater, however, they rather take the symbolic form of fire rituals. After having been drugged and raped, he burns all the bushes around and is not content until every last bit of soil has been burned clean by the flames. Similarly, after the "friend's" last temptation, Tarwater sets fire to the forked tree from which the voice seems to emanate. Erecting a wall of fire between himself and "the grinning presence" (*TVBIA*, p. 238), he exorcises once and for all his demonic double. The hour of expiation has arrived. Tarwater atones for his rebellion by accepting at last his prophetic mission. Purified by fire, he turns, in the book's last sentence, "toward the dark city, where the children of God lay sleeping" (*TVBIA*, p. 243).

According to the prototypal Christian pattern, the hero's journey leads in both novels from sinful rebellion to the recognition of sin and to penance. O'Connor would have us believe that her protagonists are responsible for their fates, that they possess freedom of choice, and are at liberty to refuse or accept their vocation: "Tarwater is certainly free and meant to be; if he appears to have a compulsion to be a prophet, I can only insist that in this compulsion there is the mystery of God's will for him, and that it is not a compulsion in the clinical sense" (*MM*, p. 116). But her readers, even those who sympathize with her Christian assumptions and are willing to make allowances for the mysterious working of grace, will hesitate to take her at her word. For in the text of the novel there is indeed little to indicate that Motes or Tarwater could have made a different choice and that events might have followed another course. Her heroes are not allowed to shape their destinies; they only *recognize* fate when it pounces upon them. Consider, for example, Tarwater's reaction at his first meeting with Rayber's child:

> Tarwater clenched his fists. He stood like one condemned, waiting at the spot of execution. Then the revelation came, silent, implacable, direct as a bullet. He did not look into the eyes of any fiery beast or see a burning bush. He only knew, with a certainty sunk in despair, that he was expected to baptize the child he saw and begin the life his great-uncle had prepared for him. (*TVBIA*, p. 91)

True, O'Connor tells us that Tarwater was "expected" to obey his great-uncle's command, not that he had to. But his attitude, in its mixture of impotent revolt and bitter resignation, as well as the similes which the author uses to describe it, point to the contrary. In the same scene, in one of those duplications which indicate her heroes' self-estrangement, Tarwater's eyes reflect "depth on depth his own stricken image of himself, trudging into the distance in the bleeding stinking mad shadow of Jesus" (*TVBIA*, p. 91). Tarwater suddenly realizes that he is forever in bondage to that shadow. He tries "to shout, 'NO!' but it [is] like trying to shout in his sleep" (*TVBIA*, p. 92). O'Connor's heroes are indeed like sleepers: they traverse life in a driven dreamlike state, and with the sense of impotence and anxiety one experiences in nightmares. They go through the motions of revolt, but their violent gestures toward independence are all doomed to dissolve into unreality. They are nothing more than the starts and bounds of a hooked fish. Tarwater and Motes both act out scenarios written beforehand by someone else.

As Josephine Hendin has aptly noted, O'Connor's novels are about "the impossibility of growing up."[11] On the face of it, they develop in accordance with the three major phases of the *rite de passage*: separation, transition, and reincorporation, but they give no sense of moving forward in time and no evidence of psychological development. Instead of inner growth, there is a backward circling which takes O'Connor's heroes inexorably back to where they started. *Wise Blood* and *The Violent Bear It Away* both follow the same circular and regressive pattern made conspicuous by the close similarities between opening and final scenes. In *Wise Blood* Mrs. Hitchcock's fascination with Hazel's eyes in the initial train scene anticipates Mrs. Flood's perplexed watching of his burnt-out eye sockets at the close of the novel. In much the same way the punishment he inflicts upon himself at ten — walking through the woods, his shoes filled with pebbles — prefigures the penitential rites preceding his near-suicidal death. In *The Violent Bear It Away*, on the other hand, the parallelism is emphasized by the use of the same setting; the novel starts with Tarwater's departure from Powderhead and closes with his return to it. "I guess you're going home" (*WB*, p. 10), Mrs. Hitchcock says to Hazel Motes on the train; in symbolic terms, his journey is indeed a journey home, and Tarwater's is quite literally a homecoming. These repetitions, to be true, are repetitions with a difference, and one could say that the movement is spiral-like rather than circular: there are intimations that through his harrowing ordeals Motes has moved toward a state of saintliness, and his physical blindness may be taken for an index to the spiritual insight he has at last achieved. It is obvious too that in *The Violent Bear It Away* the fire symbolism of the closing scenes reverses the meaning it was given in the first chapter. And it might be argued finally that recurring situations, settings, and imagery are part of the author's elaborate technique of foreshadowing.

But this is perhaps precisely where the shoe pinches: O'Connor's foreshadowing is so dense as to become constrictive; the signs and signals of destiny clutter so thickly around the protagonists of her novels that no breathing space is left to them. The author plays God to her creatures, and foreshadowing becomes the fictional equivalent of predestination. Everything propels her heroes toward submission to their predetermined fates and, at the same time, pushes them back to their childhood allegiances. Not only does their rebellion fail, it also ends each time in unconditional surrender to the parental powers from which they had attempted to escape.

In *Wise Blood* the prophetic mission is anticipated in the haunting figure of the grandfather, but Hazel's backward journey is essentially a return to the mother. The return motif is already adumbrated in the remembered episode of his visit to Eastrod after his release from the army. The only familiar object Hazel then found in his parents' deserted house was his mother's walnut chifforobe, and before leaving he put warning notes in every drawer: "This shiffer-robe belongs to Hazel Motes. Do not steal it or you will be hunted down and killed" (*WB*, p. 26). In the claustrophobic dream touched off by this reminiscence, the chifforobe is metamorphosed into his mother's coffin, while the coffin itself is fused with the berth in the train where Hazel is sleeping. What is more, Hazel, in his dream, identifies with his dead mother (see *WB*, pp. 26–27). This dream is significantly related to another one, in which Motes dreams that he is buried alive and exposed through an oval window to the curiosity of various onlookers, one of whom is a woman who would apparently like to "climb in and keep him company for a while" (WB, p. 160). Furthermore, these two coffin dreams relate back to the traumatic childhood scene of Motes's initiation into evil: the disturbing sight of a nude blonde in a black casket, exhibited in the carnival tent where the ten-year-old boy had secretly followed his father. At his return from the country fair, his mother (whose image he superimposed mentally on that of the woman in the casket) knows, after one look at him, that he has sinned, and it is her accusing look that induces his first penitential rite. In the visual symbolism of the novel, the urge to see and the fear of being seen are recurrent motifs, and in this scene as in several others they both point to sin and guilt.[12] What also appears through the interrelated imagery of these oneiric and actual scenes is the close conjunction of sex and death. But the most remarkable feature is that the themes of sin and guilt, sex and death, all coalesce around the mother figure and its surrogates.[13] Motes's mother, while being deviously linked to his sordid sexual experiences, is at the same time a haunting reminder of the demands of religion: when he goes into the army, the only things he takes with him are "a black Bible and a pair of silver-rimmed spectacles that had belonged to his mother" (WB, p. 23). It is through her glasses that he reads the Bible, and later, when he puts them on again and looks at his face in a mirror, he sees "his mother's face in his" (WB, p. 187). It is no surprise then that Motes's erratic quest should end in oedipal self-blinding and self-destruction. His tragic end completes identification with the dead mother: it is both fulfillment and expiation of the same desire.

In *Wise Blood* Motes is finally reabsorbed into his mother. In *The Violent Bear It Away* Tarwater is likewise reabsorbed into his great-uncle. Raising the orphan boy to be a prophet like himself, the tyrannical old man has molded him in his own image and conditioned him for a destiny similar to his. When he dies, young Tarwater does his utmost to assert his own separate self through repeated acts of defiance, but what the novel seems to demonstrate is that there can be no escape from the self-ordained prophet's posthumous grip. In the concluding scene the repentant boy submits to what he so fiercely rejected, and his act of submission reminds one of the etymological origin of "humility" (humus = soil): prostrate on old Tarwater's grave, smearing his forehead with earth from his burial place, he acknowledges at last the absolute power of the past over the present, of the dead over the living or, to put it in terms of kinship, of the father over the son. The story comes full circle: otherness is resolved into sameness, difference into repetition. Having forever renounced his desire for autonomous selfhood, young Tarwater is now willing to become a faithful replica of old Tarwater, and in all likelihood his ulterior fate will be nothing more than a reenactment of the dead prophet's.

For neither protagonist of O'Connor's novels, then, is true separateness possible. Nor can they ever achieve true relatedness. Theirs is a demented mirror world of doubles, where the self is always experienced as other, and the other apprehended as a reflection of self. The schizophrenic dilemma they are both confronted with is either the madness of extreme isolation or the deadness of total engulfment.[14] In both cases, the failure to define a viable identity leads ultimately to complete self-cancelation; in both cases, the inability to grow up provokes helpless surrender to an omnipotent and all-devouring parent figure.

Such a reading is of course likely to be dismissed as reductive psychologizing by those of O'Connor's critics who insist on interpreting her on her own terms. Old Tarwater, they would object, was intended metaphorically as a representative of God, and the boy's final submission to the old man's will as a symbol of his surrender to the power of Christ. But it is at this very point that ambiguity and reversibility intervene. While the Christian reader quite naturally takes his cue from the author and translates the psychological conflict into religious drama, the non-Christian reader is tempted just as naturally to discuss the religious allegory in psychological terms. The former will see in old Tarwater an analogon of the heavenly Father; the latter will reverse the metaphor and regard O'Connor's God as a magnified fantasy-projection of her overpowering parent figures. To ask which of the two approaches is the more relevant is probably an irrelevant question. Both may be considered valid insofar as they provide operational procedures of analysis which are not contradicted by the evidence of the work under consideration. And both may also become reductive to the extent that they pretend to have the monopoly of a "correct" understanding.

By whom are O'Connor's driven souls possessed? By God or by the Devil? By supernatural powers or by unconscious fantasies? Her work raises the questions; it does not give the answers. Neither is it the critic's task to provide them. He reverberates her questioning in his own language and tries to do justice to its complexities, and this is about all he can do without exceeding his prerogatives.

The Coup de Grâce

For almost all of O'Connor's characters there is a time for denial and a time for submission, a time for sin and a time for atonement. The passage from one to the other is what she has attempted to describe in her two novels, but as we have seen, she shows relatively little interest in the continuities and intricacies of inner growth. Her heroes do not change gradually; they progress — or regress — in fits and starts, through a series of switches and turnabouts rather than through a slow process of maturation. What engages most deeply O'Connor's imagination — and this, incidentally, may account for her feeling more at home in the short story than in the novel — is not so much time as the sudden encounter of time with the timeless: the decisive moments in a man's existence she would have called moments of grace. "My subject in fiction," O'Connor wrote, "is the action of grace in territory held largely by the devil" (*MM*, p. 118). Grace plays indeed a major part in her novels as in most of her stories, especially the later ones, and as a religious concept it forms the very core of her implicit theology. Left to his own devices, man, as he appears in her fiction, is totally incapable of ensuring his salvation. Whether it degrades itself in grotesque parody or exhausts itself in mad convulsions, his quest for the holy is doomed to derision and failure from the very start. Grace alone saves, and even that is perhaps going too far: reading O'Connor's tales, one rather feels that grace simply makes salvation possible. As for fallen man, he collaborates in his redemption only by default. Instead of grace coming to complete and crown nature — as the mainstream Catholic tradition would have it — it breaks in on it. Bursting like a storm, it strikes with the unpredictable suddenness of a thunderbolt. And paradoxically it is more often than not at the very last moment, at the climax of violence or at the point of death that grace manifests itself, as though these boundary situations were God's supreme snare and the sinner's ultimate chance. It is when Tarwater yields to the temptation of murder and drowns Rayber's son that the hand of God falls upon him, forcing him to baptize the child against his will, and so converting the moment of sin and death into one of rebirth for both murderer and victim. In most of the stories of *Everything That Rises Must Converge*, the flash of grace occurs in similar circumstances, and spiritual conversion is accomplished likewise through a staggering if not annihilating shock. For Mrs. May, the self-righteous widow of "Greenleaf," it is achieved through the fatal encounter with a wild bull; for others it is effected through a son's suicide ("The Lame Shall Enter First") or a mother's death ("Everything That Rises Must Converge"). In the story significantly entitled "Revelation," on the other hand, a seemingly trivial incident is enough to spark off the deep inner commotion that, in O'Connor's fiction, inevitably precedes the moment of supernatural vision: a respectable lady is abused and assaulted by a girl in a doctor's waiting room, and, with her monumental smugness forever shattered, she is eventually granted a vision of heaven in her pig parlor.

Grace takes men by surprise. It catches them unawares, stabs them in the back. Nothing heralds the passage from darkness to light. And the light of grace is so sudden and so bright that it burns and blinds before it illuminates. Consider Mrs. May on the verge of death: ". . . she had the look of a person whose sight has been suddenly restored but who finds the light unbearable" ("Greenleaf," p. 333). The impact of grace, as evoked by O'Connor, is that of a painful dazzle; it does not flood the soul with joy; her characters experience it as an instantaneous deflagration, a rending and bursting of the whole fabric of their being. For the revelation it brings is first and foremost self-revelation, the terrified recognition of one's nothingness and guilt. As each character is brutally stripped of his delusions, he sees and knows himself at last for what he is: "Asbury blanched and the last film of illusion was torn as if by a whirlwind from his eyes" ("The Enduring Chill," p. 382). Not until the soul has reached that ultimate point of searing self-knowledge does salvation become a possibility. Then begins for those who survive the fire of grace, the "enduring" death-in-life of purgatorial suffering: "[Asbury] saw that for the rest of his days, frail, racked, but enduring, he would live in the face of a purifying terror. A feeble cry, a last impossible protest escaped him. But the Holy Ghost, emblazoned in ice instead of fire, continued, implacable, to descend" ("The Enduring Chill," p. 382). For Asbury as well as for Julian, grace means "entry into the world of guilt and sorrow" ("Everything That Rises Must Converge," p. 420). For others, on the contrary, like Mrs. May or the grandmother of "A Good Man Is Hard to Find," the beginning is quite literally the end, and the price paid for spiritual rebirth is an immediate death.

In O'Connor, grace is not effusion but aggression. It is God's violence responding to Satan's violence, divine counterterror fighting the mutiny of evil. The operations of the divine and of the demonic are so disturbingly alike that the concept of God suggested by her work is in the last resort hardly more reassuring than her Devil. In fairness, one should no doubt allow for the distortions of satire, and be careful to distinguish the God of O'Connor's faith from the God-image of her characters. Her handling of point of view, however, implies no effacement on the part of the narrator, and her dramatic rendering of spiritual issues as well as the imagery she uses to evoke the actions of grace, provide enough clues to what God meant in her imaginative experience.

O'Connor's imagination is preeminently visual and visionary. Like Conrad's, her art attempts in its own way "to render the highest kind of justice to the visible universe,"[15] and far from clouding her perception, her sense of mystery rather adds to its startling clarity and sharpness. It is worth noting too how much of the action of her stories and novels is reflected in the continuous interplay of peeping or peering, prying or spying eyes, and how much importance is accorded throughout to the sheer act of seeing — or not seeing. *Wise Blood* is a prime example: a great deal of its symbolism springs from the dialectic of vision and blindness, and a similar dialectic is also at work in *The Violent Bear It Away* and in many of her stories. For O'Connor seeing is a measure of being: while the sinner gropes in utter darkness, the prophet — in O'Connor's phrase, "a realist of distances"[16] — is above all a seer. In God the faculty of vision is carried to an infinite power of penetration: God is the All-seeing, the absolute Eye, encompassing the whole universe in its eternal gaze.

The cosmic metaphor for the divine eye is the sun. Through one of those reversals of the imagination analyzed by Gaston Bachelard, the sun, in O'Connor's fiction, is not simply the primal source of light that makes all things visible, it is itself capable of vision, it is an eye. In *The Violent Bear It Away* there are few scenes to which the sun is not a benevolent or, more often, malevolent witness. After the old man's death, while Tarwater is reluctantly digging his grave, the sun moves slowly across the sky "circled by a haze of yellow" (*TVBIA*, p. 24), then becomes "a furious white blister" (p. 25) as he starts listening to the seductive voice of the "stranger." And when he resolves to deny Christian burial to his great-uncle, the sun appears "a furious white, edging its way secretly behind the tops of trees that rose over the hiding place" (p. 44). The sun is likewise a symbol of God's watchful, but this time approving presence in the two parallel scenes (see pp. 145–46, 164–65) where Bishop, the innocent child — rehearsing, as it were, the baptismal rite — jumps into the fountain of a city park:

> The sun, which had been tacking from cloud to cloud, emerged above the fountain. A blinding brightness fell on the lion's tangled marble head and gilded the stream of water rushing from his mouth. Then the light, falling more gently, rested like a hand on the child's white head. His face might have been a mirror where the sun had stopped to watch its reflection. (p. 164)

Almost obtrusive at times in its symbolic emphasis, sun imagery runs throughout the novel. Tarwater's attempted escape from Christ is a flight from God's sun/son, and the failure of the attempt is metaphorically equated with the sun's triumph: on the morning after his baptismal drowning of Bishop, the "defeated boy" watches the sun rise "majestically with a long red wingspread" (p. 217), and at the close of the novel the victory of its burning light is again proclaimed through Tarwater's "scorched eyes," which look as if "they would never be used for ordinary sights again" (p. 233).

O'Connor's sun is both cosmic eye and heavenly fire. It thus condenses two of her most pregnant symbol patterns in a single image. For fire imagery is indeed as essential in her symbolic language as eye and sight imagery: incandescent suns, flaming skies, burning houses, woods, trees, and bushes — hers is an apocalyptic world forever ablaze. Fire is the visible manifestation of the principle of violence governing the universe, and the ordeal by fire is the *rite de passage* all of O'Connor's heroes are subjected to. A symbol of destruction and death, and a reminder of hell, it is also the favorite instrument of divine wrath and, as the old prophet taught young Tarwater, "even the mercy of the Lord burns" (*TVBIA*, p. 20). Associated with purification and regeneration as well as evil, fire is the ambiguous sign of the elect and the damned, and its voracity is God's as much as Satan's.

That eye, sun, and fire are all emblems of the sacred is confirmed by another symbolic figure which both unites and multiplies them in animal form: the peacock. In "The Displaced Person," instead of being associated with human pride and ostentatiousness, the peacock becomes a symbol of the Second Coming, evoking the unearthly splendor of Christ at the Last Judgment. His tail, in O'Connor's description, expands into a cosmic wonder: ". . . his tail hung in front of her, full of fierce planets with *eyes* that were each ringed in green and set against a *sun* that was gold in one second's light and salmon-colored in the next" ("The Displaced Person," p. 200; italics added). Later in the same story the peacock reappears, with his ocellated tail gorgeously fanned out against the vastness of the sky: ". . . a gigantic figure stood facing her. It was the color of the *sun* in the early afternoon, white-gold. It was of no definite shape but there were *fiery* wheels with fierce dark *eyes* in them, spinning rapidly all around it" ("The Displaced Person," p. 210; italics added).

Immensity, brilliance, splendor, a dizzying profusion of eyes and suns, such are the features O'Connor chooses to celebrate God's power and glory. And one can hardly refrain from the suspicion that power and glory are in her imagination if not in her belief the essential attributes of divinity. In cosmic terms, her God is sun and fire. If one examines her bestiary, one finds birds of prey, cocks, and bulls — animal metaphors which all suggest phallic potency and male aggressiveness. O'Connor's God is Christ the Tiger rather than Christ the Lamb, a God infinitely distant who confronts us with the agonizing mystery of absolute otherness and whose abrupt transcendence is manifested in sudden deflagrations of power. He is the Most High and the Wholly Other. Man's relation to Him is one of vertical tension precluding any form of reciprocity. Small wonder then that the spiritual errancy of O'Connor's heroes turns into a paranoid nightmare: aware of being watched and scrutinized by the relentless eye of the almighty Judge, they are unable ever to see their remote and silent persecutor. Not until grace descends to seize and possess their tormented souls is the infinite distance separating them abolished. Now the celestial Watcher, now a God of prey; first hovering, motionless, above his victim, then swooping with terrible speed to devour it.

One might have expected so fervent a Catholic as O'Connor to focus her fiction on the figure of Christ. In a sense, to be true, she does: whether in prayer or profanity, his name is obsessively referred to, and the question of whether Jesus suffered and died for our sins is indeed of vital concern to many of her characters. Yet her work is not so much Christ-centered as Christ-haunted. Unlike T. S. Eliot's later poetry, it is by no means a reaffirmation of the Christian mystery of the Incarnation. O'Connor's divisive vision perpetuates the idealistic cleavage between spirit and body, eternity and time, God and man, and Christ is likewise split into two irreconcilable halves. His image in her work constantly oscillates between the extremes of radical humanity and radical divinity. Now he is the mythical paradigm of human suffering, as Christ crucified and recrucified,[17] now he appears in the plenitude of his majesty as Christ the King, most startlingly represented in the image of the Byzantine Pantocrator tattooed on Parker's back. Or, to put it otherwise, he is alternately the impotent victimized Son and the omnipotent Father. These are images quite common in Christian literature and iconography. The point is that in O'Connor they never meet and merge in the dual unity of Christ, the God become man, the Word become flesh. The mediating function associated with Jesus by the Christian and particularly the Catholic tradition is hardly acknowledged, and what characterizes O'Connor's fictional world is precisely the absence of all mediation, of all intercession. On the one hand, there is the utter darkness of evil, on the other, the white radiance of divine transcendence. Between the two: man, battered and blinded, the victim of Satan or the prey of God, doomed to be defeated and dispossessed whatever the outcome of the dubious battle fought over his wretched soul.

O'Connor identified her vision as a fiction writer with the vision of her faith: "I see from the standpoint of Christian orthodoxy. This means that for me the meaning of life is centered in our Redemption by Christ and what I see in the world I see in its relation to that" (*MM*, p. 32). It is a far cry, however, from the reassuring bluntness of her public statements to the puzzling evidence of her tales. O'Connor envisioned the writer's relation to his work on the same pattern as God's relation to his creation, as if art were simply the fulfillment of preexisting intentions, the embodiment of a fixed vision prior to the writing process. In defining herself as a writer, she failed to acknowledge the insight so admirably dramatized in her fiction: that the self is not even master in its own house. For the writing self is certainly not exempted from the common lot: its imaginative constructs escape its mastery both in their deeper motivations and in their ultimate effects.

The truth of O'Connor's work is the truth of her art, not that of her church. Her fiction does refer to an implicit theology, but if we rely, as we should, on its testimony rather than on the author's comments, we shall have to admit that the Catholic orthodoxy of her work is at least debatable. O'Connor is definitely on the darker fringe of Christianity, and to find antecedents one has to go back to the paradoxical theology of early church fathers like Tertullian, or to the negative theology of stern mystics like St. John of the Cross. Pitting the supernatural against the natural in fierce antagonism, her theology holds nothing but scorn for everything human, and it is significant that in her work satanic evildoers (the "Misfit," Rufus Johnson) are far less harshly dealt with than humanistic do-gooders (Rayber, Sheppard). What is more, of the two mysteries — or myths — which are central to Christianity, the Fall and the Redemption, only the first seems to have engaged her imagination as a creative writer. Gnawed by old Calvinistic ferments and at the same time corroded by a very modern sense of the absurd, O'Connor's version of Christianity is emphatically and exclusively her own. Her fallen world, it is true, is visited by grace, but is grace, as she evokes it in her last stories, anything other than the vertigo of the *nada* and the encounter with death? And who is this God whose very mercy is terror?

It may be argued of course that these are the paradoxes of faith, or that O'Connor's rhetoric of violence was the shock therapy which her benumbed audience needed. There is little doubt that there will be many further exercises in exegetical ingenuity to establish her orthodoxy. Yet her work is not content with illustrating Christian paradoxes. It stretches them to the breaking point, leaving us with Christian truths gone mad, the still incandescent fragments of a shattered system of belief.

Flannery O'Connor was a Catholic. She was not a Catholic novelist. She was a writer, and as a writer she belongs to no other parish than literature.

Notes

1. Quoted by John Hawkes, in "Flannery O'Connor's Devil," *Sewanee Review* 70 (Summer 1962): 400.

2. On the theme of the child-parent conflict, see the stimulating essay by Claire Katz, "Flannery O'Connor's Rage of Vision," *American Literature* 46 (March 1974): 54–67.

3. "My own feeling is that writers who see by the light of their Christian faith will have, in these times, the sharpest eyes for the grotesque, for the perverse, and for the unacceptable." In "The Fiction Writer and His Country," *Mystery and Manners* (New York: Farrar, Straus & Giroux, 1969), p. 33. Subsequent quotations from O'Connor's essays will be identified with the abbreviation *MM* and a page number in parentheses.

4. See "A Good Man Is Hard to Find," in *Flannery O'Connor: The Complete Stories* (New York: Farrar, Straus & Giroux, 1971), p. 117. Subsequent quotations from the stories are from this edition. References will be parenthetically indicated in the text.

5. *Wise Blood* (New York: Farrar, Straus & Cudahy, 1962), p. 39. Subsequent quotations are from this edition; they will be identified with the abbreviation *WB* and a page number in parentheses.

6. See "Flannery O'Connor's Devil," pp. 395–407.

7. "L'Univers de Flannery O'Connor," *Nouvelle Revue Française* 13 (September 1965): 488. My translation.

8. "I am more and more impressed with the amount of Catholicism that fundamentalist Protestants have been able to retain. Theologically our differences with them are on the nature of the Church, not on the nature of God or our obligations to Him." Letter to Sister Mariella Gable, May 4, 1963, as quoted by Carter W. Martin, in *The True Country: Themes in the Fiction of Flannery O'Connor* (Nashville: Vanderbilt University Press, 1969), p. 20.

9. See, for example, O'Connor's statement on old Tarwater: "[He] is the hero of *The Violent Bear It Away*, and I'm right behind him 100 per cent," as quoted by Granville Hicks in "A Writer at Home with Her Heritage," *Saturday Review* (May 12, 1962), p. 22.

10. *The Violent Bear It Away* (New York: Farrar, Straus & Cudahy, 1960), p. 39. Subsequent quotations are from this edition; they will be identified with the abbreviation *TVBIA* and a page number in parentheses.

11. *The World of Flannery O'Connor* (Bloomington: Indiana University Press, 1970), p. 43.

12. On this point, see my essay "Aveugles et voyants: Le Thème du regard dans *Wise Blood*," *Bulletin de la Faculté des Lettres de Strasbourg* 40 (January 1969): 291–301.

13. It is interesting to note that the two women with whom Motes has sexual intercourse are both perverse and parodic mother figures: "Momma" Watts, the prostitute, treats Motes like a child; Sabbath Lily becomes a travesty of the Virgin Mary in the mummy scene. It is remarkable too that most female characters in the novel are associated with castration symbols: Motes's mother appears with a stick (p. 63); Mrs. Watts uses a "large pair of scissors" (p. 33), her grin is "as curved and sharp as the blade of a sickle" (p. 60), and her teeth are pointed like those of the woman with the cadaverous face Motes sees in the swimming pool (cf. pp. 33 and 84).

14. On the schizophrenic's sense of engulfment, see, for example, R. D. Laing, *The Divided Self* (London: Tavistock Publications, 1959).

15. Joseph Conrad, preface to *The Nigger of the Narcissus* [1897] (London: J. M. Dent & Sons, 1945), p. 3.

16. "The Role of the Catholic Novelist," *Greyfriar*, Siena Studies in Literature 7 (1964): 9.

17. The theme of Christ recrucified is developed in "The Displaced Person," and, even more ambiguously, in *Wise Blood*.

Rural Gothic: The Stories of Flannery O'Connor
Ronald Schleifer*

> There are two qualities that make fiction. One is the sense of mystery
> and the other is the sense of manners. You get manners from the texture
> of existence that surrounds you. The great advantage of being a
> Southern writer is that we don't have to go anywhere to look for
> manners. . . . We in the South live in a society that is rich in contradic-
> tion, rich in irony, rich in contrast, and particularly rich in speech.

I

In *A Portrait of the Artist*, that most ungothic of literary works, Stephen Dedalus explains to his friend Lynch that although Aristotle had not defined pity and terror in the *Poetics*, he, Stephen, had:

> Pity is the feeling which arrests the mind in the presence of whatsoever
> is grave and constant in human sufferings and unites it with the human
> sufferer. Terror is the feeling which arrests the mind in the presence of
> whatsoever is grave and constant in human sufferings and unites it with
> the secret cause.[1]

Stephen is attempting to define tragic art, yet his definitions are useful in developing a sense of the larger movements of Gothic fiction — of the serious contemplation of the supernatural in literature. The novel, I would

*Reprinted from *Modern Fiction Studies*, 28 (1982), 475–85. © 1982 by Purdue Research Foundation, West Lafayette, Indiana.

argue, seeks to achieve some sense of Stephen's "pity," to create the texture of a social world in which we can join in sympathy with its human sufferers. What has characterized the great novelists in English—from Defoe through Fielding and George Eliot to the human comedy of *Ulysses* itself—is an abiding sense of sympathy for the human sufferer, or its opposite, a sense of irony toward him. Another way to say this is to argue that the novel seeks to hide and to erase its own origins, to present itself and its characters on their own terms within the context of "the texture of existence that surrounds" them,[2] whereas the Gothic romance seeks to reveal its hidden origins. The novel deals with the middle between apocalyptic ends; it deals with ongoing life, with what William Spanos, following Kierkegaard, calls the "interesting," "the intentionality of *inter esse* 'meaning (i) "to be between," (ii) "to be a matter of concern." ' "[3]

The Gothic romance, on the other hand, seeks extremes; it proceeds, as Peter Brooks has noted, by means of the logic of the excluded middle.[4] "It is not made from the mean average or the typical," Flannery O'Connor has written, "but from the hidden and often the most extreme" (*MM*, p. 58); "it is the extreme situation that best reveals what we are essentially" (*MM*, p. 113). The Gothic romance, when it is serious, seeks essences; it seeks origins—both its own and its characters'. That is, it seeks Joyce's "secret cause" and achieves, in the course of that quest, the terror Stephen talks of. Origins are always supernatural; they are always beyond what can be known in a rational, logical way. That is why Stephen talks of the "mystical estate" of fatherhood as the basis of the Catholic Church in *Ulysses*, because "it is founded, like the world, macro- and microcosm, upon the void."[5] Origins are always what O'Connor calls "mystery," the manifestation and apprehension of the Sacred within quotidian reality. The Gothic tradition arose, Brooks argues, "at the dead end of the Age of Reason, [when] the Sacred reasserted its claim to attention, but in the most primitive possible manifestations, as taboo and interdiction. . . . [The Gothic tradition] reasserts the presence in the world of forces which cannot be accounted for by the daylight self and the self-sufficient mind."[6] The daylight self and the self-sufficient mind are inhabitants of novels, where union with the human sufferer is enough and supernatural origins are beside the point: we need not know Moll Flanders' real parentage and name to feel the sympathetic understanding she occasions; and although Tom Jones's parentage is of some importance, it is precisely his indifference to such questions that makes him so appealing.

The Gothic novel, however, presents precisely the need to discover origins: its characters, from *The Castle of Otranto* on, seek to find (or find thrust upon themselves) their parentage and their origins. The Gothic is a haunted literature (it is no accident that both Joyce and O'Connor come from a Catholic tradition that takes the presence of the supernatural seriously), and what haunts it—whether it be Count Dracula, the Frankenstein monster, or the governess' ghosts in "The Turn of the Screw"—is some supernatural origin, some inhuman silence, forces beyond the self-sufficiency of the daylight self. These forces raise the question of identity and origin for the characters of Gothic romance: "who and what am I?" ask Frankenstein's monster and Lewis' Monk and Kafka's K.; "how can I discover those forces beyond myself that originate myself, my own 'secret cause'?" To put these questions in literary terms especially appropriate to Flannery O'Connor, how can we discover the origins of the power of literature, the originary force of metaphorical language? Such discoveries, as Stephen suggests, are made in terror, made in the loss of self within its secret cause. "To know oneself," O'Connor has written, "is, above all, to know what one lacks" (*MM*, p. 35): it is a way of exploring the self and the world in a manner different from sympathetic understanding, through terror, violence, and encounter with the supernatural. O'Connor goes on to say,

> St. Cyril of Jerusalem, in instructing catechumens, wrote: "The dragon sits by the side of the road, watching those who pass. Beware lest he devour you. We go to the Father of Souls, but it is necessary to pass by the dragon." No matter what form the dragon may take, it is of this mysterious passage past him, or into his jaws, that stories of any depth will always be concerned to tell, and this being the case, it requires considerable courage at any time, in any country, not to turn away from the storyteller. (*MM*, p. 35)

Seeking the Father of Souls—the secret cause and origin of identity and the "rich speech" that manifests identity—the writer and the reader must pass the dragon outside; they must, as O'Connor continually insists, recognize the literal reality of the Devil, the poverty of our self-sufficiency, and the necessity of grace. Such self-knowledge is a form of agony; as O'Connor says in what I believe is her best story, "The Artificial Nigger"—a story whose plot literally repeats the plot of St. Cyril's parable, with the artificial nigger a silent figure on the side of the road—such knowledge grows "out of agony, which is not denied to any man and which is given in strange ways to children."[7] It is this "mysterious passage" that the Gothic tradition offers us when it is most serious, a passage to and through origin and identity to their secret cause.

Nowhere are origins and identity such pressing problems, as Roy Male has recently shown,[8] than on the frontier, where one continually encounters "mysterious strangers" who raise questions about one's own as well as others' identity. One such modern frontier is O'Connor's South: it is especially a "frontier" for a Catholic writer in the predominantly fundamentalist Protestant South. Like the Gothic romance Brooks describes, O'Connor seeks in her work to "reassert" the Sacred in the quotidian world, to situate her characters on the mysterious passage between the "manners" of novels and the "mystery" of union with secret causes. Tzvetan Todorov's study, *The Fantastic*, situates Gothic fiction on the "frontier" between natural and supernatural understandings of experience. In fact, although he does not use it, "frontier" itself is an apt metaphor for the situation of the Gothic as Todorov defines it: "the fantastic is that hesitation experienced by a person who knows only the laws of nature, confronting an apparently supernatural event."[9] This is O'Connor's "frontier," that of a fiction which is always "pushing its own limits outward toward the limits of mystery, because . . . the meaning of a story does not begin except at a depth where adequate motivation and adequate psychology and the various determinations have been exhausted. Such a writer . . . will be interested in possibility rather than in probability. He will be interested in characters who are forced out to meet evil and grace and who act on a trust beyond themselves" (*MM*, pp. 41–42). The Gothic, that is, presents a world beyond the understandings of metaphor, a world of mysterious inhuman forces that cannot adequately be explained by the metaphors of psychology or sociology or well-meaning humanism. It is a literature of *presence* unmediated by the substitutions of language, presences which are inhuman, terrifying, *secret*.

Yet O'Connor's frontier is more literal than this: her constant gesture is to place her characters between the natural and the supernatural by locating them, often on a literal journey, between the cities and the rural country of the South. "What the Southern Catholic writer is apt to find, when he descends within his imagination," she notes, "is not Catholic life but the life of this region in which he is both native and alien" (*MM*, p. 197). Rufus Johnson in "The Lame Shall Enter First"—a character who embodies, as many of O'Connor's characters do, the *reality* of the Devil— has a history of "senseless destruction, windows smashed, city trash boxes set afire, tires slashed—the kind of thing . . . found where boys had been transplanted abruptly from the country to the city as this one had" (*CS*, p. 449). This is where the supernatural is most clearly and terrifyingly encountered—on those frontiers between the country and the city, faith and faithlessness, Protestant fundamentalism and cosmopolitan skepticism. Yet Rufus Johnson, as the well-meaning humanist-protagonist of the story learns, cannot be explained: he is simply a literal force, the force of the Devil, to be encountered on this "frontier." "I have found," O'Connor writes, "that anything that comes out of the South is going to be called grotesque by the Northern reader" (*MM*, p. 40), and she found this because the *strangeness* of that frontier in our culture—that location of the clashes between terror and pity—forces upon her characters confrontations with themselves and origins beyond themselves. "While the South is hardly Christ-centered," O'Connor says, "it is most certainly Christ-haunted" (*MM*, p. 40).

II

"The problem of the novelist who wishes to write about a man's encounter with this God," O'Connor has written, "is how he shall make the experience—which is both natural and supernatural—understandable, and credible, to his reader" (*MM*, p. 161). This is O'Connor's literary problem, to make the Sacred literal in a world in which it seems at best metaphorical, originating in a mode of perception rather than in the created world. Her problem, then, is the problem of the Gothic. Perhaps the best place to see her struggling with the problem is in one of her less successful stories, one that comes close to parodying the more powerful expressions of her repeated theme and plot, "The Enduring Chill." This story relates the return to rural Georgia from New York of Asbury Fox. Asbury, a twenty-five-year-old man, had gone to New York to become a literary artist, but now he is returning home to his mother without having written anything because he finds himself dying. Asbury is one of the characters in O'Connor's works—Hulga in "Good Country People," Julian in "Everything that Rises," Calhoun in "The Partridge Festival" are others—who has come to believe in nothing but himself and his own powers of perception. He, like the others, wants to teach his mother a lesson before he dies, to teach her of a realm beyond what he calls "her literal mind" of larger, sophisticated, metaphorical values. Thus on earlier visits home he had smoked and drunk warm milk with the Negro workers in his mother's dairy farm in order to shock her out of her complacencies. His mother, like so many other characters in O'Connor, lives in a self-satisfied, cliché-ridden world, a world where the metaphors of cliché are never examined at all. Asbury, like Hulga and Julian, participates in the egocentric life of his mother even while he is unaware of it: his mode of shocking her is to face her with the reality of his own dying, to counter her mindless optimism with his own brand of mindless, melodramatic pessimism. He wants her to understand the meaning—the metaphorical significance—of his death. To open her eyes he has left her a letter to be opened after his approaching death:

> If reading it would be painful to her, writing it had sometimes been unbearable to him—for in order to face her, he had had to face himself. "I came here to escape the slave's atmosphere of home," he had written, "to find freedom, to liberate my imagination, to take it like a hawk from its cage and set it 'whirling off into the widening gyre' (Yeats) and what did I find? It was incapable of flight. It was some bird you had domesticated, sitting huffy in its pen, refusing to come out!" The next words were underscored twice. "I have no imagination. I have no talent. I can't create. I have nothing but the desire for these things. Why didn't you kill that too? Woman, why did you pinion me?" (*CS*, p. 364)

Asbury's language, with its incessant "I's," is as egocentric as that of any character in O'Connor's stories. He fails to "face himself" in his letter because he himself is simply a cliché—of a writer and a son. He can only speak of himself in the tired metaphors of "freedom" and "birds," and his "desires" are projections of himself rather than desires for things in the world. He even misquotes Yeats in order to humanize Yeats's metaphor for the presence of inhuman powers and to make it the narrated description of his own imagination.

Nevertheless, the act of "facing oneself" is the recurrent action of O'Connor's stories, the action of Gothic romance. Perhaps the most striking example of this is that of O. E. Parker in "Parker's Back," who literally "faces" his own back with a giant tattoo of Jesus, the eyes of which "continued to look at him — still, straight, all-demanding, enclosed in silence" (*CS*, p. 526). This is a representative Gothic gesture: to make the metaphorical literal. Gothic romance does this, as Todorov and others have shown, [10] by narrating dream and nightmare as reality and projecting our deepest impulses and fears onto the landscape. The face on Parker's back — its "all-demanding" eyes — made Parker feel "that his dissatisfaction was gone, but he felt not quite like himself. It was as if he were himself but a stranger to himself, driving into a new country though everything he saw was familiar to him, even at night" (*CS*, p. 527). Such a feeling — a feeling that the reader is never sure Asbury achieves or not, hence the relative failure of "The Enduring Chill" — is what Freud calls the "uncanny," "that class of terrifying which leads back to something long known to us, once very familiar"; "the uncanny," Freud says, "would always be that in which one does not know where one is, as it were."[11] The uncanny is familiar and strange, just as Parker is both familiar and strange to himself with God's constant eyes literally *upon* him, and he is in a country in which he is both native and alien.

That country is the country of the frontier, between the familiar and strange, the natural and supernatural. One gets there in O'Connor by "facing" oneself, by seeking origins and seeing oneself, as Mr. Head does, with God's own eyes, with God's eyes *upon* one. The Gothic, I have said, makes the metaphorical literal, and in this action we can see why O'Connor's backwoods characters so often use country clichés in their speech: her act is to make us see the familiar as strange, to make us see literally and thus strangely what we usually don't see at all because it is so familiar. "Christ!" someone says in the pool hall when Parker reveals his tattoo (*CS*, p. 526), and suddenly — almost supernaturally — O'Connor creates Christ's presence, as literal as it is for Parker, by means of the cliché of astonishment. In "The River," Bevel learns of Jesus:

> He had found out already this morning that he had been made by a carpenter named Jesus Christ. Before he had thought it had been a doctor named Sladewall, a fat man with a yellow mustache who gave him shots and thought his name was Herbert. . . . If he had thought about it before, he would have thought Jesus Christ was a word like "oh" or "damn" or "God," or maybe somebody who had cheated them out of something sometime. . . . (*CS*, p. 163)

Such a discovery is the terrifying revelation of what we already knew: "carpenter" in this context takes on the full presence of its literal meaning of a maker, and Bevel (something a carpenter makes) is faced with the terrifying prospect of seeing himself anew.

Such confrontations with the literal — the literal self, its literal origin, a literal meaning — are the repeated actions in Flannery O'Connor, and they take place in what John Hawkes has called "her almost luridly bright pastoral world,"[12] on borderlines between the city and the country or between day and night. This is why so often O'Connor's stories end at sunset, as in "Revelation," when Mrs. Turpin watches her hogs as the sun goes down:

> Then like a monumental statue coming to life, she bent her head slowly and gazed, as if through the very heart of mystery, down into the pig parlor at the hogs. They had settled all in one corner around the old sow who was grunting softly. A red glow suffused them. They appeared to pant with a secret life. (CS, p. 508)

From this sight she looks up as the sun goes down and sees her vision of a vast horde of souls going to heaven, "whole companies of white-trash, clean for the first time in their lives, and bands of black niggers in white robes, and battalions of freaks and lunatics shouting and clapping and leaping like frogs" (CS, p. 508). The metaphor O'Connor uses is almost an allusion to Otranto with its giant statue coming to life, but the language is that of Mrs. Turpin, another in O'Connor's procession of good country people. That language informs a rural vision, Hawkes's lurid pastoral world, with a sense of supernatural force so that the whole is seen in a new light. Here again O'Connor creates the *presence* of the supernatural, of mysterious forces beyond the daylight self, in pig and sunset. "Revelation" begins with Mrs. Turpin's confrontation with a Wellesley student in a doctor's office, yet it ends with her own uncouthness — her own rural sensibility — miraculously transformed in the presence of a secret life.

That life is Mrs. Turpin's life, but dark, unknown, strange: it is the life revealed in the college girl's fierce remark: "Go back to hell where you came from, you old wart hog" (CS, p. 500). It is the inhuman life of wart hogs from hell that, literalized, leads strangely to Mrs. Turpin's vision of heaven. Mrs. Turpin "faces" herself with the hog; she sees her own secret life in the elemental life of her farm and discovers, as Parker had, the presence of God in and beyond His creation, in and beyond the hogs, the people, the peculiar light of the setting sun.

This is the light of grace, and it appears again at another sunset situated between the city and the country at the end of "The Artificial Nigger." There Mr. Head and his grandson, Nelson, after the small Inferno of their day in Atlanta, discover in the accidental image of suffering in a delapidated statue of a Negro the "action of mercy." What is powerful in O'Connor is her ability to create the *presence* of Christ and grace felt through and beyond the world of nature. How she does this is the problem and the secret of her art, and it is an art that is Gothic and that depends, fully, on its situation on one of the frontiers of our culture. Herman Melville wrote in *The Confidence-Man*, "it is with fiction as with religion: it should present another world, and yet one to which we feel the tie."[13] O'Connor, like Melville, presents another world of white trash, black niggers, freaks, lunatics — in a word, a world of "good country people" — which is tied to ours yet strangely literal in its very landscape and language. That tie with our world is the tie with what she calls the "action of mercy," and in her best work it is "tied" through her metaphoric language becoming literal.[14] Love is the burden of "The Artificial Nigger": face to face with a broken-down statue of a Negro, Mr. Head and his grandson are "faced with some great mystery, some monument to another's victory that brought them together in their common defeat" so that they "both feel it dissolving their differences *like an action of mercy*" (*CS*, p. 269). This encounter creates a sense of humility for Mr. Head until, three paragraphs later, "he stood appalled . . . while *the action of mercy* covered his pride like a flame and consumed it." In the course of these paragraphs (and in the course of Mr. Head's experience), simile is rendered as assertion until, before our eyes, grace manifests itself, the action of mercy, the secret cause, appears:

> [Mr. Head] stood appalled, judging himself with the thoroughness of God, while the action of mercy covered his pride like a flame and consumed it. He had never thought himself a great sinner before but he saw now that his true depravity had been hidden from him lest it cause him despair. He realized that he was forgiven for sins from the beginning of time, when he had conceived in his own heart the sin of Adam, until the present, when he had denied poor Nelson. He saw that no sin was too monstrous for him to claim as his own, and since God loved in proportion as He forgave, he felt ready at that instant to enter Paradise. (*CS*, pp. 269–270)

This is the "secret cause" that Joyce speaks of, a sense of God's presence and love in the heart of Mr. Head. But what is remarkable about this passage, I believe, is that we never question the fact that the realization described — its language and its theology — is simply beyond the frontier language and evangelical Christianity of Mr. Head. (Head, hick that he is, believes that an inferno underlies Atlanta and fears to be sucked down the sewer: he literalizes his own metaphor — see *CS*, pp. 259, 267.) What reveals itself here is grace, and, like the Mormon's magical glasses, grace includes the ability to see and to understand another language.

This language is that of sympathy: the passage suggests that Head can only understand the "secret cause" — here the sin of Adam — by experiencing the agony of his own egocentric denial of "poor Nelson." Mr. Head is not truly a part of the world he lives in — neither is Mrs. Turpin, O. E. Parker, Asbury Fox, and most of O'Connor's protagonists — and his struggle, like that of the others and like our own, is to find some connection in a world that simply seems alien, other, without human response. It is a world, as the Misfit says in "A Good Man is Hard to Find," in which, without an answering Jesus, there's no pleasure but meanness, "no real pleasure in life" (*CS*, p. 133) — a world in which, as O'Connor says, we are native and alien. How to discover a human response in such a world is the great problem: Mr. Head can, as he has done all his life, depend on himself and his ability to give "lessons" and be a "suitable guide for the young" (*CS*, p. 249), or he can discover, in terror or in love, but above all in humility, supernatural forces outside himself that lead him to other human sufferers who can respond to himself. Most of O'Connor's heroes fall into terror: they find, as Parker does, the terrifying cost of God's enduring eye; or they find, as the Misfit does, the senselessness of not knowing God is there. As O'Connor herself says, "Often the nature of grace can be made plain only by describing its absence" (*MM*, p. 204), and such absence *is* inhuman; it leaves our world literally senseless and results in the senseless violence — the inhuman violence — of all those who do not fit: the Misfit, Rufus, Shiftlet, and all the rest. But others — Mrs. Turpin, Mr. Head, Bailey's mother — discover love amid their terror: they discover the literal language of God already in their own Southern slang. They achieve humility when they realize that they are not fully self-possessed, that their "calm understanding," as it is said of Head, leaves out their own mysterious origins and forces beyond themselves. "An artificial nigger!" Mr. Head said to Nelson: "They ain't got enough real ones here. They got to have an artificial one" (*CS*, pp. 268, 269). Face to face with suffering — face to face with himself — Head recognizes forces outside himself.

What the action of mercy finally does is offer a sense of grace, a sense of the supernatural, in the world in which O'Connor characters, both native and alien, do not quite fit. "The Enduring Chill" is a parody of the kind of story — the Gothic romance — O'Connor writes. In the end we discover Asbury is not dying at all, despite all his histrionics: he had simply poisoned himself with the unpasteurized milk he had drunk during his last visit. But meanwhile, much as Tanner orchestrates his own funeral in "Judgement Day," imagining himself shipped home to Georgia from New York in his casket out of which he would jump on his arrival, shouting: "Judgement Day! Judgement Day! . . . Don't you two fools know it is Judgement Day?" (*CS*, p. 546), so Asbury orchestrates his own end. He calls for a Catholic priest, hoping to engage him in a literary debate, only to find the priest is as ignorant as his mother; he insults the family doctor; and he calls the household Negroes to his deathbed for a touching farewell. In the end, however, he learns he is not going to die, and, as he lies in bed at the end of the story with his nonfatal fever, he looks at a discoloration on the ceiling of his room that had always reminded him of a bird.

> The boy fell back on his pillow and stared at the ceiling. His limbs that had been racked for so many weeks by fever and chill were numb now. The old life in him was exhausted. He awaited the coming of new. It was

then that he felt the beginning of a chill, a chill so peculiar, so light, that it was like a warm ripple across a deeper sea of cold. His breath came short. The fierce bird which through the years of his childhood and the days of his illness had been poised over his head, waiting mysteriously, appeared all at once to be in motion. Asbury blanched and the last film of illusion was torn as if by a whirlwind from his eyes. He saw that for the rest of his days, frail, racked, but enduring, he would live in the face of a purifying terror. A feeble cry, a last impossible protest escaped him. But the Holy Ghost, emblazoned in ice instead of fire, continued, implacable, to descend. (CS, p. 382)

This is a far cry from the "action of mercy" in "The Artificial Nigger": here nothing appears in this story of a pseudo-sophisticated, spiteful boy to prepare for this supernatural intervention. Yet it is precisely because "The Enduring Chill" ends so abruptly that we can trace the "action" of grace in the story. Grace is occasioned by its own absence, by the despair, leading to rage or to humility, that all of O'Connor's characters, saved or not, fall into. Rage is always present, always seemingly a supernatural force. Humility translates this Gothic rage into rage against the daylight self and the self-sufficient mind to allow the apprehension not of projections of self but of the self itself, originating elsewhere. That is, to quote Yeats (correctly this time), "Where there is nothing—there is God." The grandmother in "A Good Man is Hard to Find" finally sees, literally, that she is responsible for the Misfit *because* God literally loves her, despite the apparent terrible, murderous, absence of love; she sees that her clichés about Jesus are literally true, even though she has used them throughout the story when she had nothing to say. "The Enduring Chill" does not create the sense of the presence of God, I think, because its transformation from the metaphoric absence of grace to the literal presence of the Holy Ghost is not convincing: Asbury's "defeat" does not fully succeed, and his vision, unlike that of Mrs. Turpin and the grandmother, isn't grounded in his own backwoods belief.

What the rural Southern frontier finally offers O'Connor is that position in the world—that situation—where the strangers you meet can be anyone, can, in fact, be supernatural: Jesus, the Devil, the Holy Ghost.

"I can tell you my name is Tom T. Shiftlet and I come from Tarwater, Tennessee, but you never have seen me before: how you know I ain't lying? How you know my name ain't Aaron Sparks, lady, and I come from Singleberry, Georgia, or how you know it's not George Speeds and I come from Lucy, Alabama, or how you know I ain't Thompson Bright from Toolafalls, Mississippi?" (CS, pp. 147–48)

All these names, as Roy Male has suggested, are filled with light,[15] and they set forth the action—sometimes the failed action—of O'Connor's Gothic fiction: to discover or create light out of the dark frontier of rural Georgia. "I think," O'Connor wrote, "[the Catholic writer] will feel a good deal more kinship with backwoods prophets and shouting fundamentalists than he will with those politer elements for whom the supernatural is an embarrassment . . ." (*MM*, p. 207). That sense of supernatural force that the backwoods prophets feel in the world repeats itself in the uncanny force and presence O'Connor achieves within the cliché-ridden language of her fiction. Both acknowledge the supernatural and discover that it can be found on the edges of our culture, dark and empty as they may be, on the rural frontier.

Notes

1. James Joyce, *A Portrait of the Artist as a Young Man* (New York: Viking, 1969), p. 204.

2. Flannery O'Connor, *Mystery and Manners: Occasional Prose*, ed. Sally and Robert Fitzgerald (New York: Farrar, Straus, and Giroux, 1969), p. 103; further references, abbreviated *MM*, will be included parenthetically within the text.

3. William V. Spanos, "Hermeneutics and Memory: Destroying T. S. Eliot's *Four Quartets*," *Genre*, 11 (1978), 532.

4. Peter Brooks, "Virtue and Terror: *The Monk*," *ELH*, 40 (1973), 252. For a complementary treatment of the Gothic tradition, see my "The Trap of the Imagination: The Gothic Tradition, Fiction, and 'The Turn of the Screw,' " *Criticism*, 22 (1980), 297–319.

5. James Joyce, *Ulysses* (New York: Random House, 1961), p. 207.

6. Brooks, p. 249.

7. *The Complete Stories of Flannery O'Connor* (New York: Modern Library, 1974), p. 269. Further references to O'Connor's stories will be to this edition, abbreviated *CS* and included parenthetically in the text.

8. Roy Male, *Enter, Mysterious Stranger* (Norman: University of Oklahoma Press, 1979).

9. Tzvetan Todorov, *The Fantastic*, trans. Richard Howard (Ithaca, NY: Cornell University Press, 1975), p. 25.

10. *The Fantastic* treats this throughout; see also Leslie Fiedler, *Love and Death in the American Novel* (New York: Stein and Day, 1966).

11. Sigmund Freud, "The Uncanny," in *Studies in Parapsychology* (New York: Collier Books, 1963), p. 21.

12. John Hawkes, "Flannery O'Connor's Devil," *Sewanee Review*, 70 (1962), 399.

13. Herman Melville, *The Confidence-Man* (Indianapolis, IN: Bobbs-Merrill, 1967), p. 260.

14. For Blake's similar transformation of simile to metaphor, see my "Simile, Metaphor, and Vision: Blake's Narration of Prophecy in *America*," *Studies in English Literature*, 19 (1979), 569–88.

15. Male, p. 30.

O'Connor's Unfinished Novel

Marian Burns*

During the last few years of her life, Flannery O'Connor worked intermittently on a third novel, which she intended calling "Why Do the Heathen Rage?" This novel was never completed, but from the fragments available to us[1] it is possible to construct an idea of the novel, and to see in what ways it resembles the first two novels, in what ways it differs, and how it posed many technical problems for the author.

Wise Blood, Flannery O'Connor's first novel, was about "a Christian *malgré lui*," Hazel Motes, as O'Connor says in the preface to the second edition in 1962.[2] Her second novel, *The Violent Bear It Away*, can be seen in this light as the story of a prophet *malgré lui*, the young Tarwater who at first rejected his calling, but in the end submitted to it. O'Connor's unfinished third novel follows this pattern in its conception, I believe, and is again about a Christian "in spite of himself," a hero struggling against his vocation as much as Haze or Tarwater. The protagonist of "The Heathen," Walter Tilman, will find Christ just like the other two heroes, but in this case his belief is that of a distinctly pre-Reformation Christianity. That is to say that, whereas Hazel Motes and Francis Marion Tarwater were contemporary Southern Protestants, this time O'Connor's hero — while superficially a disaffected Southerner and an atheist — is in essence a European medieval Catholic. Haze turned out to be a Christian martyr. Tarwater turned out to be a Christian prophet. Walter, it is implied, will turn out to be a Christian monk. This essay will give the reasons for such an interpretation and go on to examine the nature of the novel and the problems that impeded its progress.

Despite Walter's professed agnosticism, the image of him as a monk recurs throughout the manuscripts. In one early piece, in which he is called Julian, the hero appears to have the equivalent of the Roman or St. Peter's tonsure: his father, who is seventy-five, has a full head of hair, while Julian, who is not yet thirty, has "a bald spot the size of a half-dollar" on the crown of his head. In another manuscript Walter's mother reads with irritation her son's copy of the letters of St. Jerome: "My fellow monk Chrysogonous. Her mouth pursed. This was an example of the sort of junk he read—something to do with when there were monks." She is unaware that her son is a living example of the old monastic life: even when he is on duty in the liquor store in which he works at night (much to his mother's social disgrace), Walter can be seen "reading with all the concentration of a monk in his cell." He even tells his distraught mother that he is "a secular contemplative."

Just as the imagery of monasticism informs the manuscript of "The Heathen," so does the suggestion of medievalism, as in Walter's name. One thinks of Walter the Penniless in the eleventh century; Hubert Walter,

*Reprinted, by permission, from the *Flannery O'Connor Bulletin*, 11 (1982), 76–93.

Archbishop of Canterbury, and Walter of Coutances, both in the twelfth century; or Walter of Coventry in the thirteenth — all of them priests, the last a monk and friar. Readers may object that Walter is a popular name even now, but I think it was O'Connor's intention that the name should remind us for her purposes of the clergy of the Middle Ages. In the early drafts of O'Connor's third novel, those closely associated with the short story "The Enduring Chill," the hero was called Asbury. This name brings to mind Francis Asbury, Wesley's assistant, and is consequently suggestive of American Methodist and Episcopal belief. The change to the name Walter emerged, I believe, with O'Connor's image of the hero as a medieval monastic, and the need for a consonant name.

Walter's reading matter is exclusively and orthodoxly pre-Reformation, as if, like St. Jerome, he had made a vow never to read or possess "pagan" literature. The letters of St. Jerome in fact become a sort of ironic framework for the projected novel: Walter owns a cheap paperback copy of the Letters, which features often in "The Heathen," and O'Connor thereby sustains a tacit parallel between the epistles of the early Christian saint writing in the fourth and fifth centuries, and the humorously perverse correspondence which Walter engages in with total strangers in the twentieth century. It is partly through this whimsical correspondence that Walter is to be converted, as I shall explain later. But from the beginning Walter at least intellectually assents to a pre-Reformation Christianity congenial to his sensibility. He is familiar with patristics and constantly reads the works of medieval saints and philosophers: "Walter knew the Fathers of the Church, he had assisted at Nicaea and at Chalcedon. He had explored the intricasies [sic] of Light with Bonaventure; he knew where Aquinas and Duns Scotus would part company. He had seen the path turn downward with Abelard and illogic enter, grotesquely eloquent, with Luther. He had been active at Trent. He had always adhered to the most orthodox line but never once, never for the slightest moment, had it occurred to him, even remotely, to believe any of it." Walter is intellectually fascinated by the political intrigue and dogmatic controversy of the Catholic Church from its beginnings to its most turbulent period in history, the Reformation. His minute knowledge of the politics and philosophy of the Church from the first to the nineteenth ecumenical councils demonstrates that Walter is not only a monk but a scholar.

So, in the nineteen-sixties, in the American South, among Baptists and Methodists, Presbyterians and Episcopalians, among Fundamentalists, atheists and Laodiceans, the reader comes upon Walter Tilman, a closet medieval Catholic monk. He is not so eccentric or unique in O'Connor's work, however, if one recalls that Hazel Motes, toward the end of his life, assumed an ascetic and penitent existence, not unlike severe monasticism: "He might as well be one of them monks [Mrs. Flood the landlady] thought, he might as well be in a monkery" (p. 218). One also remembers how Rayber in the second novel led a quasi-monastic life after his wife's desertion, and was likened to "some desert prophet or pole-sitter"[3] — a reference to the early Fathers and medieval stylites. And one thinks of Thomas in "The Comforts of Home" who studied early Christian history and (in a manuscript version) wrote a thesis on Anthony of Egypt, the founder of Christian monasticism. Sheppard too in "The Lame Shall Enter First" lived ascetically, at home and in his priest-like office.

These points illustrate O'Connor's abiding interest in the figure of the monk, but Walter of "The Heathen" is distinguished broadly from these incidentally monkish characters in that his Catholicism and medievalism are what determine him in the novel, and what ultimately determine the shape of the novel, its structure and theme. Walter is a late full-length exploration in O'Connor's work of a particular type of sensibility, and of the theme of conversion to a now specifically Catholic religion. And while the other characters mentioned above assimilate their culture, Walter's sensibility is alien to the social and cultural milieu in which he finds himself. His response is to ridicule his society and its predominant religion: "For anything he could be a minister, but he acted as if the Methodist Church were a joke; [Mrs. Tilman, his mother] could not even get him to picnic suppers." There are many other such small jokes about Protestant religions in "The Heathen," as if O'Connor at last felt free to treat Southern Methodism and the Baptist Church in a primarily comic mode. For it is certainly as much O'Connor as Walter who is laughing here. The story and theme of "Why Do the Heathen Rage?" (the title of which was taken from the name of a Fundamentalist column in the Atlanta *Journal* which particularly amused O'Connor's sophisticated Catholic sensibilities) was to have been that of Walter's recognition that his ironic aversion to modern, post-Reformation Christianity and his intellectual interest in Catholic doctrine are founded on real spiritual belief in Roman Catholicism. How this revelation was to be effected in fictional terms seemed to prove a problem, or at least an opportunity to experiment, for O'Connor and was one of the factors which combined to slow down the progress of the work — factors I would now like to discuss.

First of all was this problem created by Walter's nature, the fact that he is a Catholic contemplative? This central dilemma can be explained by O'Connor's own words on the subject elsewhere:

> About the fanatics. People make a judgment of fanaticism by what they are themselves. To a lot of Protestants I know, monks and nuns are fanatics, none greater. And to a lot of the monks and nuns I know, my Protestant prophets are fanatics. For my part, I think the only difference between them is that if you are a Catholic and have this intensity of belief you join the convent and are heard from no more; whereas if you are a Protestant and have it, there is no convent for you to join and you go about in the world getting into all sorts of trouble and drawing the

wrath of people who don't believe anything much at all down on your head.

This is one reason why I can write about Protestant believers better than Catholic believers—because they express their belief in diverse kinds of dramatic action which is obvious enough for me to catch. I can't write about anything subtle.[4]

In "The Heathen" O'Connor was inverting her usual formula of the dramatic Protestant fanatic, but this brought its own problems. Her two earlier novels were about freebooting Fundamentalists: Haze, an itinerant Protestant preacher of sorts, who retired to a private religious life only at the end; Tarwater, a roving prophet. Both characters encountered different towns and people, and experienced singular events in the course of what were essentially active and public lives.

Walter, on the other hand, is restricted like the monk or nun O'Connor describes within the confines of his very private life on the dairy farm and in his study. Only once before had O'Connor written a story with a Catholic protagonist, in "A Temple of the Holy Ghost," which was not so much a drama as a meditation on the mystery of human suffering. The convent in this story, a central image, tends to reduce it to stasis, as O'Connor herself might have predicted. Although "A Temple" is one of O'Connor's most beautifully written stories, it contains little action, and the main character actually does nothing other than observe, dream and contemplate. Similarly with Walter, in his role as a monk, there is little that he can *do*. He is not a modern Catholic priest like those in the fiction of J.F. Powers, who are mobile and powerful, public figures. Walter is a *rara avis* in modern fiction—a medieval contemplative and scholar. O'Connor had of course created non-Catholic characters similar to Walter—Hulga Hopewell and Thomas for example—who remained at home and lived an intellectual life. But she had dealt with them only in short stories, all of which ended in the violent disruption of their quiet way of life. To sustain interest in such an undramatic, immobile character for the length of a novel would doubtless cause problems for O'Connor—"I can't write about anything subtle," as she put it.

After the problem of Walter's Catholicism was that of how best to describe the revelation of his Christianity, which, as we shall see, was in effect both a structural problem and a question of mode. Looking back to *Wise Blood*, one can see that its structure was climactic. Though the crucial conversion scene was not exactly at the end of the book, it was followed only by Haze's expiation and death, a culmination. Similarly in *The Violent Bear It Away* O'Connor worked toward a climax, the final scene in which Tarwater was compelled to accept his prophetic mission, as Haze had been forced to accept his Christianity and martyrdom. The fact is that O'Connor's imagination was apocalyptic and that her fictional expression was consonantly catastrophic; thus her novels as well as her short stories end abruptly and violently. The epiphanies (which are always religious conversions) experienced by her characters are always climactic and irreversible, both in the novels and the stories. And once this crucial transfiguration occurs, there is no longer any story for O'Connor. There can be no coda to the stories of Hazel Motes or Francis Marion Tarwater. Haze's story must end with his death; Tarwater must disappear into the night; many characters in the stories must die on receiving grace; and all the stories must end on a conclusive and dramatic note.

One is surprised, therefore, on examining the manuscripts for "The Heathen," to discover that the intended third novel started out as a sequel to the story "The Enduring Chill," and was to feature Asbury, whose conversion—so climactic in the tale—was originally to have been the premise of the third novel. This was indeed an unusual structural strategy for O'Connor, to have the spiritual revelation at the start. Predictably, she dropped the idea soon after. For, once having converted the main character to Christianity, what could O'Connor, within the limits of her sensibility and fictional imagination, do with him? For her the conversion had to be the crux and end of the narrative; hers was the fiction of crisis, not of quotidian experience. So, more characteristically, for the rest of the manuscripts of "The Heathen," Walter is only a susceptible personality, already intellectually converted to an early form of Christianity, but yet to undergo spiritual conversion.

But the moment of revelation may not have been at the end either, as one would expect. In a departure from her normal structural habits, "The Heathen" shows O'Connor experimenting with several different instances of revelation—and simultaneously trying various narrative modes. One moment of grace occurs as Walter is sitting on a rock reading a letter from his cousin whom he had never met, Sarah (or Oona, as she is sometimes called). He had written to her as a stranger under an assumed name, intrigued by her Northern, radical view of life. But now the fashionable and vague philosophizing in her letter no longer amuses him. He sees that "The woman had abrogated the place of God and set herself up where it had been. Her error was theological." In another draft of this scene where Walter reads the significant letter, he looks up at the sky which is dappled with small clouds: "he had not up until that moment been a believer. He realized now, with a shudder, that he was. He was a Christian, bound for hell." This is evidently an early draft of the crucial "scene," not yet dramatized. It is a letter, the written work, an argument, which has wrought this change in Walter, and his conversion is explained in terms of logic. One does not expect O'Connor characters to experience conversion in such a muted and cerebral fashion. The only signature of God's grace and of O'Connor's habitual dramatic and symbolic mode is the presence of the clouds, which in Christian symbolism suggests the unseen God, and the hint that Walter is sitting on a *rock*. One does not expect to be told, in so many words, that Walter has been converted to Christianity, which is what O'Connor repeatedly does: "He felt the thorn in his side that was discovered belief"; "The corollary came with a deadly blow: he believed in God." This is very far from O'Connor's mode in the two novels and in stories like, for instance, "Parker's Back." O'Connor must be consciously trying another approach here, one feels. In one piece the narrator actually comments that Walter's conversion has not been dramatic: "Unlike Paul he had not been thrown to the ground and blinded." His conversion is not then like Haze's violent apocalypse, or Tarwater's trial by murder, rape, and fire. In fact it has not been at all in the common run of O'Connor revelations, which is to say gratuitous, violent, and biblical in style.

In another fragment, the same scene is rendered more dramatically: Walter "looked as if the country-side had dropped away from the rock he sat on and he and the rock were suspended over nothing." Added by hand to the typescript is this: "while a bolt of lightning flashed from the cloud and turned everything around him to glaring white." Considering the frequency of lightning storms in Georgia, this detail is quite naturalistic, but with the sense of the sudden disappearance of the countryside, there is a strong supernatural, quasi-biblical effect here that is more in keeping with O'Connor's usual mode. Walter has effectively been struck by lightning, the external supernatural agent of God's grace, rather than, as in the first piece, by a logical thought process.

Another version of Walter's revelation will be familiar to readers of "Parker's Back." In one manuscript Mr. Gunnels, the farm help, who is tattooed all over his body, reveals to Walter the face of Christ on his back. Walter experiences "a kind of smarting repulsion and attraction" for this face, but when he tries to take a picture of it, his hand trembles, and this photograph is the only one to come out blurred: "The face was visible but as through a veil." Walter is so disturbed by the face of Christ at the time that he runs the car into a ditch on the way home, and is badly shaken up. Like Parker, who is a composite of Walter and Gunnels, Walter encounters the face of God. It is not clear whether this scene was to have been an alternative version of Walter's revelation or whether in fact both scenes, the rock scene and the tattoo scene, were to have been retained together. It is possible that O'Connor intended to portray Walter undergoing a sequence of such violent visions, and struggling between grace and the devil. It is probable that the structure of "The Heathen" was to have been more complex than that of the first two novels, since Walter's conversion was not to have been instant or unalterable.

Here then O'Connor was trying a new approach, the effect of incremental spiritual growth, and is offering both scenes dramatized by violence, and the reasons for these illuminations, by retaining some of the explicatory asides (like "What appealed to his intellect in theory did not appeal to his taste in fact" or "his vision was as clear as Satans [sic]. It was his will that was out of kilter"), and by the device of the correspondence. In both *Wise Blood* and *The Violent Bear It Away* O'Connor had avoided any internalization of the spiritual conflicts involved. In the first novel

Haze's conversion happened suddenly — and for some readers, obscurely — when the cop pushed Haze's car over the edge of the embankment. In purely symbolic terms, this made sense, but the change in the protagonist was never explained in moral or psychological terms. Haze's subsequent decision to martyr himself was also seen at a distance and mysteriously. In the second novel, although the reader was permitted some insight into the emotional and spiritual state of Tarwater, in the end the author offered no more moral rationale for the hero's actions than she did in the first. It was not the logic of Christianity or ethical compunction which seemed to drive Tarwater forth as a prophet, but his rape by a passing homosexual (the devil, that is) and his burning of the woods at Powderhead. Again this was potent on the symbolic level and in dramatic effect, but still O'Connor allowed no explication, and no corollary to Tarwater's conversion was glimpsed. This is not a criticism; it is merely a statement of O'Connor's habitual narrative mode. It points up the similarity between O'Connor's method and that of the ancients who composed the stories of the Bible. There is no psychological or moral reason given for St. Paul's conversion, for instance, only the narrative of a violent manifestation. O'Connor's heroes experience their epiphanies in the old biblical sense, and virtually in the old biblical style. It is probably also due to O'Connor's orthodox belief in a divine grace which acts unwarrantedly and mysteriously that her fiction (always about grace) is always rendered by an objective and implicit technique: by an unusual or magical event; by a gesture; by another person, a stranger or freak; by physical violence; or solely by the violence of grace. Explanation is out of the question in what O'Connor sees as a mysterious occurrence; and to extend a story beyond this would be to lessen its power.

Walter in "Why Do the Heathen Rage?" is in this way a development. O'Connor intended to balance her habitual violent, external accesses of grace with occasional philosophical argument at least, if not moral or psychological explanation. O'Connor had experimented with two forms of violent epiphany: being struck by lightning, and running a car into a ditch. Neither of these events matches the violence of her other two novels, but then Walter is not one to mow someone down with a car or put his own eyes out with lime, or to drown an idiot child or get raped by a strange homosexual or set fire to a wood. These things are beyond his characterization and his role as a monk. His experiences are less violent and always tempered by his reflective personality. In the discursive mode, O'Connor employs the motif of the letters as a convenient vehicle to indulge Walter's theological arguments, and in this way she certainly approximates a more traditional novelistic form than the form of *Wise Blood* or *The Violent*. "Why Do the Heathen Rage?" does not become exactly an epistolary novel, but a large part of the manuscript consists of monologues written by Walter and Sarah proposing diametrical theological points of view — a contrivance unthinkable in the first two novels.

O'Connor wanted to try this—for her—unusual tactic, but she also realized the possible danger of such a lengthy expository device overwhelming the dramatic and symbolic component of the novel. One can see her correcting excesses in the manuscripts, excising expatiatory passages, and over-philosophical language.

This problem can be seen to rise again in the matter of the framework of symbolism for the third novel. In *Wise Blood*, Haze's spiritual struggle was portrayed variously through the symbolism of the New Testament and Greek myth, amid surrealistic imagery and allusions to contemporary existentialist philosophy. In *The Violent Bear It Away*, Tarwater's submission to his vocation was rendered through his own and his great-uncle's Hebraic sensibilities, with a heavy reliance on both Old and New Testament symbolism. In "The Heathen" O'Connor portrays a sensibility that is neither classical-cum-modern like Haze's nor biblical like Tarwater's, but pre-Reformation, and she therefore employs a frame of reference taken from the patristic period and medieval doctrine. In the first two novels, the symbolism was familiar to most: the Gospels, Revelation, and Greek drama in *Wise Blood*; the traditional paradigms and rhetoric of the Bible in *The Violent*. By comparison, O'Connor's use of the writings of early Christians and medieval saints and philosophers, and images taken from specifically Catholic sources, in "The Heathen," would prove less accessible and potent for the average reader. For example, the published excerpt from the third novel contains a lengthy allusion to the writings of St. Jerome. It quotes some seven sentences of a letter from Jerome to Heliodorus, and goes on to explain the historical background to this correspondence. Furthermore, the narrator eventually has to resort to a full explication of the central image: "Then it came to her, with an unpleasant little jolt, that the General with the sword in his mouth, marching to do violence, was Jesus."[5] The entire published piece is only four pages long, of which almost one page is taken up by this exegesis. O'Connor must have realized that such unfamiliar references might have to be explained, in a way that Greek myth or biblical analogy might not, for the full impact of the image to be felt. Or simply she decided that she would employ a discursive mode on occasion. But if the entire novel were to be written in such a manner, it would probably grow tedious to those readers who expect a more dramatic and implicit style from O'Connor.

Apart from the questions of characterization and theme, structure, mode and symbolism, another predicament for the author was that of plot. In "The Heathen" Walter writes letters to strangers, in each correspondence assuming a different, imaginary personality and name. When he tires of a particular correspondence, he simply writes "Deceased" across any replies, and returns them. It is a brilliant and appealing comic idea. The central correspondence of the novel is between Walter in the invented persona of June William, a black manservant on the farm, and Sarah. This correspondence is important in the major theme, that of

Walter's conversion, since it is the surprisingly erudite "June William" who argues over theological points with Sarah. It also allows scope for the minor themes of the novel: that of Walter as a failed writer, who sees his letters as "prolegomena to the writing of a novel," with June William and the rest as fictional characters he has created; and that of racial inequality and unrest in the South.

The dramatic irony involved in this correspondence, that Sarah thinks Walter to be someone he is not, was to have been the central plot of the novel, the device which initiated action on all levels. But the development of this plot seems to elude O'Connor's fictional imagination. The girl, having read the letters of "June William" indicting the social system of the South (and incidentally demolishing the argument of Calvin), is angered by injustice and sexually intrigued by her correspondent, and decides to come down from New York to visit him on the farm. Walter vacillates between dreading the crisis and trying to avert it, and looking forward eagerly to the catastrophic encounter to enliven his dull days. This complication has many comic possibilities. But O'Connor never seems to come to any decision about what should happen at the dénouement. She seems to avoid the issue, instead repeatedly revising and expanding the details of the situation, the letters, and the characters. Sarah appears in many manuscripts, suspended forever on the highway in her little red car speeding toward the South. O'Connor lavishes so much comic attention on Walter's letters that she loses sight of the plot. It is unusual that with such a good comic idea the momentum was not sufficient to carry it to a conclusion.

I cannot explain why this should have happened to O'Connor at this stage in her life; this essay is not biographical or psychoanalytical. I am merely pointing out *how* O'Connor's novel seemed to be stalling. I could suggest, however, that in structural terms O'Connor was again reverting to a basically short-story concept. Once having composed the resolution of the plot and disclosed Walter's true identity to the girl, how would the story go on? This plot, which is essentially a joke-structure like so many of O'Connor's short stories, must end there. Any extension of the comic dénouement would be an anticlimax. Since this is the main action of the novel, which bears the weight of all the themes and sub-themes, the question was crucial, and its irresolution impeded the progress of the novel.

To recapitulate: the characterization of Walter, the main theme and its attendant symbolism, O'Connor's habitual structural and narrative techniques and limitations of sensibility, and an uncongenial story-line all conspired against the completion of the third novel. There are reasons enough to suppose that, even had O'Connor lived much longer, "Why Do the Heathen Rage?" would never have been published as a novel.

It is a loss to the reading public that the brilliant comedy of "The Heathen" was never finished, and that the gentle, monkish Walter Tilman never achieved consummation in novel form. But by way of a postscript it is interesting to observe the appearance in print of another fictional figure who was almost lost to the public, that of Ignatius J. Reilly in John Kennedy Toole's posthumously published novel *A Confederacy of Dunces*. There are many similarities of characterization between Toole's mother and son and O'Connor's families, such as those in "Everything That Rises Must Converge," "Greenleaf" or "The Comforts of Home," all of whom could be the direct ancestors of Mrs. Reilly and Ignatius in Toole's book. There are further incidental similarities between *A Confederacy of Dunces* and "Why Do the Heathen Rage?" For instance, Ignatius' correspondence with Myrna Minkoff in New York is a device remarkably like Walter's correspondence with his female cousin Sarah. In its theme too, this correspondence is strikingly like that in "The Heathen." Both women, Myrna and Sarah, represent a *Weltanschauung* alien to the men: living among liberals in the North's most sophisticated city, they are saturated with modern ideology, while Ignatius and Walter cling to an orthodox medieval worldview.

The most arresting coincidence between the two works is this shared philosophy of the two main figures. Toole's Ignatius, like O'Connor's Walter, feels alienated from modern society, and takes refuge in medieval Christian writings. He considers himself a "medievalist,"[6] whose criteria are ever "theology and geometry" (p. 1). He is currently writing "an indictment against our century" (p. 6). Other people also see him as an anachronism: "This strange medieval mind in its cloister" (p. 334), as Myrna describes him. Ignatius, again like Walter, "cannot support the Church" (p. 53), but is intellectually drawn to the philosophy of pre-Reformation Christianity. He writes, for example, in his cheap notebooks: "With the breakdown of the Medieval system, the gods of Chaos, Lunacy, and Bad Taste gained ascendancy. . . . After a period in which the western world had enjoyed order, tranquility, unity, and oneness with its True God and Trinity, there appeared winds of change which spelled evil days ahead. An ill wind blows no one good. The luminous years of Abélard, Thomas à Becket, and Everyman dimmed into dross . . ." (p. 25).

Toole wrote his novel in the early sixties, when O'Connor was working on "The Heathen," but there can be no question of the two writers being aware of each other's work. O'Connor could not have known about Toole's book, which was not discovered by Walker Percy until 1976, and Toole could not have had access to anything other than the small extract of O'Connor's novel published in *Esquire* in 1963,[7] which does not suggest the hero's medieval role to any significant degree. It is even more remarkable then that two young Southern novelists in the early sixties should simultaneously decide to write about a faith and system of philosophy from such a distant age — for neither of them was writing about modern Catholicism in the South, as Percy was doing.

That both should write about pre-Reformation Christianity in a conspicuously comic mode is a further coincidence. The main comic difference between O'Connor's fictional characters and Toole's is one that points up the singularity of the third novel among O'Connor's opus: Walter is comic, certainly, but in a subtle way; he is not offensive or ridiculous like Toole's character. Whereas Ignatius J. Reilly is perverse and grotesque, at least physically, O'Connor's Walter Tilman is — a rarity among her heroes and villains — *not* grotesque, *not* perverse, and *not* violent. Unlike the heroes of her first two novels, who must be considered at all events socially grotesque in their background and behavior, Walter is superficially quite normal.

It is this that makes "The Heathen" such a leap of the imagination for O'Connor, in that she chooses as hero not the violent, primitive, evangelistic type of Haze and Tarwater, but a figure closer to the intellectual Raybers of the world, as she saw them. For the spiritual distance between Walter and his inventor is initially much greater than that between the author and Haze or Tarwater. *Their* fierceness in belief and disbelief, their strictly Christian education and idiom, is closer to O'Connor's. Walter's mother is a Laodicean, his upbringing religiously indifferent, his temperament mild and ironic. That O'Connor endowed such a character with an attractive, warm personality is a tribute to the increasing breadth of her imagination.

For Walter is not unpleasant or embittered like Asbury or Hulga or Julian. In the end it is his sense of humor that makes him the most "normal" of her heroes and the most likeable of her atheistic villains. His pervasive self-irony saves him from appearing ridiculous or mad, and makes a refreshing change from the hubris of Haze and Tarwater and the arrogance of Hulga and Julian. In Walter Tilman, O'Connor had at last found a protagonist who was both tragic and comic, and who could achieve heroism without violence or grotesquerie.

Notes

1. I have based my interpretation on the manuscripts of "Why Do the Heathen Rage?" in the Flannery O'Connor Collection in the Ina Dillard Russell Library of Georgia College, Milledgeville. Quotation from the manuscripts is permitted by the Estate of Flannery O'Connor. All quotations in the text are from these manuscripts unless otherwise indicated.

2. Flannery O'Connor, *Wise Blood* (New York: Farrar, Straus & Cudahy, 1962). Subsequent references to this edition will appear in the text.

3. Flannery O'Connor, *The Violent Bear It Away* (New York: Farrar, Straus & Cudahy, 1960), p. 114.

4. Letter to Sister Mariella Gable, 4 May 1963, *The Habit of Being: Letters of Flannery O'Connor*, ed. Sally Fitzgerald (New York: Farrar, Straus & Giroux, 1979), p. 517.

5. Flannery O'Connor, "Why Do the Heathen Rage?" *The Complete Stories* (New York: Farrar, Straus & Giroux, 1971), p. 487.

6. John Kennedy Toole, *A Confederacy of Dunces* (Baton Rouge and London:

Louisiana State University Press, 1980), p. 27. Subsequent references to this edition will appear in the text.

7. The excerpt now available in *The Complete Stories* was originally published as "Why Do the Heathens Rage?" in *Esquire*, 60 (July 1963), 60–61.

Singular Visions: "The Partridge Festival"
Irving Malin*

Calhoun, the hero of this relatively neglected story, parks his "small pod-shaped" car in the driveway of his great-aunts' house. The "pod-shaped" car, like Hazel Motes's "high rat-colored car" in *Wise Blood*, is somewhat alien, fantastic, unreal. Why *pod*? Perhaps O'Connor is trying to alert us to the seed-container, the beginning of things. Her story deals with origins, transformations, and deliveries — and the "pod-shape" immediately suggests these possibilities; the story is, indeed, about spiritual possibilities and mundane facts (and their marriage).

Calhoun acts oddly. (What would one expect from the driver of this car?) He gets out "cautiously"; he believes the azalea blossoms will have a "lethal effect" on him; he notes that the house is "imposing" and "unpainted." If we look closely at the various adjectives O'Connor uses, we see that Calhoun fears (and seeks?) death and suffocation and enclosure; his view of nature including, as we shall soon read, human nature, is obsessive, imaginative, and perverse.

Calhoun is partially right about his aunts. They are "good country people." They are a bit overbearing; they smother him with affection. Their kisses and rambling words cannot completely disguise — the story deals with various deceptions — their "box-jaws," their rigidity, their black suits.

But Calhoun, disturbed as he may be by their "normality," looks past them. His visit to the "festival" of the town arises not out of love for his aunts, who believe that he is returning as an act of family affection, but out of an interest in the mass murder that has recently taken place. He really comes to see Singleton, the murderer, because he is his "brother" in spirit. Calhoun believes that the murderer is an interesting "character" for a novel. Thus the various turns of "love" are put on display in these few pages. Is he in love with his aunts (his family), Singleton, or himself? Does he remain loyal to everyday life or to bizarre fictions?

Calhoun is shown a "box" in which there is a "miniature of his great-grandfather."[1] The ancestor was a "master merchant"; he sold the idea of

*This essay was written specifically for this volume and is published here with the permission of the author.

the annual festival to the town. Calhoun flinches at the picture because he doesn't like the resemblance — one aunt says, "You look very like Father" (p. 422) — and the enclosure in family affairs. He again asserts, at least to himself, that he is special, artistic, "single" (to play with the murderer's name).

It is ironic, of course, that right after he looks at the "miniature" — is he, by the way, a "miniature" version of his ancestor or Singleton? — he remembers, even more vividly, another picture — of the murderer: "Singleton's was the only distinctive face in the lot. . . . A calculating contempt lurked in the regular eye but in the general expression there was the tortured look of the man who becomes maddened finally by the madness around him. The other six faces [of the victims] were of the same general stamp as his great-grandfather's" (p. 423). The symbolism is subtle: he must choose between the murderer and the victims. The victims, linked to his ancestor, are "too normal"; Singleton is too "crazy" — "peculiar" is the word spoken by his aunt — to inspire affection. He must make a decision — he is, we must remember, in a "pod-stage" — but he loses (or wins) if he moves in either direction.

Calhoun is not alone as observer. He is, surprisingly, being observed not only by his self-centered aunts but by a "spectacled" girl sitting next door. The effect is vertiginous; he is the seer seen — his awkward, poisonous comments are commented upon by the girl. She seems to know him (his situation). She smirks — as *he* does in displaying his secret wit for his aunts. O'Connor suggests here — and, of course, in the rest of the story — that there is always *an unseen presence* — a mysterious force looking through events, words, and objects. The story is "comic" because Calhoun, the aunts, the girl — even Singleton and the ancestor — are acting roles; they think that they have *created* these roles, but the Director hovers behind the stage. We may elaborate upon this metaphor. Although Calhoun, for example, will choose to look at reality from his warped, selfish perspective — "I am different" — he refuses to understand, except at the end (of his fictional life), that he cannot simply break through jails of self-conception, that he cannot triumph over natural creation. Art, psychology, plant growth — these worlds have *limits*; they cannot flourish without designed borders.

Calhoun escapes from his aunts and the girl, but he cannot — nor does he want to — escape from Singleton. He is under the madman's spell, the "shadow." And, this shadow is somehow enlightening — O'Connor uses light and dark; she intermingles them — because it is so "pure," uncontaminated by the crass commercialism of the aunts and town life. We are told at this point that Calhoun himself is a two-sided creature. For most of the year he sells boats and air conditioners (and lives with his parents), and for the rest of the year he creates fiction. He sees himself as "rebel-artist-mystic" and, we may add, creator, who uses routine life for his artistic ends. Although he does not acknowledge his own freakishness — he is, after all, a young man—he dimly recognizes that he is, to use another O'Connor title, a "displaced person."

Calhoun finds freaks everywhere—he thinks the girl next door is one. He even regards the popular azaleas as monstrous—they wash in "tides of color" across the lawns and his consciousness. They cannot be controlled; they drown him. They are fresh and fertile—so unlike his dead art.

Calhoun tries to avoid the flowers because their natural beauty forces him to see his own limited powers as writer, man, creator. He seeks another *sign*; he gravitates toward the demonic and the decadent. He celebrates festive darkness, not recognizing that light and dark are mixed. It is little wonder that he admires Singleton, his "brother," and condemns the Partridge normality.

Calhoun "worships" the jailhouse shrine. He stretches his imagination here. He feels that he, like Singleton, has been "padlocked" in the "privy." There is a barrier, of course, between the murderer and himself—which he refuses to acknowledge!—and this barrier creates unbearable tension. Calhoun does not comprehend the grim comedy of this situation. O'Connor does. There is a limit to self-expression—one does not kill six people to prove individualism; one does not celebrate murder. Calhoun's "indignation swathed his vision in a kind of haze" (p. 429). He cannot see clearly; he cannot thus create truly distinctive fictions. He is unbalanced, blurred, unformed (and uninformed).

There is a fascinating scene in the barber shop. Calhoun faces the mirror; he is confronted suddenly with an "image that was round-faced, unremarkable-looking and innocent" (p. 429). This unforeseen image angers him; he does not want to be *unremarkable*. Indeed, he wants, as I have suggested, to be a *marked* man, not another face in the crowd, not a miniature version (vision) of his ancestor.

But Calhoun, unlike the real killer, lacks the strength to destroy others—except through nasty language. The barber, however, is so folksy that he has few ideas about murder or art. The disturbing thing, of course, is that even *he* misjudges reality (or "fictionalizes" it). He calls Calhoun "reverend." Then he calls him "lawyer." Then he adds "writer"—after Calhoun's use of the word. The passage suggests that professions, roles, labels—language itself?—are distortions of inner being, of soul life. Calhoun is caught in the bib "as if it were a net" (p. 432). The enclosure image returns; here its meaning includes everyday, well-meaning discourse. When he escapes—like a prisoner?—he rushes back to the aunts' house. The escape is not particularly liberating. The aunts are still there; the azaleas are even more threatening—their colors have "deepened with the approach of sundown" (p. 432). And there is another, even more ominous "spirit."

Calhoun, who finally is pulled by his aunt, is introduced to a "rangy-looking" girl seated on the sofa. Mary Elizabeth, the smirking observer from next door, is now scowling. She is said to be a "real scholar." (Will she continue to study him?) She looks through him. It is typical of O'Connor to compound the ironies. Mary Elizabeth is so cool that she appears "retarded." The word — together with "childish" — applies in a sense to Calhoun himself, who, after all, has never completely left the nest (despite all his claims).

Mary Elizabeth is "several inches taller than he"; she walks "slightly in advance of him" to the festival beauty contest (p. 433). She proceeds to take out a note pad. Appearances prove deceptive once more: Mary Elizabeth is not "retarded" or "childish" — at least in the usual senses. The fact that she is a writer surprises Calhoun; perhaps even more astounding is the realization that they are secret doubles. She also hates the festival; she writes out of the need to attack the whole town, which she hastens to add is "false and rotten to the core" (p. 434).

Despite their resemblances, Calhoun and Mary Elizabeth are hostile again. She calls him "Baby Lamb," echoing the aunts' pet expression; she refuses to go to the contest — especially with him. O'Connor underlines the "Baby Lamb" expression. She intends to alert us not only to Calhoun's innocence — which is, as we have seen, "rotten" — but to the fact that he has sacrificed "normality" for the sake of self-deceptive art. There are, indeed, several "lambs" or "victims" in the story — Singleton, Mary Elizabeth, the aunts. But the question of real victim is clouded; often the *victims are victimizers* as well. It is difficult to know how the turnabout begins or ends. Even in this apparently hostile relationship of Mary Elizabeth and Calhoun, we are never completely certain who is victim or victimizer.

Calhoun follows Mary Elizabeth through the courthouse door (a "side" door). He passes the spot where Singleton "had stood to shoot" the citizens of Partridge. There is a sense of enclosure again because he and the murderer occupy the same position — at least geographically. But Calhoun is too much of an observer to act; he is somewhat passive — at the mercy of others or invisible (subconscious?) forces. Although he looks at Mary Elizabeth, who, in turn, looks at the scene below, he cannot find her. We are told that he "stared at her so long that he was afraid her image would be etched forever on his retina" (p. 435). The etched image recalls the photograph of Singleton and the ancestor. Calhoun is hemmed in by images; they are more powerful than he; they are, if you will, constantly stamping, destroying, photographing him. The usual distinctions between object and subject are suspended, creating comedy and terror.

Mary Elizabeth calls Singleton a "Christ-figure." She simplifies in a "literary" way his life; she uses him as a reflection of her academic, distorted views. She insists that Singleton is the object of her "non-fiction study," but in this story the line between fiction and non-fiction is quite thin and surprising. By calling Singleton a "scapegoat," she goes against her own belief in truth; she lies. Thus she is not the clear-sighted thinker she maintains that she is.

Calhoun partially sees through her grandiose objectivity. He under-stands the murderer is not a symbol—a mythic archetype. He informs Mary Elizabeth that she is "afraid" to "look at" Singleton, the "real object." But Calhoun, who rails against abstractions, is also an unreliable observer—his whole life has abided in abstractions. When he hears from Mary Elizabeth, who is more hostile than ever, that he (they) can interview Singleton, he is shaken. Her words fall "on his head like a sack of rocks" (p. 436).

Calhoun and Mary Elizabeth are "sunk" in "some mammoth private problem." (Another enclosure!) They part ways, for the time being, because although they share a vague, textual love for Singleton, they cannot cross over—they cannot be Singleton; they cannot give up singular views of the "other."

Calhoun is obviously reaching a turning point (as is the story itself). He seeks salvation for his misguided misery; he yearns for Singleton as a kind of "new Jesus." We are informed by O'Connor that "the sight of Singleton in his misery might cause him suffering sufficient to raise him once and for all from his commercial instincts. Selling was the only thing he had proved himself good at; yet it was impossible for him to believe that every man was not created equally an artist if he could but suffer and achieve it" (p. 437). Calhoun is more fanatical than ever; he dreams of the "low red buildings with rough heads sticking out of barred windows" (p. 437). Singleton is the demonic savior—a fear-inspiring figure in all the would-be writer's nightmares. Yet Calhoun is ambivalent; he longs for—and fears—the actual encounter with the murderer.

When the time approaches for the pilgrimage to Singleton—the final, hair-raising end—Calhoun loses whatever nerve (will) he has once had. The rainfall blurs his vision; the girl's return hampers self-assertion; the promised apocalypse "destroys" him. He cannot retain any useful, clear image of Singleton; instead, it seems to fall apart and it makes the writer a mere ghost. He is truly "left with nothing."

When they approach the tomb, as it were, of Singleton, we are reminded of Calhoun's first entry into Partridge. O'Connor implies that no "house" is ever safe, peaceful, unviolated. The dangers are compounded by Mary Elizabeth's statement: "Abandon hope all ye who enter here" (p. 439). The entrance to Singleton is full of hellish and crazy signs, warnings, portents.

Finally Calhoun gets a permission slip. So does Mary Elizabeth. Both slips indicate that the bearers are "relatives": "For a moment they stared at the slips, then at each other. Both appeared to recognize that in their common kinship with him, a kinship with each other was unavoidable" (pp. 440–41).

They enter the "big house." They are now trapped (or liberated?). They wait for the revelation, some "momentous event in their lives—a marriage or instantaneous deaths" (p. 442). They seem joined in a "predestined convergence." (The words suggest the governing pattern of events, that pattern Calhoun and Mary Elizabeth wanted to avoid or simplify or use for narcissistic, artistic ends.)

Singleton emerges. His eyes are "mismatched" (like his worshipers). His body is guarded by twin-like attendants who have "identical looks of good-natured stupidity" (p. 442). (Perhaps the twin quality refers us back to the various doublings we have already considered; reality is always obscure and duplicitous.) Singleton "seduces" Mary Elizabeth — and Calhoun; he takes off his "gown" and reveals his unmistakable evil spirit and body. His actions are so contrary to the (non) fictional portraits created by his worshipers that Mary Elizabeth and Calhoun run for their lives.

The couple scramble into the "pod-shaped" car. Calhoun looks at the highway; it is said to stretch "like a piece of the earth's exposed nerve" (p. 443). And this "exposed nerve" reminds us that a revelation has indeed occurred; something has been "exposed" and truly seen — perhaps for the first time in the story. But they cannot bear the exposure, the truth. They try in vain to find a "more tolerable image," a more relaxed one.

In the last few lines Calhoun sees himself as "round," "innocent," "undistinguished" — and he knows that he will never worship art again. He will, in fact, become a salesman all year round; and he knows furthermore that this role, which he has tried so hard to avoid, has "been waiting there from all time to claim him" (p. 444). He is now eternally enclosed.

"The Partridge Festival" is profoundly troubling. It suggests that art can never completely capture spiritual worlds. In the "conflict" between art and theology, theology always wins. Now we can understand why O'Connor has used an "innocent" Calhoun. He may be less of a writer than the girl or anyone else, but he suggestively stands for not only the mixed-up, false worshiper but any creative writer. I take it that O'Connor implies the ultimate limitations of art; it always tries to capture the invisible, underlying pattern of life, but it is doomed to failure. Yet, oddly enough, "The Partridge Festival" is also a celebration of this very failure. It is festive because it accepts limitations, enclosures, and delusions, and at the same time, it tells us to search elsewhere. It is, if you will, a celebration of earthly (artistic) defeat — and supernatural victory.

Note

1. *The Complete Stories* (New York: Farrar, Straus and Giroux, 1971), p. 422. All subsequent references, included parenthetically in the text, will be to this edition.

Previous critics have paid little attention to "The Partridge Festival." In " 'Parker's Back' vs. 'The Partridge Festival': Flannery O'Connor's Critical Choice," *Georgia Review*, 21 (1967), 476–90, Leon Driskell discusses why O'Connor omitted "The Partridge Festival" from *Everything That Rises Must Converge*, arguing that the pessimistic carnality in the story was thematically unsuitable for the collection. In "The Genesis of O'Connor's 'The Partridge

Festival,' " *Flannery O'Connor Bulletin*, 10 (1981), 46–53, Carter Martin examines early drafts to explore O'Connor's creative process. But the story has received very little detailed exegesis. [Ed.]

A Particular History: Black and White in Flannery O'Connor's Short Fiction

Janet Egleson Dunleavy*

Flannery O'Connor's South was a world on the edge of transition.[1] Born in 1925 in Savannah, Georgia, and moved, in her twelfth year, to Milledgeville, former capital of the state, she was brought up in the Old South — a land traditionally segregated in its institutions yet integrated in its daily life, except for pockets of white poverty where no black man or woman dared venture. The North was another country: to a Southerner, a land of hypocrisy that lured Southern blacks with promises of equality and rewarded them with menial, low-paying, industrial jobs to replace the menial, low-paying, agricultural work they had left — segregating them, moreover, by Northern restrictive codes more pernicious than Southern laws, in overcrowded, substandard housing. Europe was across an ocean, across an eternity; Africa was a dark continent; history was the stuff of parades, commencement addresses, political speeches, and courthouse square debates.

Not many blacks were lured from Southern farm employment during Flannery O'Connor's childhood: the Depression hit hardest among unskilled workers in industrial areas, and menial jobs were especially scarce in factories, North and South. Not many people she knew traveled to Europe, which, not yet a tourist playground, held attractions only for the most adventuresome or the very rich. Civil rights, racial equality, repeal of miscegenation laws and restrictive covenants — yes, there was talk of these, a distant rumble like summer thunder from beyond the horizon, the work of Communists and other strange people unknown to Milledgeville. Outsiders who came to Georgia stirring up trouble went, for the most part, to places like Atlanta; in any case, they were managed offstage, by organizations such as the Klan — they did not disturb the peace or disrupt the order of Milledgeville life. Within the confines of Flannery O'Connor's Milledgeville society — a comfortable Old South society that easily tolerated misfits, grotesques, and freaks, not just because they were all children of God with their place in the scheme of things, but also because such tolerance is easier in an agricultural community[2] — a code of manners governed relationships. Increasingly rendered obsolete by change during

*This essay was written specifically for this volume and is published here with the permission of the author.

the last years of her life, that code was based on mutual charity, according to Flannery O'Connor; it preserved, she believed, individual privacy and protected members of each race from small intrusions on each other.[3]

Change began almost imperceptibly in Flannery O'Connor's South when, with the end of the Depression and the beginning of World War II, a settled population began to move — toward the cities, where defense factories with insatiable appetites for a growing work force promised unheard-of wages; toward military camps, where local young men became soldiers who were shipped to unheard-of places. At first proportionately few Southern black agricultural workers were affected: few Southern black schools had prepared them to qualify for defense jobs or to pass the literacy test required of military inductees. But as the war continued and the need for factory workers and military manpower increased, more and more left the farms to return with smart Army uniforms, new attitudes, and more spending money than they ever had seen in their lives. Overseas, black soldiers discovered that the social mores of Paris, London, and other European cities were not what they had learned at home, South or North; in Europe a different and less prejudicial code of manners prevailed. Rumors of marriage between black American soldiers and white Europeans, of conflict between black and white American soldiers, reached the communities from which they had come, raising questions that never before had been asked, requiring answers that never before had been considered.

By the time the war ended in 1945 (the year Flannery O'Connor was graduated from Georgia State College for Women, now Georgia College, in Milledgeville), the scene had been set for the demonstrations and legal challenges that were to rock Southern society in the last decade of her life. In 1946 she published her first short story, "The Geranium." By the time a fledgling New South had been recognized formally by the Federal government, through the Civil Rights Act of 1964, Flannery O'Connor was dead, and "Judgement Day," a radical revision of "The Geranium," was awaiting publication. The period in between is reflected not only in differences between these two stories but in other examples of her short fiction.

As many critics have noted, similarities between "The Geranium" and "Judgement Day" survived the long process of revision and the years that separate their dates of composition. Both stories focus on the plight of an old man who has been taken by his daughter from his native South to live with her in New York City. The situation they explore remains the same: unhappy in this strange, new environment, the old man not only yearns to return home but often *is* there, it seems, in memories so vivid that he actually talks out loud to an old black companion of many years, left behind in Georgia. Jarred from these reveries by his daughter's voice, he tries to adapt by recreating, as much as possible, the world he had relinquished so lightly (in retrospect, so mistakenly). His spirits soar, therefore, when a black man appears in the apartment building (a rabbit hutch it seems to him) in which he, his daughter, and her family share a few crowded rooms. Employing the code of manners that has been second nature to him throughout his long life, he will approach the black man, he thinks — perhaps with a little flattery and some loose change he can persuade him that they might fish or hunt together. In each story the Northern Negro's reaction to the old white Southerner is, although different, both predictable and unhappy.

Within this broad outline, marked differences of character and situation establish each story's tragic inevitability. Old Dudley of "The Geranium" has not been forced to move North to live with his daughter: whimsy, a sense of adventure (he had once seen New York in a movie) — perhaps some unacknowledged response to his daughter's warnings that he might sicken and die without his children near, with no one to care for him — had persuaded him to accept her invitation. In the boardinghouse where he had lived since the death of his wife (doing odd jobs not only to help pay for his room but also to strengthen his feeling of belonging, of being needed) an established hierarchy had prevailed: the old ladies who crocheted in the parlor each evening had regarded him, the only white male, as head of the household and therefore their protector; Rabie, the black man who cleaned and tended the vegetable garden, and his wife, Lutish, the cook, lived in the basement. Outdoors was common ground where the two races observed the Southern code referred to by Flannery O'Connor: it allowed Rabie and Old Dudley to work together on Old Dudley's various painting and carpentry projects and to join in fishing, 'possum hunting, gun talk, and similar forms of male companionship; it permitted Lutish the luxury of her admirable flower garden enjoyed by all. Remembering Lutish's garden, Old Dudley recalls also that her flowers were always bright and healthy, not pale and sickly like the New York geranium put out on a window still across the alley each morning and taken in each night. Deeply, painfully homesick — confined to the small apartment he shares with his dutiful but uncompanionable daughter, her husband, and their uncommunicative sixteen-year-old son — afraid of getting lost in the halls beyond the apartment door, of being pushed and shoved in street or subway where "black and white and yellow [are] all mixed up like vegetables in soup"[4] — Old Dudley spends his waking hours staring mournfully at the sick geranium, a lump in his throat, daydreaming himself home.

Relief appears possible when a new neighbor moves in, down the hall — a neighbor with a black servant whom Old Dudley plans to approach (employing his best Southern manners appropriate to the situation) in hopes of finding another Rabie. Shocked by his daughter's assertion that the black man is not the neighbor's servant but the neighbor himself, that his daughter is living "tight with niggers that think they're just as good as you" (p. 9), he retreats to his room and once again takes refuge in his memories. These memories occupy his mind as, on an errand for his daughter, he goes to another apartment in the building, three floors down; they provide the courage he needs to encounter the cold-eyed residents who pass him in the halls without a single word of greeting. Returning to his daughter's apartment, his mission accomplished—his mind still far away, shooting pigeons with Rabie, his arms raised to reenact the familiar scene—he is startled by the sound of a voice: the new black neighbor asking, "What are you hunting, old-timer?" (p. 12). The patronizing tone and jocular manner, the condescension implied in the way he is addressed, and (worse to come) a pat on the back as a strong brown arm assists him to his daughter's door are too much for Old Dudley. In the relative privacy of his small room, unaware that he is being watched by the owner of the geranium across the alley, the old man throws back his head and cries silently and uncontrollably. Meanwhile, having fallen from the sill, the sick geranium lies, uprooted, far below, among the shards of its broken pot.

Tanner of "Judgement Day," a much tougher bird than Old Dudley in some respects, is much frailer in others. Certainly he is poorer and much less respectable. Moving North to live with his daughter had been, for him, a devil's choice: "Dr." Foley (Corinth, Georgia's black pharmacist, undertaker, general counsel, and realtor to the black community) had bought the land on which Tanner and his black companion, Coleman, had been living in a squatter's shack. Foley had given Tanner but two options—operate the still Foley knew Tanner had hidden on the property for Foley's profit (that is, become a "nigger's white nigger" [p. 540]) or clear out. That very morning Tanner's daughter, visiting from New York, had been appalled to find that her father not only had been reduced to becoming a squatter but was sheltering on equal and intimate terms with a Negro: "If you don't have any pride I have and I know my duty and I was raised to do it," she had told him, insisting that he accompany her to New York "to live like decent people" with herself and her family (p. 534). Her proposition had had its attractions: it had enabled Tanner to spurn Foley and thereby recover, under the old Southern code that he long since had abandoned, some small measure of the dignity due him. (He was, after all, an elderly white man who once had owned his own land, the kind of person whose status later concerned Mrs. Turpin of "Revelation.") At the very least, the move provided assurance that he would slide no further down the Southern hierarchical scale still fixed, despite her New York address, in his daughter's mind.

In New York, however, Tanner regrets the choice he has made. Down South, his shack at least had had air around it: in his daughter's "pigeon-hutch of a building," the halls are narrow and dark; the other apartments are occupied by "all stripes of foreigner"; and beyond the front door there are intimidating crowds, a frightening underground railway, stairs that move beneath your feet, and elevators that shoot you to the thirty-fourth floor (p. 541). Three weeks after his arrival, he observes that the next apartment has been rented by a black couple. (Unlike Old Dudley, Tanner sizes up the situation immediately.) At first, he is amused that his high-and-mighty daughter, who had shamed *him* for living with Coleman, now has to accept Negro neighbors herself. Priding himself on his lifelong ability to "handle niggers," however, he also sees opportunity in this new development: he will try to befriend the man, he decides, using the techniques that years ago had won over Coleman and earned the respect of the black laborers at the sawmill; he will get the upper hand over New York; he will find himself a new fishing companion. In a reversal of the situation in "The Geranium" the old white Southerner (cocky in his approach because, to date, Foley is the only black man he has been unable to manipulate) is both patronizing in manner and condescending in tone; it is the black neighbor, a Northerner and an actor, who tries to ignore the presumptuous old man until, exasperated by Tanner's persistence (both in regarding him as a Southern black and in calling him "Preacher"), he loses self-control. Meanwhile, oblivious to his black neighbor's reactions (over-confidence based on bias and limited experience has dulled his percep-tions), Tanner assures himself that such "flattery" is the way to "handle" Negroes. He is therefore astonished when the actor grabs him roughly and shoves him through the doorway into his daughter's apartment; he falls, injuring himself, and suffers a disabling but not fatal stroke.

From that moment on, all Tanner's thoughts and energies are directed toward one goal: to gather his strength and arrange that, dead or alive, he be returned to Corinth, Georgia. For weeks he dreams and plans, sometimes imagining Coleman's reception of his corpse in a coffin, sometimes thinking that, as a joke, he might send the coffin, with himself alive and well inside it, to Coleman. His greatest worry is that he might die and be buried in the Northern city he yearns to escape. His greatest fear is that, if he does not manage to get to Corinth in time to be buried there, he will find himself, as he is now, among strangers when the dead are called to rise again on Judgement Day. Through daily pestering he succeeds in extracting from his daughter a promise that she will bury him in Corinth should he die in New York City; overhearing a conversation between her and her husband, he learns that she has lied to him — she intends to bury him in the cemetery plot she owns in New York, to save the expense of shipping his body to Georgia. Although still weak and shaky from his stroke, Tanner avows that he will wait no longer but set out for Corinth that very day, as soon as his daughter goes shopping. A note pinned inside his pocket instructs the finder to send his body express collect to Coleman, should he die en route, but he gets no further than the stairs outside his daughter's apartment. There he falls and for a while lies partially conscious, ⁀ot sure where he is, until he sees a black face hovering over him. ⁀ıep me up, Preacher," he says jauntily, "I'm on my way home." By the time his daughter finds him, "dangled over the stairwell like . . . a man in the stocks," he has been dead for about an hour (p. 549).

As Old Dudley and Tanner are different from each other, so Rabie and Coleman are different, too. Old Dudley may be so poor that he has to do odd jobs in the boardinghouse in order to keep his room, but he is respectable, he is a resident; the other boarders, all white, elderly, and female, accord him the position they regard as proper for a Southern white male. Rabie, the Negro companion of Old Dudley's old age, is respectable, too. He is, however, a worker about the place, an employee from below stairs in the boardinghouse. Both maintain the hierarchical values of the Old South, meeting only on common ground: outside in the yard, where there is man's work to be done; on the river, fishing; in the woods, hunting. As they conduct it, their companionship not only is permitted but sanctioned by Southern tradition. The white man respects the black man's appropriate areas of expertise; they concern such matters as where the fish are biting, where the birds are roosting. In return, following the code of manners to which they both subscribe, the black man exhibits appropriate awe of the white man's knowledge of the inner workings of guns and the inner streets of Atlanta. Remembered incidents reveal the extent to which, through this code, Old Dudley has been able to count on Rabie to bolster his sense of himself. Wishing Rabie there with him now, in New York, Old Dudley thinks, "If he could have showed it to Rabie, it wouldn't have been so big—he wouldn't have felt pressed down every time he went out in it. 'It ain't so big,' he would have said. 'Don't let it get you down, Rabie. It's just like any other city and cities ain't all that complicated' " (p. 6). It does not even occur to him to wonder what Rabie might have replied. By contrast, although they maintain a pretense of conforming to the traditional Southern social order when it seems expedient to do so, both Tanner and Coleman have abandoned the code that governs Old Dudley and Rabie's relationship in favor of a different, Darwinian set of values: they have experienced the struggle for existence; they have joined forces to survive. Indeed, when their relationship was established long ago, it was not in accordance with Old South hierarchies but in a showdown between two aggressive, dangerous males—behavior usually associated with frontier rather than Southern life. Its ominous aspects provide the first suggestion of potential violence, of savagery just beneath a civilized veneer. Tanner may tell his daughter, who asserts that she still has her pride (meaning, she still observes the hierarchy), that Coleman is his personal servant, a man "paroled" (in the sense of 'promised') to him for whom he has accepted responsibility for the past thirty years, but it is clear that this is not true. Even in Tanner's daydreams, Coleman is assertive, equal, an alter ego: "What we doing here? Where you get this fool idea coming here?" Tanner imagines Coleman asking, if the black man were with him in New York. "I come to show you it was no kind of place. Now you know you were well off where you were," he hears himself replying. Coleman, however, would be too wise to accept such an explanation: "I knowed it before. . . . Was you didn't know it" (p. 541). Foley's introduction into the story is but further evidence that the old code has been destroyed. "The day coming . . . when the white folks IS going to be working for the colored and you mights well to git ahead of the crowd," he tells Tanner in "Judgement Day" (p. 540). Such a reversal of the hierarchy within which Old Dudley and Rabie had developed a harmonious relationship, comfortable for each of them, never would have been accepted by either.[5]

Like Old Dudley, Tanner, of course, has been schooled in the code of manners of the Old South, the code that still dictates right and wrong to Tanner's daughter; he does not respect it, but when it serves his purpose, he exploits it — to account to his daughter for Coleman's presence, asleep on the floor of the shack that he and Coleman share; to approach the new black neighbor in New York, whom he mistakenly identifies as also a Southerner. The black neighbor's negative response distresses Tanner, in fact, not because the code has failed but because *he* has failed: for the first time in his life his ability to "handle niggers" is in question. It is this evidence that he no longer is in control, that he has lost his ability to live by bluff and by wit, that he no longer can manipulate others, that leaves him feeling lost and confused. The problem, he believes, is New York. If he can but return to Corinth — to Coleman, who will turn his world right-side-up again, who will affirm his identity — all will be well. Within the illusion, however, there is a persistent reality that even Tanner cannot ignore: greatly weakened by his stroke, he has little hope of reaching the South alive or, if he does, of living very long after he gets there. With death clearly not far off, he focuses on Judgement Day. Corinth, the Corinth he knows, is where he wants to be buried so that he will be there, himself once more, with Coleman beside him, when he wakes again to eternal life.

Among the O'Connor stories that belong to the same period as "The Geranium," "The Train" also depicts a Southern white male under stress and unable to conceal his emotional dependency on a former black companion.[6] In this story, however, the principal character is not elderly; indeed, Hazel Wickers' insecurities stem from an opposite condition — he is very young, barely more than a boy, and a very inexperienced traveler. A soldier on furlough, he is on the train because he is going to his sister's home (now, perforce, his own home) in Taulkinham. For him, however, home never really will be Taulkinham; it always will remain Eastrod, Tennessee, his birthplace and the village in which he had lived all his life before joining the Army. But the Eastrod he knew no longer exists: his mother is dead, Cash Simmons is dead, his own home has been abandoned, and the village — two houses, a barn, a store, and a cluster of shacks — is derelict. Members of the two white Eastrod families — his own and one other — have scattered both locally and afar; members of the more numerous black families — the "gulch niggers," as Haze defines and describes them — have moved to Memphis or Murfreesboro. Although Haze had been told that everything had been abandoned, that everyone had gone, he had insisted on spending his last leave in Eastrod, sleeping on the kitchen floor of the deserted house, in preference to going to his sister's. Now, even as the train races toward Taulkinham, memories of Eastrod fill his senses, superimposing remembered perceptions on present reality. This is his state of mind when he first sees the railroad porter, a black man he identifies immediately as a son of Cash Simmons, the "gulch nigger" from Eastrod whose image comes before him, in his attempt to hold on to the past, as often as that of his mother.

Rebuffing the strange young man's attempts to establish a communality of personal experience for which he recognizes no basis, the porter tells Haze that he knows nothing of Eastrod, that he himself is from Chicago, and that his father before him was not someone called "Cash" from Haze's native village but a "railroad man" like himself. Haze snickers at this phrase (he is not used to a Negro being referred to as a man) and assures himself that the porter is lying: the resemblance, he believes, is too strong to be mistaken. (Like Tanner of "Judgement Day," Haze has absolute confidence in the validity of the stereotypes that pass in his mind for observation and opinion.) Remembering a rumor heard in childhood, that Cash had had a son who had run away long before Haze was born, he convinces himself that the porter is the runaway son. Continuing to find excuses to talk with him, Haze tries to trap him into acknowledging their mutual origins. The porter's brusque denials simply strengthen Haze's convictions and magnify the dependencies that leave him sick and exhausted in his coffinlike upper berth. As the train continues toward Taulkinham, the dead of Eastrod on Haze's mind, this simile becomes less a mere figure of speech, more a nightmarish transformation. Pale and trembling, Haze finds the opening in the heavy curtains and leans out, seeking help. Unmoved and unmoving, the porter is transformed, too: "a white shape in the darkness" (p. 62), he stands guard at the end of the car.[7]

Although, in an interview conducted toward the end of her life, Flannery O'Connor declared that she did not feel competent to create the subjective reality of black characters or to use their dialogue as a chief means of forwarding plot ("In my stories they're seen from the outside," she explained),[8] another story from the same early period of her work as "The Geranium" and "The Train" is told through the indirect internal monologue of an elderly, blind, black man and the dialogue exchanged between himself and other black characters. Called "Wildcat," it is an account of old Gabriel's terror when he is left alone in his cabin a short distance from the other cabins of his small black community; meanwhile, the young men of the house go out to hunt the predator that has been killing their cows. Certain that the wildcat is after human blood, that it is coming for *him*, at first old Gabriel tries unsuccessfully to persuade the young men either to stay nearby or to take him with them into the woods. In their absence he recalls the last time their small community was harassed by a wildcat: he was only a boy then, kept home with the women because he was blind, while the others went out, just as now, to set a trap for the cat. In that incident the wildcat found its way into the cabin of old Hezuh, just a few yards down the road, and killed him; he fears that now he is the old man for whom the wildcat will come. Trying to keep his terror under control, to stay alert and thus avoid old Hezuh's fate, old Gabriel exercises all his talents: for hours he sits, turning this way and that, using his blind man's sense of smell to try to ascertain the direction from which the wildcat will come; he counts (he is the only Negro for miles around, he assures himself, who can count as well or as high as he can) to keep his mind calm and clear. Noise of an animal attacked, an animal attacking, temporarily relieves his terror; the wildcat has killed a cow (he has both heard and smelled the incident) in a field scarcely half a mile away: he is safe. For perhaps twenty-four hours or more the animal will be satisfied. Exhausted, old Gabriel falls into bed and sleeps soundly—through the rest of the evening, through the noisy return of the young men, through the whole night. Next morning once again he tries to convince the hunters to stay close, not to go to the woods, to guard the cabin against the wildcat's certain return. Once again he is unsuccessful; the young men go off, and he is left to face another night of terror, perhaps death.

Unpublished until six years after the author's death, neglected by some critics and unfairly criticized by others,[9] "Wildcat" has received little attention. Yet it is unique in Flannery O'Connor's canon, her only story to employ a black protagonist. Critical neglect may be explained as a response to the author's own implied rejection of this work, in the interview referred to above. But the question of why she doubted her own ability to create a black protagonist after having written "Wildcat" (a better story than the few commentators who have expressed their opinion of it would have readers believe) invites reconsideration. Was it because, given the changes that were affecting black/white relations in the 1950s and 1960s, she felt less sure in those years of what Southern blacks were thinking and feeling than in the 1940s, when she wrote "The Geranium," "The Train," and "Wildcat"? Was it because increasingly during the 1950s and 1960s the credibility of white writers who portrayed blacks in their fiction was being challenged? Or was it because she declined to present as an evocation of the inner consciousness of blacks images she regarded as protective masks?

Whatever the answers to these questions (deserving of a separate essay, but significant at least to raise here), Flannery O'Connor had no scruples about her ability to enter the minds of another set of characters in the changing Georgia landscape whose inner consciousness apparently was truly alien to her: Southern white advocates of civil rights for blacks. For the most part the entire civil-rights movement was, in Flannery O'Connor's opinion, wrongheaded. She did not question the need to improve the social, political, and economic status of Negroes; she did object to the way improvement was sought — mostly, in her opinion, by Northerners who did not understand what she regarded as the "particular history" of both races in the American South.[10] It was a subject on which obviously she felt strongly, for it comes up not only in her letters but in an interview published the year before she died:

> For the rest of the country, the race problem is settled when the Negro has his rights, but for the Southerner, whether he's white or colored, that's only the beginning. The South has to evolve a way of life in which the two races can live together with mutual forebearance. You don't form a committee to do this or pass a resolution; both races have to work it out the hard way.[11]

Flannery O'Connor's opinion of Southerners unwilling to "work it out the hard way" is reflected in the humor and the tragedy, the satire and the empathy, of such stories as "The Barber" (written before June 1947 and included in the author's M.F.A. thesis), "The Enduring Chill" (written approximately ten years after "The Barber" and first published in 1958), and "Everything That Rises Must Converge" (written and first published in 1961, three years before she died).

Rayber, a teacher who later plays a major role in Flannery O'Connor's second novel, *The Violent Bear It Away* (1960), is the civil-rights advocate of "The Barber." The kind of person the author mockingly refers to in her letters as an "interleckchul," he finds it "trying" to be a liberal in Dilton, a college town not unlike Milledgeville, for no one seems to take him seriously, and in the barbershop he is continually being called upon to defend his position in support of the Democratic White Primary liberal candidate when he is least prepared. Most uncomfortable to him is the fact that he is unable to provide a quick rebuttal to the barber's racist arguments in favor of the conservative candidate in front of George, the young black man who cleans and does odd jobs around the shop and whom Rayber would like to impress. After two exchanges with the barber in which Rayber uses the excuse of a pressing appointment to avoid being drawn into a political duel without appropriate ammunition, he returns to the barbershop for a third appointment armed with a speech he has written out and practiced for oral delivery. Inappropriately rhetorical, the speech goes badly, leaving Rayber feeling more than ever the fool. The barber is patronizingly kind; the other men in the barbershop amuse each other with gentle barbs directed toward Rayber in particular, all "Mother Hubbards" in general. Furious with himself for appearing so foolish, angry at being mocked, his face still half-lathered, the barber's bib still around his neck, Rayber strikes the barber, knocks him down, and strides out into the Dilton courthouse square to the astonishment of the populace.

Evidence that Rayber's liberal position is a pose rather than a conviction is introduced subtly throughout the story. When George first appears, Rayber's mental note is that he is "a trim-looking *boy*" (p. 16, italics mine); George is in fact old enough to be asked for whom he is going to vote in the primary. When Rayber observes "three colored *boys* in zoot suits" (italics mine) lounging against the window outside the barbershop, his irritable reaction is "Why the hell can't they park somewhere else?" (p. 20). When Rayber insists that George be brought in from the back room of the barbershop to listen to his speech, the barber looks at him knowingly and says, "He can hear what he hears and he can hear two times that much. He can hear what you don't say as well as what you do" (p. 24). George's response to Rayber is cautious, noncommittal. He is skilled at getting along with his employer: he simply says what the barber wants to hear, in the fewest possible words, in the way the barber wants to hear it ("sho' nuff," "wouldn't like that," "I don't know is they gonna let me vote. . . . Do, I gonna vote for Mr. Hawkson"). George has neither the dignity of Rabie (the barber would have regarded it as sass), the self-assertiveness of the Pullman porter (the barber would have regarded it as insubordination), nor the clever tongue of Coleman (the barber would have fired him on the spot, as a troublemaker). Yet, despite his "sho' nuff" responses to the barber, George is no Uncle Tom. Rayber's observation that he is "trim-looking" indicates a more positive self-image than his taciturn responses to his employer would suggest. The barber's recognition of George's ability to weigh what he hears without revealing his perceptions in what he says and does indicates that the young black man is both wary and self-protective, especially in encounters with Southern white advocates of Negro rights.

Like Rayber, Asbury of "The Enduring Chill" and Julian in "Everything That Rises Must Converge" also regard themselves as liberals and intellectuals, superior to the white people around them, especially such smug, self-satisfied representatives of the Old South as their own widowed mothers. Younger than Rayber, they are both economically dependent on their mothers, however, a situation they both deplore. Both fancy themselves to be literary men, great authors in the making. Both assume a stance of commitment to Negro rights that is contradicted by their romantic attitude toward black people in the abstract and their patronizing manner toward blacks in the flesh.

During the summer before the events of "The Enduring Chill," Asbury was at work on a play in which all the central characters were black; he had come home from New York to work in the dairy, he said, in order to be close to the black farmhands and discover their interests, that he might better portray them in his drama. In the dairy he had tried to ingratiate himself with the two Negroes regularly employed there, Morgan and Randall, by showing contempt for his mother's rules. When they allowed themselves to be persuaded to smoke with him (the next day two cans were returned from the creamery because the milk had absorbed the odor of tobacco), it was, for him, "one of those moments of communion

when the difference between black and white is absorbed into nothing"
(p. 368). But try as he would—to the extent of filling an old jelly glass,
Morgan and Randall's drinking cup, with warm milk that he himself
drained to the last drop—he could not get them to take the communal sip
of the forbidden milk from the milk room that would repeat for him the
exhilarating experience. "She don't 'low that," Randall had warned him;
"that *the* thing she don't 'low" (p. 369). Now back from New York again,
with an undiagnosed illness from which he is sure he will die, he has
written but not yet delivered to his mother "such a letter as Kafka had
addressed to his father," expressed through literary allusions she is sure not
to understand, about his New South attitudes and the artistic spirit within
him, which she has pinioned and thus rendered impotent (p. 364). He also
has refused to see the local doctor (his mother sends for him anyway) and
the local Methodist minister; he has asked instead for a Jesuit priest
(because he wants someone near with whom he can discuss James Joyce),
and he has invited Morgan and Randall to his bedside for a last farewell.
Uncomfortable in their employer's house but unwilling to refuse the
invitation, the two farmhands assure Asbury that he looks "just fine" and
misunderstand, to his dismay, his attempt to re-create the communion he
felt they had achieved when they all had smoked together in the dairy.
Shortly after they leave, the local doctor arrives with the mystery of
Asbury's illness solved: it is undulant fever, contracted from drinking
unpasteurized milk; he will not die, but the "enduring chill" will recur
throughout his life, both actually and (as Flannery O'Connor makes clear)
metaphorically.

Less affluent than Asbury, Julian of "Everything That Rises Must
Converge" has not been able to support his image of himself as an author
by moving to such a two-room, five-floor walk-up in New York, with
garbage on each landing, that Asbury enjoyed, nor is he able to boast of
having worked alongside black farmhands in a dairy. His apprenticeship
in literary art has consisted of selling typewriters. Nevertheless, he is as
disdainful of the white Southerners around him as Asbury, as eager to
show the black Southerners he encounters (when he accompanies his
mother downtown on the bus, to the exercise class ordered by the doctor to
help control her high blood pressure) that he does not share white
Southern attitudes and values. His greatest embarrassment is his mother,
who persists in reminding him that his great-grandfather had owned a
plantation and two hundred slaves; who reminisces about her own
childhood when Caroline, "the old darky," was her nurse; and who
commiserates with other white passengers over the fact that the buses are
now integrated. In retaliation Julian makes a point of sitting next to the
first Negro to board the bus and daydreams about calling a black doctor to
attend to his mother on her deathbed (or, better still, bringing her *to* her
deathbed by introducing a beautiful black woman as his intended wife).
Meanwhile, a large, sullen-looking black woman boards the bus with a

little boy and squeezes herself into the small space next to Julian; the little boy clambers into the seat next to Julian's mother and initiates the kind of flirtation often engaged in by older women and small children. Julian's mother responds (to her all children are cute) and, turning to the mother of the child, who makes no attempt to conceal her irritation, she flashes "the smile she used when she was being particularly gracious to an inferior" (p. 417). The four dismount the bus at the same stop. As the black woman jerks the boy toward her, Julian's mother, still smiling, offers the child a penny. "He don't take nobody's pennies," shouts the woman, slapping Julian's mother's outstretched arm with such force as to knock her off balance (p. 418). Hauling his mother to her feet, Julian tells her that she got what she deserved: "Don't think that was just an uppity Negro woman. . . . That was the whole colored race which will no longer take your condescending pennies . . . the old world is gone. The old manners are obsolete and your graciousness is not worth a damn" (p. 419). Without replying, his mother staggers along the sidewalk, muttering "Home"; "Tell Grandpa to come get me"; and then, before she collapses and dies on the pavement, "Tell Caroline to come get me" (p. 420).

If the two mothers of these stories depict the Old South at its obtuse, unreconstructed, patronizing worst, the two sons present the New South as infantile, incompetent, insincere, and self-aggrandizing. Asbury of "The Enduring Chill," like Rayber of "The Barber," reveals that his position on racial equality is but a pose when he offers Morgan the forbidden milk: "Here *boy*, have a drink of this," he says (p. 369, italics mine), repeating Rayber's telltale slip. Like George, Randall and Morgan are aware even without such evidence that Asbury's behavior reflects no genuine commitment to the freedom he urges upon them but is simply his way of discharging his resentments against his mother: "Howcome he talks so ugly about his ma?" asks Morgan; "She ain't whup him enough when he was little," Randall replies (p. 370). Asbury might play at being one of them in the dairy barn, but when Morgan tries to recommend his own home remedy for Asbury's illness, Randall tells him to shut his mouth: "He don't take what you take" (p. 380), he says fiercely. Like Asbury, Julian of "Everything That Rises" seethes with resentment against his mother, but for different reasons. Her talk of the wealth enjoyed by his grandparents and great-grandparents, the social status his family once knew as descendants of a governor of Georgia, and her own pampered childhood infuriates him: he has had none of this; to be told that his ancestors confer status when he himself must live in a slowly decaying neighborhood, sell typewriters for a weekly salary, and take his mother to the Y on a city bus is, to him, an insupportable injustice for which he holds her responsible. His position as advocate for civil rights and the New South therefore serves two purposes, both related to his feelings toward his mother in particular and all his ancestors in general: first, it relieves the frustration he feels at belonging to an Old South that had everything and preserved nothing for him; second, it punishes his mother for her personal culpability in not having something of the Old South to pass on to him. Clues to Julian's personality and attitudes are revealed not only in the indirect internal monologue through which Flannery O'Connor enters his mind but also through his responses to outer reality: he exploits the opportunity to sit next to a black man (first making sure that he is the proper class of black man, well dressed and carrying a briefcase) in order to irritate his mother; his own irritation when a large black woman squeezes into the seat beside him is dissipated only when he realizes that the juxtaposition troubles his mother more than it troubles him; if he could he would use a black doctor or a black wife to punish her. However, although Julian may have fantasies about marrying a black woman or bringing home "some distinguished Negro professor or lawyer . . . to spend the evening," the truth is that, riding the bus, he often has tried to "strike up an acquaintance . . . with some of the better types" but has "never been successful at making any Negro friends" (p. 414).

Flannery O'Connor leaves no doubt that Julian would have been equally unsuccessful in *any* attempt to befriend less advantaged Southern blacks: "The uneducated Southern Negro is not the clown he's made out to be," she declared in an interview. "He's a man of very elaborate manners and great formality which he uses superbly for his own protection and to insure his own privacy."[12] The statement is reaffirmed in her fiction not only by George, Randall, and Morgan, but also by Astor and Sulk of "The Displaced Person." Mrs. Shortley, whose economic position is little better than the Negroes' and whose status is derived only from the fact that her family is white and therefore (in accordance with Southern hierarchy) her husband supervises the Negroes, quotes her employer as saying, "This is going to put the Fear of the Lord into those shiftless niggers." When Mrs. Shortley hears that Mr. Guizac, a displaced person from Poland, has been hired to work on the farm (p. 199), it is she who worries about being displaced by "ten million billion" displaced persons who "ain't where they were born at." "She say something like that every now and then. . . . Ha. Ha. Yes indeed," is Astor's unperturbed reply, even though, having thought through the situation with a logic that surpasses Mrs. Shortley's, he has concluded, "If they here, they somewhere" (p. 199). Understanding, like Rabie, the mutual dependence inherent in the Southern code, Astor later reassures Sulk, who has grown nervous in the face of Mrs. Shortley's repeated warnings, "Never mind, . . . your place too low for anybody to dispute with you for it" (p. 206). What Rabie, George, Randall, Morgan, and Astor all have accepted may appear "low" in the Southern hierarchy but in fact provides them, in Flannery O'Connor's fiction, with greater respect and more security than that accorded poor whites.

The Negro's position in relation to whites in Flannery O'Connor's transitional South, whether the latter are poor and landless or moderately comfortable and rich, is made clear by the Boethian soliloquy of Mrs. Turpin of "Revelation," who sometimes wondered "who she would have chosen to be if she couldn't have been herself" (p. 491). Schooled like Old Dudley in the hierarchies of the Old South, unlike him she perceived that the obsolescence of the old code was everywhere evident. In fact, she often

> occupied herself at night naming the classes of people. On the bottom of the heap were most colored people, not the kind she would have been if she had been one, but most of them; then next to them — not above, just away from — were the white-trash; then above them were the home-owners, and above them the home-and-land owners, to which she and Claud belonged. Above she and Claud were people with a lot of money and much bigger houses and much more land. But here the complexity of it would begin to bear in on her, for some of the people with a lot of money were common and ought to be below she and Claud and some of the people who had good blood had lost their money and had to rent and then there were colored people who owned their homes and land as well. (p. 491)

"Moiling and roiling around" all the classes of people of the South in Mrs. Turpin's head (p. 492), the New South was coming. No longer would the blacks walk half a mile to a job in the cotton fields: her husband picked them up and took them home in his truck. She, herself, calling out "Hi yawl this evening?" greeted the farmhands with a bucket of ice water when they finished their day's work (p. 503). Mrs. Turpin, better than any civil-rights worker, understood the necessity for daily change. She even had the strength to think the unthinkable, to imagine herself black (albeit a "neat clean respectable Negro woman," p. 491). Transitions from Old South to New were possible for her because her relationship with God was both personal and friendly. Comfortable in her own spiritual superiority, confident that God would never make her "white trash," she sings to herself, "And wona these days I know I'll we-eara crown" (p. 490). Thoroughly unprepared for the attack by the emotionally disturbed girl in the doctor's office, Mrs. Turpin therefore is deeply shaken to find herself (like the "white trash" she herself loathes) an object of loathing. Her first reaction is to seek solace from the Negro farmhands whom she prides herself on having befriended. The insincerity of their exaggerated response disgusts her, even though it is but a mirror of her own insincere expressions of friendship. Next, she rails against her God, who has singled her out for special favor, creating her neat, respectable, fat, lovable, and white-skinned, only to humiliate her through the instrument of a lunatic girl: "Who do you think you are?" (p. 507), she shouts at Him. The echo of her own question "returned like an answer from beyond the wood" and the sunset vision of the New Jerusalem reveal to her what is in store:

> a vast horde of souls were rumbling toward heaven. There were whole companies of white-trash, clean for the first time in their lives, and bands of black niggers in white robes, and battalions of freaks and

lunatics shouting and clapping and leaping like frogs. And bringing up the end of the procession was a tribe of people whom she recognized at once as those who, like herself and Claud, had always had a little of everything and the God-given wit to use it right. . . . They were marching behind the others with great dignity, accountable as they had always been for good order and common sense and respectable behavior. (p. 508)

Although it seldom made the papers, "in a very satisfactory way," according to Flannery O'Connor, the South's particular history was evolving a new code of manners.[13]

Notes

1. I am grateful to Myra M. Baker for refining and correcting the historical perspective essential to this discussion. A Southerner by birth, Dr. Baker also has studied closely the work of a number of Southern writers, including Flannery O'Connor.

2. Cf. Irish society, as depicted by its writers of short fiction, e.g., Frank O'Connor, Sean O'Faolain, Liam O'Flaherty, Mary Lavin, Benedict Kiely, et al.

3. "Flannery O'Connor, An Interview" by C. Ross Mullins, *Jubilee*, 11 (June, 1963), 33–34, quoted in Dorothy Walters, *Flannery O'Connor* (New York: Twayne, 1973), p. 135.

4. *The Complete Stories* (New York: Farrar, Straus and Giroux, 1971), p. 7. All references in the text to O'Connor's stories are to this edition.

5. Cf. Thady Quirk of Maria Edgeworth's *Castle Rackrent* (1800), who is shocked by his son Jason's exploitation of the new economic and social order that has followed the Act of Union.

6. "The Geranium" was the title story of a collection that included "The Train," "Wildcat," "The Barber," "The Crop," and "The Turkey," submitted by Flannery O'Connor in partial fulfillment of the degree of Master of Fine Arts, University of Iowa, 1947. Published first in the *Sewanee Review*, "The Train" later became chapter one of Flannery O'Connor's first novel, *Wise Blood* (1952).

7. In *The Question of Flannery O'Connor* (Baton Rouge: Louisiana State University Press, 1973), Martha Stephens writes, "[Hazel] recognizes the porter as from an Eastrod Negro family, but the porter insists he is from Chicago" (p. 91). I base my different interpretation on the fact that nothing in Flannery O'Connor's story confirms Hazel's identification, which seems especially specious – based only on a general physical resemblance – given the fact that Hazel never has known Cash's runaway son (he had left Eastrod before Hazel was born). It seems more accurate to assume that Hazel's identification is mere wishful thinking; that more than anything else in the world, he needs either his mother or his old friend Cash as the train takes him to his new "home"; that because both are dead, perceiving the porter as Cash's son provides at least a surrogate at this stressful moment.

8. Quoted in Stephens, p. 91, from Katherine Fugin, Faye Rivard, and Margaret Sieh, "An Interview with Flannery O'Connor," *Censer* (College of St. Teresa, Winona, Minnesota), Fall 1960, p. 30.

9. Cf. Kathleen Feeley, S.S.N.D., *Flannery O'Connor: Voice of the Peacock* (New Brunswick: Rutgers University Press, 1972), pp. 90–91: "Although the story is imaginatively conceived, it does not possess 'felt life.' It is filtered through the consciousness of the old man, with both dialogue and narration written in idiomatic language. The story is largely told by dialogue, which makes it difficult to read."

10. Cf. *The Habit of Being*, to "A.," January 19, 1963, p. 506; to "A.," September 1, 1963, p. 537; to Janet McKane, October 11, 1963, p. 542; to "A.," October 26, 1963, p. 543; to Maryat Lee, January 18, 1964, p. 562; to Maryat Lee, May 21, 1964, p. 580; to Maryat Lee, June 16, 1964, p. 584; to Catharine Carver, July 15, 1964, p. 593; to Maryat Lee, July 26, 1964, p. 595.

11. Mullins, quoted by Walters, p. 135.

12. Mullins, p. 135.

13. Mullins, p. 135.

A Review of O'Connor
Criticism   Beverly Lyon Clark and Caroline M. Brown*

This bibliography annotates in depth some of the best and most innovative criticism on Flannery O'Connor. We hope that it can help to initiate novices at the same time that it provides reference and insight for those more familiar with O'Connor criticism. It complements the essays included in the present volume by giving a detailed account of what other critics have said.

We have tried to include the best-conceived criticism, but we have also aimed for diversity, including the sociological as well as the religious, the feminist as well as the formal. The annotations appear in the order in which the criticism was first published.

Joselyn, M., Sr. "Thematic Centers in 'The Displaced Person.' " *Studies in Short Fiction*, 1 (1964), 85–92.

Following G. M. Hopkins' distinction between "overthought" and "underthought," Joselyn examines the peacock and the "displaced person" to show how "symbolization" can be both a means and an end. The two thematic centers embody theological themes: respectively, the Incarnation and Christian love. The peacock is an ancient symbol for the divinity and rebirth of Christ. The "displaced person," for Joselyn, represents the poor, homeless, and hungry of Matthew 25: "Inasmuch as ye did [or did not] do this for one of the least of these my brethren, ye did [or did not] do it for Me."

Unlike most O'Connor stories, "The Displaced Person" has no demoniac: "Evil is not defined in a person nor in an action but in an absence, the absence of love" (p. 86). The attitudes of each character toward the peacock, the "displaced" Guizacs, and Christ often coincide. The priest, who brings the Guizacs, sees the peacock's spreading tail as an embodiment of the Transfiguration. Mrs. McIntyre sees the peacock as only

*This essay was written specifically for this volume and is published here with the permission of the authors.

another mouth to feed. To her, Christ is just another displaced person; she cannot see Christ *in* the displaced person.

The two thematic centers — and the "overthought" and "under-thought" — are brought together in the final description of the frugal, pragmatic Mrs. McIntyre, alone and bedridden, her only visitor the priest, who always brings breadcrumbs for the peacock. "By a variation of the displaced person motif, O'Connor shows that it is the displacer who is truly displaced," Joselyn comments (p. 92). Although Joselyn does examine the theological aspects of the story more deeply than Robert Fitzgerald did (*Sewanee Review*, 1962), nevertheless the concept of "overthought" and "underthought" could be developed more to clarify its value in an analysis of this story.

Holman, C. Hugh. "Her Rue with a Difference: Flannery O'Connor and the Southern Literary Tradition." In *The Added Dimension: The Art and Mind of Flannery O'Connor*. Ed. Melvin J. Friedman and Lewis A. Lawson. 1966; rpt. New York: Fordham Univ. Press, 1977, pp. 73–87.

Is O'Connor simply another Southern Gothic writer? Certainly not. She may be a Southern writer, quarrying the manners of the South for her fiction, yet she is not simply a novelist of manners. Holman's essay defines her relationship to the Southern literary tradition.

O'Connor's South was, first of all, neither the Deep South nor the aristocratic Tidewater. Her Georgia foothills were settled by the Scotch-Irish, who "were joined by the refugees and malcontents of the established seaboard society to form a harsh and unmannered world" (p. 76). Other writers have condescended to these people, have judged them grotesque. O'Connor likewise has portrayed grotesques, but hers derive from "other sources than the heat of social anger which warms Erskine Caldwell's [work] or the sense of the absurdity of human existence which shapes the grotesqueries of our young existentialists" (p. 78).

O'Connor's "passion for order" is related to the Southern tradition too, for "[t]he Southerner, predisposed to look backward as a result of his concern with the past, has tended to impose a desire for a social structure that reflects moral principles and he has tried to see in the past of his region at least the shadowy outlines of a viable and admirable moral-social world" (pp. 78–79). Like other Southern writers, O'Connor treats the family as the basic social unit, expresses meaning in small actions, is aware of caste structures.

Yet she diverges from contemporary Southern writers in one impor-tant respect: her religious belief, specifically her Catholicism. Her gro-tesques seek an order that the individualistic, Protestant South lacks. Thus while she uses the Southern setting, and the Southern hunger for order, her "anti-existentialist message" is the presence and power of God: "what she said transcends her region and speaks with the authority of art to the great world outside" (p. 86).

Hyman, Stanley Edgar. *Flannery O'Connor*. University of Minnesota Pamphlets on American Writers, No. 54. Minneapolis: Univ. of Minnesota Press, 1966.

Hyman's influential early monograph quickly covers a lot of ground, from a biographical sketch through examinations of O'Connor's work to glances at a context that includes Twain, West, Dostoevsky. Hyman touches briefly on many topics that later critics examine in detail, these critics often taking issue with Hyman.

When examining individual works Hyman concentrates on networks of imagery, symbol, theme. Although good at pointing to false prophecy in *Wise Blood* and the importance of sight and blindness, Hyman is a little too intent on symbol-hunting, as when miscellaneous references to rocks become "tokens of the Rock, Peter's Church" (p. 12). He notes the paradoxical, negative presentation of Christian themes yet concludes that, without an institutional channel, Hazel Motes's "call can only destroy him" (p. 15): Hyman ignores the possibility of the negative way, the possibility that destroying the worldly is an avenue to the otherworldly. Hyman also does not care for O'Connor's vivid (he calls it garish) early style.

He prefers the later plain style, and he considers *The Violent Bear It Away* O'Connor's masterpiece. He traces imagery of burning and feeding, and here he is willing to admit the unworldly: he considers the homosexual rape "at once the ultimate violation of the untouchable anointed of the Lord, a naturalistic explanation for the shaman's spirit possession, and a shocking and effective metaphor for seizure by divine purpose" (p. 23). It burns away Tarwater's reason, yet "in his madness he will preach the truth" (p. 25).

Hyman makes brief comments on the stories, but he feels O'Connor was primarily a novelist. He concludes by pointing to themes and images recurring throughout her work, convincingly pointing out the function of flaming suns, convincingly showing the importance in O'Connor's characters of God-intoxication and self-intoxication, less convincingly waxing anthropological in discoursing of mothers' brothers and sisters' sons. Hyman discusses too O'Connor's radical Christian dualism, in which sinfulness leads to sanctity: "In a time of desperate unbelief, in Miss O'Connor's view, the Christian sacraments must be understood to be equally desperate, and the language of desperation is violence and crime" (p. 38). And as for her penchant for the grotesque, it is far from gratuitous: "All art, to the extent that it is new and serious, is shocking and disturbing, and one way of dismissing those truths that get through to us is as 'grotesque' " (p. 44).

Stephens, Martha. "Flannery O'Connor and the Sanctified-Sinner Tradition." *Arizona Quarterly*, 24 (1968), 223–39.

Stephens postulates that the theological explanation for the "warped" and "insane" behavior of O'Connor's characters lies not in O'Connor's Southern roots but in "the sanctified-sinner tradition of modern-day European Christians," such as Eliot, Mauriac, Bernanos, and Greene (p. 224). In fact, little in Southern literature illuminates her theology. O'Connor shares with the European writers a traditionalist, conservative, "Christian dualist" viewpoint: "For them sin . . . [is] a reality of human life not to be denied" (p. 226). Therefore, the person who believes that good and evil exist yet chooses to do evil is closer to sanctification than the evader of belief.

Sanctified sinners fall into two categories: the believer who defies God, and the nonbeliever who recognizes the importance of belief but, not believing, sees no personal necessity to choose good. The latter group includes Hazel Motes, The Misfit, and Rufus Johnson. Stephens quotes Eliot: "It is better, in a paradoxical way, to do evil than to do nothing." Haze and Johnson are also like Pinkie of Greene's *Brighton Rock*, as sinners whose superiority to "good" nonbelievers is based on inhabiting a world not of "good and evil" but of "right and wrong." Admitting differences between the authors, Stephens suggests that O'Connor may even have "felt a certain hostility to Greene's work" (p. 231), but she gives no supporting evidence.

Eliot's influence is manifest both in O'Connor's general belief and in her work. Stephens notes in both *Wise Blood* and Eliot's *The Family Reunion* the theme of conflicting views of reality, and each contains variations of the Eliot paradox quoted above. Likewise, Stephens considers Mauriac's *Thérèse Desqueyroux* (1927) an early exemplar of the sanctified-sinner tradition. Yet Mauriac hesitated to show his heroine redeemed; O'Connor did not. Her heroes ultimately cannot resist divine grace.

The triumphant affirmation of "essential heroism" in the final pages of O'Connor's novels ought to overcome the numbing effects of earlier violence. Stephens insists that readers are projecting when they find spiritual deformity in O'Connor's heroes. The author's intent, her concern with the conflict between "the religious-intuitive and the non-religious rationalistic," is elucidated in her published letters and conversations (p. 238). Her treatment of sanctified sinners is thus part of her strategy to shock and outrage—and thereby to communicate with—her hostile rationalist audience. On the whole, this article provides a plausible and perceptive alternative to the "warped religion" strand of criticism.

Asals, Frederick. "Flannery O'Connor's 'The Lame Shall Enter First.'" *Mississippi Quarterly*, 23 (1970), 103–20.

In his discussion of "The Lame Shall Enter First," Asals asserts that "the richness and coherence of language and imagery . . . not only . . . demonstrate the fineness and complexity of [O'Connor's] art but further . . . suggest . . . the larger meanings of her 'poetically' conceived fiction" (p. 104). His careful textual analysis highlights O'Connor's use of subtle imagery to project the story's outcome and its metaphysical focus.

The climax of the story is projected throughout "in terms of eating and digestion" (p. 107). Sheppard's do-goodery feeds only his own ego; it revolts the other characters. Although a "self-appointed savior" (p. 110), Sheppard fails the Shepherd's basic command, "Feed my sheep." His pastoral role, ironically, is partly fulfilled by the wolflike Johnson. Asals delineates the biblical metaphor of the shepherd, like other biblical allusions, in a dispassionate tone, not forcing it on the reader.

Asals sees lameness as "a metaphor of human limitation and suffering," with which "all men are afflicted" (pp. 117, 118). Sheppard's reliance on the power of intellect denies the reality of evil as well as his own "lameness," his pride. Johnson admits that Sheppard is "good" but denies that he is "right"; O'Connor would suggest that "rightness" is necessary for intended good to fulfill its purpose. Asals concludes that "the true focus of 'The Lame' is . . . metaphysical or theological rather than moral" (p. 118). We can transcend nature's deformities only by first accepting them; denial will only lead us into a maze of illusory "intellectual concepts" (p. 120). Asals' thoughtful reading thus combines textual analysis and thematic interpretation with a grace and subtlety worthy of his subject.

Hendin, Josephine. *The World of Flannery O'Connor.* Bloomington: Indiana Univ. Press, 1970.

Hendin has written an iconoclastic counterbalance to the volumes of criticism by the spiritual exegetes. Yet in trying to balance the weight of the many volumes on the spiritual side, Hendin moves too far out on the material arm of the scale. Nevertheless she has written a thought-provoking study that has helped other critics define their own positions, when they do not casually dismiss her.

Hendin starts by providing biographical background and evoking the atmosphere of her own visit to Milledgeville. She hypothesizes that, while living the code of the Southern lady, O'Connor was raging inside, suffering from the disease that would kill her, but showed this rage and suffering only in her writing: "Flannery O'Connor seems to have lived out a fiction and written down her life" (p. 13). Hendin further questions the centrality of O'Connor's Catholicism. Sometimes Hendin implies that O'Connor's fiction works both religiously and therapeutically — is both "about Redemption" and is "a redemptive process" (p. 17) — but more often Hendin wants to deny the religious perspective altogether. And she becomes guilty of too much psychologizing. She rightly finds O'Connor's

characters distanced from their emotions, isolated and imagistically entrapped, but wrongly insists that O'Connor was similarly distanced.
Mightn't O'Connor simply have recognized a potential in herself, a
potential in any of us? Hendin is perceptive to note the literalization of
symbols in such stories as "The River," situating O'Connor between the
modernists and the New Novelists. But does such literalization entirely
negate, as Hendin claims, the significance and affect of the symbols?

Hendin then explores the relationship of mind and matter in early
stories and the conflicts between generations in later ones, perceptively
mapping constellations of imagery. She finds, further, that the novels are
about initiation and growing up, or rather about the impossibility of
growing up and confronting adult complexities, about rejecting adulthood
and passion and turning to rigidity and pain. Hendin finds O'Connor
reductive. But Hendin herself is reductive, avoiding complexity, as she
claims O'Connor's heroes do. She reduces all to the physically sordid and
refuses to acknowledge the possibility that the flatness of the characters
may intimate something beyond the physical. Often she gives good partial
interpretations, just failing to recognize a possible extra dimension. Even a
reader who is not Christian, who does not bear witness to the transform-
ing power of grace, can at least see O'Connor hinting at the extra-ordinary
in the violence she wreaks on the ordinary. Hendin, however, does not.

Hendin concludes by comparing O'Connor to other Southern writers.
In a striking analysis of murder scenes she contrasts Faulkner's and
Styron's mythologizing with Capote's and O'Connor's affectless, ahistori-
cal "murders without creation, murders without mythology" (p. 140). In
O'Connor's flat, affectless scenes, "it is what is left out that says most" (p.
148). Yes, indeed. But even if Hendin tends to be dogmatic in filling that
lacuna, she has added a challenging perspective to discussions of what has
been left out.

Feeley, Sister Kathleen. *Flannery O'Connor: Voice of the Peacock.* New
Brunswick: Rutgers Univ. Press, 1972.

O'Connor once said that the Catholic fiction writer need not play
God, only show this world exactly as he sees it. On the evidence provided
by this study, the same could be said of the Catholic literary critic. Since
Feeley and O'Connor share the same dogma, Feeley need not reiterate,
much less rediscover, the laws of O'Connor's universe. She is free to move
beyond the dogmatic questions that impale most critics and — through
investigating the marked passages in O'Connor's personal books — examine
the theological foundations for O'Connor's stories.

Feeley centers her study on six recurring themes, which are reflected
in her chapter titles: O'Connor's vision, the creation of a false self,
alienated modern man, death in the context of history, the numinous
quality of reality, and a prophet's view of reality. O'Connor's art and belief

formed an integral whole. Aware of her own limitations, O'Connor delved deep within her sphere rather than trying to reach beyond it.

Many of O'Connor's characters build up false images, which time and again are broken, usually by violent means: after their pretensions have been destroyed, can these characters live truly? In discussing modern alienation, Feeley points out that faith and reason conflict only when man won't accept the existence of the incomprehensible — the intellectuals in O'Connor's stories don't accept mystery because their minds can't encompass it. Significantly, where other critics have seen the disparity between O'Connor's professed belief and her actual production as a flaw, Feeley sees the one as a natural result of the other: because she sees man as "totally integrated into the world of the spirit" (p. 84), O'Connor depicts alienation, the absence of that integration, so vividly.

Feeley handles complex themes masterfully, examining the separate components of each from various perspectives. Perhaps her best exegesis is the chapter on "the numinous quality of reality," in which she discusses O'Connor's sense of "the essential glory of matter" (p. 113). O'Connor draws her reader toward a "penetration of the visible world [to reveal] ultimate reality" (p. 120), one of the great strengths of the fiction. In conjunction with this Feeley discusses O'Connor's affinity with Teilhard de Chardin, whose views on the relation between the natural and supernatural parallel O'Connor's own. Feeley draws many of her examples from stories in which children are the protagonists: they are more sensitive than adults to the numinous.

At the end, Feeley considers O'Connor's view of reality as akin to that of a prophet, and she proceeds from studies of Old Testament prophets, studies found in O'Connor's library, to a survey of the prophets in O'Connor's stories. Occasionally (usually at the end of a chapter) Feeley slips into strings of adjectives as her admiration for O'Connor overrides her scholarly restraint. For the most part, however, she gracefully and unobstrusively presents her thoughtful interpretations.

Orvell, Miles. *Invisible Parade: The Fiction of Flannery O'Connor.* Philadelphia: Temple Univ. Press, 1972.

Orvell's superb study begins by providing contexts for O'Connor. O'Connor often uses Southern materials, for instance, but she is less interested in social and political ramifications than in an individual's self-deceptions. Another context is of course her Christianity, "socially conservative and culturally enlightened" (p. 19). Orvell argues that at her best O'Connor fuses the spiritual and the aesthetic, and reveals a paradoxical tension between mystery and fact; a story such as "Greenleaf," for example, "culminate[s] in an image that is true dramatically, psychologically, and morally" (p. 27). Literature provides another context, and Orvell discusses European Catholic writers and the American romance tradition, making perceptive comparisons with Melville, Hawthorne, Poe. He discusses too the grotesque and the comic, including the cartoon and the tradition of popular American humor, and he notes the vividness and range of O'Connor's style.

In examining individual works, Orvell suggests that the protagonists of the novels are actively seeking and fleeing God, while those of the short stories are typically passive, intruded upon. He discusses imagery of sight and entrapment in *Wise Blood*, suggests that occasionally O'Connor is too eager to point a moral, and notes that the Christianity of the book "may represent a version of reality without demanding a belief in the image itself" (p. 92). *The Violent Bear It Away*, Orvell finds, is more concerned with portraying an inner struggle and with wresting meaning from history through multiple perspective. Again Orvell traces themes and images, and he judges the portrayal of Rayber too forced, sees Rayber as "a victim of O'Connor's too palpable intentions" (p. 120).

Orvell feels that the short story, though, was more congenial to O'Connor's talents, to her disinterest in nonessential detail. In the stories the protagonists are likely to be passive, "normal" characters, acted upon by agents resembling the heroes of the novels, but the agents are failed prophets. Orvell elucidates six stories, grouping them, a little awkwardly, into tales where a single figure is intruded upon and tales where two are.

Orvell concludes by considering the importance of the reader's beliefs. He occasionally finds the narrator intrusive yet feels that at her best O'Connor balances realism and mystery — and hence the reader need not share all the tenets of her belief to enjoy her tales, even if he or she thereby misses out on larger intentions. In examining early and late versions of a story, "The Geranium" and "Judgement Day," Orvell demonstrates how O'Connor heightened the drama, so that "a spiritual significance emerges from the naturalistic level of a situation and a sense of entelechy is discovered in the present moment" (p. 181).

Orvell is particularly good at providing a literary context for O'Connor — even after the first chapter he makes frequent comparisons with other works — and at dealing with the issue of belief. His criticism is a good place for the uninitiated to start, especially for those troubled by O'Connor's insistent Catholicism.

Asals, Frederick. "Flannery O'Connor as Novelist: A Defense." *Flannery O'Connor Bulletin*, 3 (1974), 23–39.

Are O'Connor's novels better than her short stories? Asals does not directly answer this question, but he does urge "that beside Flannery O'Connor's unquestioned genius for the short story we set her considerable talent for a certain kind of novel, and that if her longer efforts are not entirely flawless — indeed, how many novels, even recognizably great novels, are? — they are nevertheless largely successful and impressive on their own terms" (p. 24). He then defines those terms, seeing both her novels as "brief, intense, poetically conceived, highly condensed works, where the modern scene (or certain aspects of it) is refracted into symbolic forms of expression rather than being observed, delineated, analyzed in all its diverse and sometimes bewildering abundance" (pp. 25–26). Her predecessors in this lyric novel include Poe, Hawthorne, Crane, Fitzgerald, West.

Is *The Violent Bear It Away* better than *Wise Blood?* Asals responds that *The Violent* is probably better, but not for the reasons previous critics have given. Perhaps because it is a more traditional novel than *Wise Blood*, with a more tightly structured narrative, critics have been more comfortable with it. Yet *Wise Blood* too is patterned, much as West's *Miss Lonelyhearts* is, and enlivened by comic playfulness. It is, in its own terms, "a genuinely sustained performance, its unity gained from the images, symbols, and motifs that flow toward its hero, Hazel Motes, rather than from a conventionally well-made plot" (p. 29). Neither book is flawless — *Wise Blood* is occasionally too explicit, Rayber not altogether convincing — but both are successful.

Do O'Connor's novels simply reiterate her short stories (as dismissive critics claim)? Not that it matters, Asals responds, but no. The protagonists of the short stories are "just folks," while the protagonists of the novels are heroes, dreadful heroes, but Christian heroes, one a saint, the other a prophet.

How good, finally, are O'Connor's novels? Not as good as the predecessors he has listed, Asals responds, but almost. In this essay Asals provides sound answers to questions important for judging O'Connor, for placing her in a literary context.

Browning, Preston M., Jr. *Flannery O'Connor.* Pref. Harry T. Moore. Crosscurrents / Modern Critiques. Carbondale: Southern Illinois Univ. Press, 1974.

Browning addresses the dialectic between the criminal and the holy, convinced "that out of this tension grew Flannery O'Connor's extraordinary creative power and unique vision" (p. 11). This is Browning's most important insight, and it appears as well in his "Flannery O'Connor and the Demonic," *Modern Fiction Studies*, 19 (1973), 29–41. Browning argues that O'Connor attempted "to recover the idea of the Holy in an age in which both the meaning and the reality of this concept have been obscured," by portraying crimes "whose ultimate motive is a desperate desire to affirm a basis for human existence which transcends the waywardness and willfulness of the individual human self" (pp. 13, 14). At the same time she satirized contemporary smugness.

Browning stresses the compatibility of the religious and experiential dimensions of O'Connor's work — that, in fact, O'Connor is religious through the experiential, portraying "the primary spiritual question of our era": the loss of faith (p. 21). He objects to the overreactions of the secular critics such as Hendin, who try to be entirely nonreligious; for Browning, any critic who does not appreciate O'Connor's religious significance misses a great deal. But surely it says a lot for O'Connor's depth if her work can also sustain secular interpretations.

In discussions of individual works Browning stresses the reliance, in *Wise Blood*, on such oppositions as sin vs. innocence, oppositions that provide a dynamic tension. He comments on the frequency of three character types — the positivist, the positive thinker, the criminal-compulsive — in *A Good Man Is Hard to Find*. He examines the clash between two ways of viewing reality, Tarwater's and Rayber's, in *The Violent Bear It Away*. He notes that the stories of *Everything That Rises Must Converge* include fewer psychopathic killers than earlier stories do, yet "what appears as a more or less harmless and humorous contest of wills detonates into a fury of destruction, and self-destruction, even as the comic surface is preserved almost to the very end" (p. 109). That is, in her later stories the conflicts are internalized, less dramatically external, but they are potent nonetheless.

Aiken, David. "Flannery O'Connor's Portrait of the Artist as a Young Failure." *Arizona Quarterly*, 32 (1976), 245–59.

David Aiken's reading of "The Enduring Chill" compares the protagonist to Joyce's Stephen Dedalus, characterizing each as a "self-conscious artist-hero" who is a "personal failure" (p. 245). Aiken argues that O'Connor satirizes Joyce's artistic techniques in the character of Asbury Porter Fox, thereby providing an index of her "own central esthetic tenets" (p. 245). Asbury, like Stephen, alienates himself from home, family, and religion "in the name of art" (p. 246) and incidentally, Aiken points out, finds in Joyce a kindred spirit — a spirit not understood by those around him.

Aiken digresses to discuss the choice of Asbury's name, which, he says, reflects the complex fox imagery in Joyce's novels. Aiken's comparison seems overdrawn, but he does admit that the correspondence between Asbury's name and those of major religious rebels may not be intentional on O'Connor's part — an admission that, frankly, relieved a reader impatient with farfetched correspondences.

More significant, however, are the correspondences between the two characters in terms of their general disposition, which Joyce termed "hyperborean," and their relationships to their mothers and their art. Asbury's isolation and lack of love exaggerate Stephen's aloofness. Again, Stephen's alienation (for which his art provides no consolation) is satirized when Asbury uses the Joycean model of "the sensitive artist at odds with his . . . surroundings to justify his own egocentricity" (p. 255). Asbury is in fact neither artistic nor intellectual but "simply at odds with everyone and everything" around him (p. 255).

For O'Connor, Aiken suggests, the point of the story is Asbury's enlightenment in regard to his own character and the actual source of his illness; his enlightenment makes him vulnerable to the "purifying chill of the Holy Ghost" (p. 255). Aiken finds the conclusion flawed by O'Connor's "heavy-handed" moral judgment (p. 257), but appreciates its satirical guise, for the ceiling stain shaped like a "fierce bird" (p. 256) recalls Stephen's hawk-god, which represented art. As Aiken points out, art is "not enough" for O'Connor: "In her theocentric world, . . . the last word is God's" (p. 259). Aiken judiciously implies thereby that, however prominent the Joycean parallels may appear, they were not O'Connor's primary concern in this story.

May, John R. *The Pruning Word: The Parables of Flannery O'Connor.*
Notre Dame: Univ. of Notre Dame Press, 1976.

May starts with a review of previous work on O'Connor, work that he groups in three overlapping stages of critical dialogue: initial interpretation, evaluation of the criticism, reevaluation of the works. He charts what he considers the emerging consensus on O'Connor and examines cruxes that still generate contradictory opinions. Parts of May's book previously appeared in the *Canadian Journal of Theology* (1970), *Southern Humanities Review* (1970), *Flannery O'Connor Bulletin* (1973), *Renascence* (1975).

May's central contribution is to apply the New Hermeneutic, which views the "word" as interpreter, to O'Connor's fiction: "her fiction achieves its distinctive dramatic impact through the power of language to interpret its listener rather than through its need to be interpreted by him" (p. xxiv). Although, in keeping with traditional hermeneutic theory, O'Connor's theoretical pronouncements primarily relate the work of art to reality, "the New Hermeneutic is the key to understanding the religious dimension of the aesthetic function of her stories, the relationship between the work and meaning" (p. 11). Mrs. Turpin of "Revelation," for instance, eventually allows the word of judgment to interpret her, shattering her illusory superiority. And the reader is likewise affected.

O'Connor's fiction, like the parable, centers on everyday experience. And like parables her stories "are not allegories but dramatic narratives involving conflicts between human beings that symbolize rather than describe man's relationship to ultimate reality" (p. 14). Her fiction focuses on "the word of revelation spoken to the protagonist that either achieves conversion or announces simple condemnation" (p. 20). Through her contemporary parables of the ordinary, the reader encounters a religious, or at least extra-ordinary, experience — "not orthodox Christian theology in its fullness but a single-minded revelation of human limitation and possibility in the face of mystery" (p. xxv).

May briefly discusses the stories and novels, elucidating major themes and imagery. He attends especially to the "revelatory power of the word," more pronounced in *Everything That Rises Must Converge*, but more effective in *A Good Man Is Hard to Find* (p. 60). In the novels too "word illumines their meaning, even fully, although *The Violent Bear It Away* is more subtly effective than *Wise Blood* as an interpretive parable" (p. 125). May's analysis of *Wise Blood* traces patterns of threes and recurring references to home, both secular and spiritual. His analysis of *The Violent* notes such themes as hunger for the word and the word as seed.

Still, May's emphasis on the power of the word undermines some of his own role as critic. For the critic should stand aside to let the words speak for themselves. But May attempts to retain his role by urging that interpretation may be necessary "where language-event is impeded for some reason or other" (p. 4). The role of the interpreter is not to spin out complex analyses of the text but to facilitate the reader's response to the words: "if, in the final analysis, man is to be interpreted by the text—the possibilities of his situation to be illumined by it—it is the task of the interpreter to place the text where it speaks to man" (p. 4).

McFarland, Dorothy Tuck. *Flannery O'Connor*. Modern Literature Monographs. New York: Ungar, 1976.

McFarland's overview makes an excellent undergraduate introduction to O'Connor criticism. After placing O'Connor in religious, geographic, and literary contexts, McFarland points out, in a short biographical sketch, that any relation between O'Connor's life and work must remain "merely speculative" (p. 5)—thereby quelling any budding psychologically inclined critics. McFarland's perceptions of O'Connor's contexts neatly elucidate the consensus of critical thought.

McFarland then discusses, briefly but comprehensively, the four volumes that comprise the bulk of the O'Connor canon. In discussing the short stories, McFarland first considers the style, technique, and imagery of each volume, then discusses a major concept of that volume, and finally describes each story individually, relating it to the title of the volume. The thesis that the central theme of each collection resides in its title is more successful with *Everything That Rises Must Converge* than with *A Good Man Is Hard to Find*. Furthermore, the evidence is rather thin; one wonders if O'Connor did in fact intend each volume to have such thematic unity.

In discussing *Wise Blood*, McFarland notes Orvell's observation of the novel's cinematic quality. With the advantage of hindsight, this reader agrees that *Wise Blood* is "more immediately effective" (p. 73) on the screen than on paper. McFarland touches on the imagery, then discusses Jesus' role in the novel. His ambiguous success as a liberator from psychological imprisonment leads McFarland to comment that O'Connor characteristically provides incidents that can be interpreted in opposite ways — and that from this device springs much of the power of her work. McFarland sees the dichotomy as "conscious and deliberate" (p. 88), not as evidence of O'Connor's indecisiveness. The "often repulsive" imagery of *Wise Blood* makes romanticization "virtually impossible" (p. 88); the reader is forced to confront both the frightening aspects of Jesus' "wild ragged figure" and the hollow absurdity of the Taulkinham world (thereby seeing the equal importance of style and content).

McFarland focuses on freedom in her discussion of *The Violent Bear It Away*. Psychological interpretations suggest that Tarwater's attempted rejection of his calling represents his bid for freedom. Even some religious interpretations, though considering prophecy viable, still find in Tarwater's inability to refuse the suggestion that he does not, after all, possess free will. McFarland's own suggestion is that the novel concerns two people with free will who have "an inborn attraction toward the Holy" (p. 108); Rayber resists it, but Tarwater finally surrenders to it.

O'Connor's personal beliefs regarding the meaning of life and of her work have concerned her critics far more than is usual in modern interpretation. Throughout her clear exegesis, McFarland unemotionally presents the diverse opinions of her fellow scholars before drawing her own conclusions. Her final comment is that, despite the harshness of O'Connor's vision, despite O'Connor's ironic and often repulsive description of the universe, there is yet beauty in her work, beauty encompassed by her vision.

Richard, Claude. "Désir et destin dans 'A Good Man Is Hard to Find.' " *Delta (Flannery O'Connor et le réalisme des lointains)*, No. 2 (1976), 61–73.

In his close reading of "A Good Man Is Hard to Find" Richard sketches "une véritable géographie du désir" (p. 61). The grandmother wants to go to Tennessee, not Florida, since Tennessee represents for her the acme of moral, intellectual, and cultural order.

The grandmother associates herself with cultural order. She aspires to dying on the highway and looking like a lady (her sense of culture is a sense of class) — but she ends up sprawled in a ditch, looking like a child. She is associated with the artificial, cloth violets mimicking real ones, cloth lace mimicking the lacework of trees. And she knows how to manipulate the vehicle of culture, language, as when she invokes the magic formula of a good man or when she whets the curiosity of her grandchildren by claiming that a mansion she wants to visit has a secret panel.

The Misfit, however, operates outside the grandmother's cultural sphere of linguistic control. He demonstrates as much when he corrects her statements and when he fails to respond to her invocation of the "good man" (at least not in the social or moral sense that she intends). She even loses her voice with him, loses language altogether. The shifting control of language underscores how the grandmother passes "de l'ordre du désir (actif) à l'ordre du destin (passif)" (p. 70), out of the social and cultural into the Christian and eternal.

At times Richard's ingenuities strike the American critic as labored, as overreading. (His association of the front and the back — of the car, of the mansion — with the real and the apparent, the natural and the cultural, seems a little contrived.) Yet he does offer keen insights, and he demonstrates how well O'Connor's work travels.

Rubin, Louis D., Jr. "Flannery O'Connor's Company of Southerners; or, 'The Artificial Nigger' Read as Fiction Rather Than Theology." *Flannery O'Connor Bulletin*, 6 (1977), 47–71.

Rubin's reading of "The Artificial Nigger" is a refreshing change from the many readings that have seen the story in theological terms. For him, O'Connor's humorous contrast of the uneducated speech of "the Georgia plain folk" with her cultured authorial voice is as important as her religion. Rubin thus pinpoints a major flaw in O'Connor criticism — one aspect of the work, her thematic concern, has been isolated from the whole: "one might as well be dealing with *Pilgrim's Progress*" (p. 49). O'Connor herself was often much concerned with specificity: if her natural world wasn't believable, how could she expect her readers to believe in the un-natural?

Rubin emphasizes O'Connor's roots in the Southern literary tradition, particularly in Southern humor, whose hallmark is the aforementioned "humorous linguistic incongruity" (p. 59). The incongruity between tones produces distance between narrator and character, leading first to the reader's amusement but then, also, to compassion for the character — essentially a viewpoint in counterpoint. The characters are thus given a niche not only in their own milieu but also in universality.

Much of O'Connor criticism displeases Rubin, being "simplistic, reductive, thin" (p. 69). Many critics are tempted to moralize, lifting the religious strands out of context, out of the complex whole. True, O'Connor was a Roman Catholic, but she was also a Middle Georgian, a modern Southern writer, "and a great many other things besides" (p. 70). She read Teilhard de Chardin, but she also read Joel Chandler Harris. As O'Connor said, a story is not an algebra problem in which one finds "X . . . and dismiss[es] the rest" (p. 71). Rubin terms such an approach "good exegetical theology" (p. 71) but wretched literary criticism. Too much criticism appears to ask, as O'Connor was asked, what a peacock was "good for" — the sort of question that needs — rather, deserves — no answer.

Kahane, Claire. "The Artificial Niggers." *Massachusetts Review*, 19 (1978), 183–98.

For O'Connor the black, the Negro, can be "a metaphor of redemptive humility" (p. 184), as Kahane argues. Yet individual black characters are more ambiguous: lazy, shiftless, lying, pilfering — her racism "mitigated only by the fact that she directs her acidic wit at all her characters" (p. 184). Still, O'Connor is aware that the roles the blacks play are social masks, "a white projection [turned] into a superb comic weapon," and she uses this weapon "to direct her own killing ridicule against both the values of Northern liberalism and a host of domineering Southern matriarchs" (p. 185). O'Connor's inability to show blacks without their masks, "her inability to portray Negroes from the inside," still doesn't prevent her from conveying "a complicated network of psychological involvement and mutual dependency between black and white" (p. 187).

Kahane examines "The Displaced Person" in some detail, exploring the implication "that the Southern whites are in fact dependent on the blacks, and that their very fear of this dependency has evolved a set of manners which totally denies it — even reverses it" (p. 189). The possibility of miscegenation threatens social boundaries, and "is a living metaphor of that confusion, blurring the distinction between black and white through sexuality, and obliterating the entire structure of defined power" (p. 190). Kahane then discusses "Everything That Rises Must Converge" and "Judgement Day," pointing out that a violent black can trigger "the day on which the roles of the powerless and the powerful are reversed" (p. 198).

Kahane is sensitive to the nuances of black-white relations in O'Connor's fiction, yet she misses some of the point. She finds O'Connor unable to portray "a viable political reality" and reduced to invoking "a magical resolution" (p. 198). Furthermore, O'Connor's fiction may emphasize "the need for the 'nigger' role to bind sexuality and aggression through manners" (p. 192) if one is to preserve the status quo. But, one could demur, preserving the status quo was not O'Connor's aim. She was attempting to show the inadequacy of any mere political reality, the need to seek beyond the secular.

Westling, Louise. "Flannery O'Connor's Mothers and Daughters." *Twentieth Century Literature*, 24 (1978), 510–22.

Westling provides a feminist reading of O'Connor by examining mother-daughter relationships within the short stories and finding "a passionate but inadvertent protest against the lot of womankind" (p. 511). Westling recognizes that O'Connor was not a feminist, that "the problems of women are not of central importance in Flannery O'Connor's view of her stories" (p. 517). Yet Westling suggests that even while focusing on religious experience O'Connor can still convey secular insights, that in fact O'Connor achieves "a rich integration of the literal and symbolic" (p. 519).

Westling, however, does not always present such a balanced view of the multiple possibilities in O'Connor's fiction. Occasionally she wants entirely to supersede religious interpretations, arguing that "within the religious context of the stories, there are no satisfactory solutions to the difficulties faced by widows like Mrs. Cope and Mrs. Hopewell and by daughters like Sally Virginia and Joy-Hulga" (p. 517). But perhaps this lack of solutions is the point — perhaps there is no secular solution, and a spiritual one can only be implied, not directly shown.

Still, Westling does offer useful insights. She points to the pattern of stranded but tough and resourceful mothers raising truculent daughters (and sons). She points to the recurring problems of the intelligent and independent daughters: the twelve year olds who imagine being adventurers but who actually are powerless voyeurs, and the thirty-two year olds betrayed by unscrupulous males. And Westling points to how difficult it is in our culture "for women to feel assured about discussing their own special experiences. Such attitudes result in portraits of women who are too strong or troubling or awkward for their assigned places in their fictional worlds" (p. 521).

O'Connor's misfits may serve a higher purpose, but in portraying them she reveals, as Westling notes, keen insights into the miseries of man — and woman.

Wasserman, Renata R. Mautner. "Backwards to Ninevah." *Renascence*, 32 (1979), 21–32.

What is the relation between "truth" and "reality"? Wasserman suggests that O'Connor's fictional world is by no means as orthodox as the dogma that she claims as the basis for her point of view. Even if it isn't orthodox, is her reality at least compatible with her theology? Wasserman suggests that although there is no coherence here of the normal kind, based on resolved conflicts, there is a coherence based on "a pattern of consistent . . . disjunctions" (p. 22). O'Connor's language provides clues to the characteristics and implications of these disjunctions.

Wasserman emphasizes O'Connor's interest in Mystery, which shows itself only where manners break down. In the two novels the breach in manners is caused by murder, which, as both a capital crime and a capital sin, has repercussions in the realm of Mystery as well. O'Connor's theology affirms not only a connection but an actual mediator between the two realms; but the novels, Wasserman says, show such great disjunction that successful mediation seems highly doubtful. The murderers go unpunished by temporal law. The repercussions under spiritual law are ambiguous: all we can see is that the murders seem to be turning points in the murderers' lives. From that act, the utter repudiation of order, the murderers return to an acceptance of order and the work they are meant to do — backwards, as Jonah returned, to Ninevah.

Wasserman finds the novels ambiguous as well as disjunct. Paradox serves O'Connor well, but appears to confuse Wasserman so that her thought becomes difficult to follow. Although she agrees with O'Connor that "the artist 'cannot move or mold reality in the interests of abstract truth' " (p. 21), she still seems distressed that O'Connor's murderers are not only unpunished but apparently furthering their spiritual lives by committing crimes. She notes that O'Connor seems to be trying to reestablish direct relations between God and his prophets, without Christ's mediation. Disturbed because the search for the source of Mystery has terror implicit in it, and requires the surrender of one's own will and reason, Wasserman despairs at the situation O'Connor presents: men are separated from each other and from God, cause from effect, absolute truth from reality. All O'Connor's critical work does is to cover the disjunction with a patina of "orthodox coherence" (p. 30).

Wasserman's elucidation of O'Connor's opposing critical and fictional viewpoints is impressive, but since the world O'Connor depicted was exactly what she was trying to depict, Wasserman's despair seems misplaced. In the face of a modern world even half as violent and senseless as O'Connor's fictional one, O'Connor's dogmatic beliefs may seem, superficially, absurd — but nevertheless the "credo" is spoken: what else have we to go on with?

Coles, Robert. *Flannery O'Connor's South.* Baton Rouge: Louisiana State Univ. Press, 1980.

Robert Coles's study is not of O'Connor's literature so much as of — as the title indicates — her South. In discussing the social, religious, and intellectual milieus of O'Connor and her characters, Coles, a social psychologist, draws on O'Connor's recently published letters and on his own extensive conversations with Southerners whose backgrounds and concerns mirror those of O'Connor's characters.

"A facility for fiction," O'Connor wrote, "depends on the ability to mimic the social scene" (p. 3). The "social scene" within which she wrote was that of a growing civil-rights movement — a movement that not only highlighted the differing viewpoints of black and white Southerners but juxtaposed with these the perceptions of the Yankee activists who came South to aid the cause. O'Connor's characters, although drawn in comic relief, still sharply illustrate contemporary class structure and racial differences. O'Connor incorporated her social comment into her stories rather than making public statements; she was a writer, not a public figure. Coles makes clear O'Connor's "debt to a people and a tradition," but adds that "Flannery O'Connor's South is Robert Frost's New England . . . — American regionalism in the service of a vision that glances toward Heaven and Hell, both" (p. 45).

O'Connor's vision was firmly rooted in her region and in its "hard, hard religion" (p. 60). Coles quotes farmhands, itinerant evangelists, and rural women, whose remarks make it clear that the religious fervor of Hazel Motes, O. E. Parker, and their ilk does not deserve the incredulity with which critics have examined it. Their fervor was not O'Connor's, of course; a "theologically sophisticated" Catholic (p. 64), she not only appreciated her neighbors' violent zeal but was also quick to discern the possibility of "practical heresies" (p. 72); Coles parallels Gnosticism and Haze Motes's dualistic search.

O'Connor's intellectual characters are as firmly rooted in reality as her rural folk, although not always as well depicted. O'Connor herself was an intellectual, but she was also a harsh critic of certain contemporary intellectual fashions, in particular liberal humanism and psychoanalysis, in which she was quick to spot the overweening pride and self-righteous "professionalism" she several times lampooned (p. 129). The confrontation of this intellectual pride with "Christ-haunted" zeal produces violence. Coles knits together his three strands — region, religion, and intellectualism — in the person of Flannery O'Connor, whose letters show that, in her, the latter strand can be considered only in conjunction with the former two.

Coles's study is not, in the strictest sense, literary criticism, and should not be taken as such. But no other study thus far has treated O'Connor's milieu with such expertise and sensitivity as Coles does here, thus providing O'Connor scholars with a fresh view of their subject.

Kahane, Claire. "Gothic Mirrors and Feminine Identity." *Centennial Review*, 24 (1980), 43–64.

This article is not primarily about O'Connor, but it provides valuable contexts. Kahane starts by identifying herself as a feminist and a psychoanalytic critic, concerned about the intersubjectivity of interpretation. She then examines Gothic fiction, pointing out how male critics focus on incest and oedipal conflicts, while a woman may locate the experience of the Gothic in the displaced mother and the heroine's identity problems. For Kahane "the real Gothic horror" is that "the heroine seems compelled either to resume a more quiescent, socially acceptable role, or to be destroyed" (p. 54). Modern radical Gothic (not the popular drugstore variety) typically allows no escape from the Gothic experience but destruction. Modern Gothic also unveils what has been cloaked in mystery, grotesque images of self-hatred: "when the unseen is given visual form, when we lose the obscurity of the Gothic center, the Gothic turns into the Grotesque, into a focus on distorted body-images, as so much of what we call Gothic illustrates" (p. 55).

And here is where O'Connor comes in, Gothic in her concern for penetrating a central truth, modern in giving the truth grotesque form. Kahane examines maternal images in *Wise Blood* and pregnancy in "A Stroke of Good Fortune." More generally, "Although [O'Connor's] various female characters continually attempt to escape by repudiating their womanhood, their flight invariably proves to be circular, nightmarishly bringing them face to face with the danger inherent in female identity—face to face—that is—with mothers" (p. 59). Kahane concludes by examining the image of the hermaphrodite, potentially grotesque (when physically described), but potentially liberating, "a Gothic emblem of the desired transgression of boundaries I experience within the Gothic space" (p. 60). Thus in "A Temple of the Holy Ghost" O'Connor "transforms the grotesque into the sublime, self-hatred into awe, by means of indirection and ambiguity" (p. 62).

Kahane elucidates some of O'Connor's mystery, even if her responses ignore the Christian perspective (that's for another reader, with other predilections). And Kahane gives an intelligent feminist reading, eloquently redefining the Gothic.

Tate, J. O. "Flannery O'Connor's Counterplot." *Southern Review*, 16 (1980), 869–78.

Tate admits that O'Connor "was an expert on sin," writing "all too knowingly of murderous impulses, or petty spite" (p. 869). Yet he does not consider her as belonging, in spite of herself, to the devil's party. Like Hawthorne's, her ambiguities are positive, not subconsciously deconstructive. And like the similar critical assault on Milton, that on O'Connor almost "seems fair, since it is in the nature of established orders, whether they are political institutions or imaginative projections, that they provoke envious wrath" (p. 870).

Critics have discussed Milton's counterplot, his subtle diminishing of Satan's greatness, through distancing, foreshortening, celebrating Creation. O'Connor too has celebrated "beauty and vitality, which we can perceive in her works when a perverse human evil does not obscure the view" (p. 871). She too has provided contexts that diminish the surface events of her fiction. In *Wise Blood*, for instance, we occasionally glimpse the larger realms of sky and planets, ordinarily ignored by the characters. In "The Lame Shall Enter First," Norton seeks to travel to the stars. O'Connor discreetly invokes distance and depth, thus preparing us for a supernatural reading. She invokes vision, seeing far things as if they were near, seeing the beauty of the peacock's tail. She also invokes harmony—hymns and choruses echoing the music of the spheres.

Like Milton's, O'Connor's narratives have a counterplot, but with a difference: "Milton's counterplot controls our response and understanding of Satan's pseudo-heroic activity with anachronistic references to 'contemporary' time and place, and denies grandeur by artfully confusing our senses of proportion and scale. O'Connor's counterplot cuts the other way, elevating our awareness from the small and shabby toward the great and grand, disorienting our sense of time with gestures toward eternity, and ensuring our mental placement of the human figure within a broad perspective of cosmological arrangements" (p. 877). Both Milton and

O'Connor recognize that good can come out of evil; both celebrate the possibility of overcoming demonic corruption.

Tate's essay provides O'Connor with a telling context. He may be too ready to dismiss secular readings, but he makes an eloquent defense of O'Connor's vision.

Tolomeo, Diane. "Home to Her True Country: The Final Trilogy of Flannery O'Connor." *Studies in Short Fiction*, 17 (1980), 335–41.

In discussing O'Connor's final stories—"Revelation," "Parker's Back," and "Judgement Day"—Tolomeo observes a shift in the placement of the climactic, consciousness-raising scenes of violence. Typically the violent action occurred near the end of an O'Connor story; in the final trilogy, however, it is shifted to an earlier position. No longer is the effect on the character left to the reader's imagination; instead, O'Connor continues the narrative, explicating the changes in the character. Therefore the reader cannot brush aside the incident, but "is confronted with the implications of what he has just encountered" (p. 336).

O'Connor's intended audience was one that did not share her Christian viewpoint. Yet since she ended her stories at the violent "moment of recognition," the burden of interpretation was put on the reader—and often only a reader who shared O'Connor's beliefs and scriptural background could be expected to perceive the religious parallels. However, in the final trilogy, "O'Connor's insistence that we understand fully contains an urgency that is not entirely present in the earlier stories, which by comparison seem to present her vision through a glass darkly" (p. 339). Tolomeo's judicious and skillful presentation of that urgency lends credibility not only to her understanding of and belief in her subject but also to her discernment of O'Connor's intent.

INDEX